A GIFT FOR

FROM

50TH ANNIVERSARY EDITION

OUR DAILY *Bread*

COUNTRYMAN

Copyright © 2005 by Discovery House Publishers.

Published by the J. Countryman division of the Thomas Nelson Book Group,
Nashville, Tennessee 37214.

This book is based upon selections from Our Daily Bread,
Copyright ©1988 to 2004 by RBC Ministries, and is published by
special arrangement with and permission of Discovery House Publishers,
3000 Kraft Avenue, SE, Grand Rapids, Michigan, 49512. All rights reserved.

Compiled and edited by Terri Gibbs.

All Scripture quotations in this book are from
The New King James Version (NKJV) ©1979, 1980, 1982, 1992,
Thomas Nelson, Inc., Publisher. Used by permission.

www.thomasnelson.com
www.jcountryman.com

Designed by LeftCoast Design, Portland, Oregon.

ISBN: 1-4041-0221-3

Printed and bound in China.

Writers

HENRY G. BOSCH
(1914–1995)

J. DAVID BRANON

DENNIS J. DE HAAN

M. R. DE HAAN, M.D.
(1891–1965)

MARTIN R. DE HAAN II

RICHARD W. DE HAAN
(1923–2002)

DAVID C. EGNER

PAUL R. VAN GORDER

VERNON C. GROUNDS

JULIE LINK

DAVID C. MCCASLAND

HADDON W. ROBINSON

DAVID H. ROPER

HERBERT VANDER LUGT

JOANIE E. YODER

In 1956, Henry G. Bosch, a Radio Bible Class staff member, proposed a daily devotional publication to help radio listeners structure a daily time of Bible reading and prayer. Dr. M. R. De Haan agreed, and the name *Our Daily Bread* was chosen for the new publication. Seventeen thousand booklets were printed and offered to the Radio Bible Class listeners. From this inauspicious beginning came a devotional book that has helped millions of people nurture their relationship with God through regular Bible reading and prayer.

The design of the devotional is simple. A down-to-earth, life-related story leads into the timeless truth of God's Word. *Our Daily Bread* writers aim to encourage reflection on biblical truth that moves readers to love and praise God, to be obedient and thankful to Him, to seek forgiveness and restoration, or to find comfort, inspiration, and encouragement in His Word.

Our Daily Bread intends to help its readers hear the Word of God in a fresh way, to see His mighty works of grace, to touch them so that they turn their hearts and minds toward Him in faith and trust, and to move them to speak of His love and bear witness to His work in their lives. If the devotional accomplishes its purpose, the truth of the writing will stay in the reader's mind long after the pages on which it was written are gone.

The original writers of *Our Daily Bread* could never have envisioned the worldwide impact of the little devotional book they published. Through the years, the *Our Daily Bread* staff has received thousands of letters from readers reporting how the daily ministry of the devotional has helped them. Many times someone will say, "How did you know that I needed that particular Scripture verse?" or "How did you know what I was facing in my life?" We didn't know. But God did, and by His grace, He placed the words in the right place to be read by the person to whom they offered comfort, encouragement, or guidance. We are thankful to be instruments He uses still, fifty years later.

MARTIN R. DEHAAN II
PRESIDENT, RBC MINISTRIES

O GOD, OUR HELP IN AGES PAST,

OUR HOPE FOR YEARS TO COME,

OUR SHELTER FROM THE STORMY BLAST,

AND OUR ETERNAL HOME!

WATTS

January

Noah walked with God.

GENESIS 6:9

*P*eople who want to feel better, reduce stress, and shed unwanted pounds are discovering that walking may be the best exercise of all. A fitness philosophy of 10,000 steps a day, which first took hold in Japan, is gaining popularity in other countries. Experts advise starting slowly and working toward a higher goal, realizing each day that every step counts.

It's even more important to stay spiritually fit by "walking with God," which the Bible describes as an intimate, growing relationship with the Lord. "Enoch walked with God three hundred years" (Gen. 5:22). "Noah was a just man, perfect in his generations. Noah walked with God" (6:9). Both men are mentioned in Hebrews 11, where they are commended for their faith.

To walk with God, we need to keep in step without running ahead or lagging behind. Along the way, we talk with the Lord, listen to Him, and enjoy His presence. We trust His guidance when we cannot see what lies ahead. It is not just the destination that's important, but the journey we take together.—D. C. M.

THERE'S NO BETTER TIME THAN NOW TO BEGIN WALKING WITH GOD.

That I may know Him . . .
and the fellowship of His sufferings.

PHILIPPIANS 3:10

At age sixteen, Madame Jeanne Guyon (1648–1717) was forced into an arranged marriage with an invalid twenty-two years older. She found her marriage to be one of utter humiliation. Her husband was often angry and melancholy. Her mother-in-law was a merciless critic. Even the maid despised her. In spite of her best attempts at devotion to her husband and family, she was subjected to relentless criticism.

Forbidden by her husband to attend church, she sought God in His Word and worshiped Him in secret. She learned that even in the midst of her dreary circumstances she was "perfectly fine—within the safe hands of God."

How can we respond to difficult circumstances with acceptance and abandonment? The only way to have that same attitude is to believe that God's will is "good and acceptable and perfect" (Rom. 12:2), and to lay down our will and patiently submit to Him day by day.—D. H. R.

HE WHO ABANDONS HIMSELF TO GOD
WILL NEVER BE ABANDONED BY GOD.

"Follow Me, and I will make you become fishers of men."

MARK 1:17

The Son of God chose His first followers at an unlikely place. He didn't search the religious schools for the most learned scholars. He didn't look among the ranks of brilliant military leaders. Rather, Jesus went to the shores of Galilee and called out four common fishermen—Peter and Andrew, James, and John.

"Bad choice," some might say. "Uneducated. Tough characters. What would they know about starting a worldwide movement? They couldn't work a crowd if they had to."

Now, on behalf of fishermen everywhere, let me say that they have many positive traits. They must be resourceful, courageous, and patient. They must plan carefully and take care of their equipment. But I don't think that's why Jesus chose those men. I believe He wanted to demonstrate how God can transform ordinary people into "fishers of men" (Mark 1:16–17). God's work is often done by unlikely people from unlikely places—people like you and me.—D. C. E.

GOD USES ORDINARY PEOPLE TO DO EXTRAORDINARY WORK.

Whatever you want men to do to you, do also to them.

MATTHEW 7:12

The owner of a company was talking with one of his managers about an employee who was stealing from the firm. The owner, who was a follower of Christ, asked, "What do you think we should do about him?"

"Give him the ax!" replied the manager.

"Suppose he admits his wrongdoing and agrees to pay for what he's stolen," said the owner. "Why not let him keep his job? Isn't that how you would want to be treated?"

"Well, yeah," said the manager, "but that's not the real world!"

Jesus calls us to follow the rules of His world, which is the real world. His rules demand our integrity, responsibility, and accountability. When they are practiced, employees become more dependable and fulfilled.—D. J. D.

THE REWARD FOR HONEST LABOR IS ALWAYS GREATER THAN THE WAGES RECEIVED.

Jesus increased in wisdom and stature,
and in favor with God and men.

LUKE 2:52

I'll never forget Jake. His legs seemed too thin and spindly to hold him against the current of the river. His patched and discolored waders looked older than he was. His fishing vest was tattered and held together with safety pins; his ancient hat was battered and sweat-stained; his antiquated fly rod was scarred and taped.

I watched as he worked his way upstream to a patch of quiet water and began to cast. Then I took notice! He was fishing the same water I had fished earlier in the day and catching trout where I had caught none. Here was a man who could teach me a thing or two. All I had to do was ask.

We gain insight when we listen to those who have gone before and who know more than we do—insight we miss when our pride stands in the way. We're able to learn from others when we humble ourselves and acknowledge how little we know. Willingness to learn is a mark of those who are truly wise.—D. H. R.

IF YOU THINK YOU KNOW EVERYTHING, YOU HAVE A LOT TO LEARN.

God is our refuge and strength,
a very present help in trouble.

PSALM 46:1

Erma Bombeck wrote a column about the conflicts that sometimes occur as siblings divide family items after a parent has died. Whether it's the mixing bowls, grandma's quilts, or the Christmas ornaments, people are often convinced that they alone should have a certain item. Bombeck said she never wanted a TV set or a tote bag to remember her parents, because their true legacy to her was the way they lived, not what they left behind.

Those comments caused me to ask, "What kind of legacy would I like to leave my children?" I've concluded that I would like my kids to feel that their dad helped them learn where to go during the storms of life.

Three times in Psalm 46, the writer refers to the Lord as "our refuge" —a place of protection during times of danger or distress (vv. 1, 7, 11). If I learn to find shelter and strength in the Lord today, then my children have an example to follow and know where to turn. I'd be pleased if someday they would all say of that refuge they've found in the Lord: "Dad wanted me to have this."—D. C. M.

LIVING FOR THE LORD LEAVES A LASTING LEGACY.

The LORD gives wisdom;
from His mouth come knowledge and understanding.

PROVERBS 2:6

*P*rofitable Bible study involves more than just opening to a chapter and reading what's there. Here are six guidelines to help you make the most of your study of the Bible.

1. Set aside a regular time. Unless you schedule it, you'll neglect it.
2. Before you start reading, ask God for help and understanding.
3. Carefully think about what you are reading.
4. Before you decide what a passage means to you, try to understand what the author was saying to the original readers.
5. Write down at least one truth or principle you can put into practice.
6. Don't get discouraged. Some parts of the Bible are difficult to understand, but there's much that you can understand. And if you apply what you've learned, it will revolutionize your life.—H. W. R.

GEMS OF TRUTH ARE FOUND IN THE BIBLE
—BUT YOU MUST DIG FOR THEM.

We are all like an unclean thing,
and all our righteousnesses are like filthy rags.

ISAIAH 64:6

Two men were talking not long after they had become
Christians. One was a poor man from a godless background;
the other was from an affluent religious environment. After each man told
of his conversion, the man with the religious background asked the
other, "Why do you suppose you responded the first time you heard the
gospel, while so many years passed before I did?"

The poor man answered, "That's easy. Suppose someone came
along and offered to give each of us a brand-new suit. I'd jump at the
offer. My clothes are old and worn. But your closet is no doubt filled with
the finest of suits. That's the way it is with salvation. You were probably
satisfied with all your goodness, so it took you a long time to see the
need for God's garment of righteousness offered to you through Christ.
But I was deeply aware of my sinful condition, and I was eager to receive
forgiveness and cleansing."—R. W. D.

NO ONE IS GOOD ENOUGH TO SAVE HIMSELF;
NO ONE IS SO BAD THAT GOD CANNOT SAVE HIM.

When you pass through the waters, I will be with you.

Isaiah 43:2

I'll never forget my first experience using an automatic car wash. Approaching it with the dread of going to the dentist, I pushed the money into the slot, nervously checked and rechecked my windows, eased the car up to the line, and waited. Powers beyond my control began moving my car forward as if on a conveyor belt. There I was, cocooned inside, when a thunderous rush of water, soap, and brushes hit my car from all directions. *What if I get stuck in here or water crashes in?* I thought irrationally. Suddenly the waters ceased. After a blow-dry, my car was propelled into the outside world again, clean and polished.

In the midst of all this, I remembered stormy times in my life when it seemed I was on a conveyor belt, a victim of forces beyond my control. "Car-wash experiences," I now call them. I remembered that whenever I passed through deep waters my Redeemer had been with me, sheltering me against the rising tide (Isa. 43:2). When I came out on the other side, which I always did, I was able to say with joy and confidence, "He is a faithful God!"—J. E. Y.

A TUNNEL OF TESTING CAN PRODUCE A SHINING TESTIMONY.

"Truly I say to you that this poor widow has put in more than all."

LUKE 21:3

*S*omeone has calculated that if the widow's two mites had been deposited in a bank at four percent interest compounded semiannually, by today it would have grown to the sum of $4.8 billion trillion. What potential there is in such a small investment when it's left to grow for a long time!

In a more significant sense, that widow's two-mite investment continues to reproduce itself to this very day. Only eternity will reveal how many of God's people have been challenged by that woman's sacrifice, and have dared to follow her example.

Like the widow, the poorest and least-talented Christians can invest in eternity when what they give represents sacrifice, devotion, and love for Christ. Let's not underestimate the potential our small contributions can make to the cause of Christ. Only in eternity will this world's true millionaires be revealed. Will we be among them?—D. J. D.

**IF YOU CANNOT GIVE A MILLION,
YOU CAN GIVE THE WIDOW'S MITE.**

"I indeed baptize you with water;
but One mightier than I is coming."

LUKE 3:16

*D*ave Thomas, founder of Wendy's restaurants, appeared in more than 800 television commercials. He offered his homespun humor and "old-fashioned hamburgers" to a worldwide audience. Viewers saw him as friendly, funny, believable, and caring. In spite of his popularity, though, Thomas always said he was "the messenger, not the message."

That's a good word to remember as we speak about Christ to our friends and family. While our behavior should always be consistent with what we say, our goal is to point others to Jesus and not to ourselves. The apostle Paul said, "We do not preach ourselves, but Christ Jesus the Lord, and ourselves your bond servants for Jesus' sake" (2 Cor. 4:5).

Through our words and actions, we testify of Jesus Christ as Savior and Lord. We are His messengers, but He is the Message.—D. C. M.

WE WITNESS BEST FOR CHRIST
WHO SAY THE LEAST ABOUT OURSELVES.

Those who desire to be rich fall into temptation and a snare,
and into many foolish and harmful lusts.

1 TIMOTHY 6:9

The ancient Greek philosopher Socrates (469–399 B.C.) believed that if you are truly wise you will not be obsessed with possessions. Practicing to an extreme what he preached, he even refused to wear shoes. He loved to visit the marketplace, though, and gaze with admiration at the great abundance of wares on display. When a friend asked why he was so allured, he replied, "I love to go there and discover how many things I am perfectly happy without."

That type of attitude runs counter to the commercial messages that continually bombard our eyes and ears. Advertisers spend millions to tell us about all the latest products that we can't be happy without.

The apostle Paul advised his spiritual son Timothy, "Godliness with contentment is great gain. For we brought nothing into this world, and it is certain we can carry nothing out. And having food and clothing, with these we shall be content" (1 Tim. 6:6–8). Let's ask ourselves, "What am I truly happy without?"—V. C. G.

CONTENTMENT COMES NOT FROM GREAT WEALTH
BUT FROM FEW WANTS.

*"I endure all things for the sake of the elect,
that they also may obtain the salvation which is in Christ."*

2 TIMOTHY 2:10

It was the kind of moment that people have nightmares about. A tanker truck filled with 2,500 gallons of propane gas caught fire while parked at a fuel storage warehouse. The flames shot 30 to 40 feet out of the back of the truck and quickly spread to a loading dock. Several large tanks nearby were in danger of exploding.

At that point, the plant manager, after helping to rescue the badly burned driver, jumped into the cab and drove the blazing truck away from the warehouse. His quick action and courage saved lives.

The apostle Paul also risked his life on behalf of others (2 Tim. 2:10). He was stoned and left for dead (Acts 14:19). On another occasion he was mobbed, whipped, and imprisoned (Acts 16:22–23). Three times he was shipwrecked, and he was beaten many times with lashes and rods (2 Cor. 11:23–28). Why did Paul willingly endure such suffering? He was thinking in terms of eternal fire and eternal life, so he gladly undertook the risk.—M. R. D. II

IT'S RISKY TO GO OUT ON A LIMB—BUT THAT'S WHERE THE FRUIT IS.

Professing to be wise, they became fools.

ROMANS 1:22

In 1636, a group of Puritans founded Harvard University. Its motto was *Christo et Ecclesiae*, which means "For Christ and the Church." One of the school's guiding principles was this: "Everyone shall consider the main end of his life and studies, to know God and Jesus Christ, which is eternal life. John 17:3."

That prestigious center of learning and culture has long since abandoned its original spiritual intent. Even many Harvard Divinity School faculty members now regard its Christ-centered goal as narrow-minded and outdated.

But three hundred fifty years after the establishment of Harvard, the chief purpose of life is still and always will be, in the words of those colonial Puritans, "to know God and Jesus Christ, which is eternal life." Let us make that the main goal of our lives.—V. C. G.

TO KNOW LIFE'S PURPOSE, WE MUST KNOW LIFE'S CREATOR.

Christ also suffered once for sins, the just for the unjust,
that He might bring us to God.

1 PETER 3:18

*D*uring his years as mayor of New York City, Fiorello La
Guardia sometimes presided as judge in a night court. In
one case, a man was found guilty of stealing a loaf of bread. He pleaded
that he had committed that theft to feed his starving family. "The law is
the law," La Guardia declared. "I must therefore fine you $10." When the
man sadly confessed that he had no money, the judge took $10 out of his
wallet and paid the fine. He also asked each person in the courtroom to
contribute 50 cents to help the man.

At the heart of the gospel stands the cross of Jesus Christ. Its
message is so plain that even a child can understand it: Jesus took my
place and died instead of me. But its truth is so awesome that the wisest
of humans can't fully fathom its meaning.

As we look at the judge's compassion, we catch at least a glimpse
of God's measureless grace. The demands of the law were satisfied. The
judge himself paid the fine. The lawbreaker was set free and even blessed
with an undeserved gift. What a profound picture of our Savior!—V. C. G.

THE WAY TO FACE CHRIST AS JUDGE IS TO KNOW HIM AS SAVIOR.

Tribulation produces perseverance; and perseverance,
character; and character, hope.

ROMANS 5:3–4

ristlecone pines are the world's oldest living trees. Several are estimated to be 3,000 to 4,000 years old. In 1957, scientist Edmund Schulman found one he named "Methuselah." This ancient, gnarled pine is nearly 5,000 years old! It was an old tree when the Egyptians were building the pyramids.

Bristlecones grow atop the mountains of the western United States at elevations of 10,000 to 11,000 feet. They've been able to survive some of the harshest living conditions on earth: arctic temperatures, fierce winds, thin air, and little rainfall. Their brutal environment is actually one of the reasons they've survived for millennia. Hardship has produced extraordinary strength and staying power.

Paul taught that "tribulation produces . . . character" (Rom. 5:3–4). Adversity is part of the process that God uses to produce good results in our lives. Trouble, if it turns us to the Lord, could actually be the best thing for us. It leaves us wholly dependent on Him.—D. H. R.

GOD USES OUR DIFFICULTIES TO DEVELOP OUR CHARACTER.

Do not lie to one another,
since you have put off the old man with his deeds.

COLOSSIANS 3:9

A college football coach resigns after admitting he falsified his academic and athletic credentials. A career military officer confesses to wearing combat decorations he did not earn. A job applicant acknowledges that her stated experience in "food and beverage oversight" was actually making coffee each morning at the office.

Within each of us is a tendency to embellish the truth in order to impress others. Whether on a job résumé or in casual conversation, exaggeration comes naturally—but we pay a price. Small lies usually grow larger as we try to avoid discovery. Then we wonder how we ever got ourselves into such a predicament.

The Bible says, "Do not lie to one another, since you have put off the old man with his deeds, and have put on the new man who is renewed in knowledge according to the image of Him who created him" (Col. 3:9–10). In other words, if we've placed our faith in Jesus as our Savior, lying is inconsistent with what God expects us to be. The antidote to the poison of self-promotion is a growing Christ likeness—a spirit of mercy, kindness, humility, patience, forgiveness, and love.—D. C. M.

HONESTY MEANS NEVER HAVING TO LOOK OVER YOUR SHOULDER.

All things work together for good to those who love God.

ROMANS 8:28

Randy Alcorn, in a book he has co-authored with his wife Nanci, offers some insights on Romans 8:28. He quotes the New American Standard Bible translation of this verse: "God causes all things to work together for good." Randy points out that it doesn't say each individual thing is good, but that God works them together for good.

Recalling his boyhood days, Randy tells how he often watched his mother bake cakes. One day when she had all the ingredients set out—flour, sugar, baking powder, raw egg, vanilla—he sneaked a taste of each one. Except for the sugar, they all tasted horrible. Then his mother stirred them together and put the batter in the oven. "It didn't make sense to me," he recalls, "that the combination of individually distasteful things produced such a tasty product."

Randy concludes that God likewise "takes all the undesirable stresses in our lives, mixes them together, puts them under the heat of crisis, and produces a perfect result."—J. E. Y.

WHEN THINGS LOOK BAD, DON'T FORGET: GOD IS GOOD.

The tongue of the wise promotes health.

PROVERBS 12:18

A Greek philosopher asked his servant to cook the best dish possible. The servant, who was very wise, prepared a dish of tongue, saying, "It's the best of all dishes, for it reminds us that we may use the tongue to bless and express happiness, dispel sorrow, remove despair, and spread cheer."

Later the servant was asked to cook the worst dish possible. Again, he prepared a dish of tongue, saying, "It's the worst dish, for it reminds us that we may use the tongue to curse and break hearts, destroy reputations, create strife, and set families and nations at war."

Solomon wrote: "The tongue of the wise promotes health" (Prov. 12:18). It affirms and encourages others. The key word in that verse isn't *tongue* but *wise*. The tongue is not in control, but the person behind it is.—J. E. Y.

**WISDOM IS KNOWING WHEN TO SPEAK YOUR MIND
AND WHEN TO MIND YOUR SPEECH.**

*If anyone loves the world,
the love of the Father is not in him.*

1 JOHN 2:15

once read about an interesting method used by people in North Africa to catch monkeys. A hunter hollows out a gourd and makes a hole in its side just large enough for a monkey to insert his open hand. The gourd is then filled with nuts and tied to a tree.

The curious monkey is attracted by the smell of the nuts and reaches inside and grasps them. The hole in the gourd is too small, however, for the animal to withdraw his fist as long as it is tightly closed around the nuts. Because he refuses to release his prize, the unsuspecting monkey falls easy prey to his captor. Unwilling to relax his grasp, he actually traps himself!

Satan uses a similar method to ensnare us. He tempts us to grasp after more and more material possessions, which we think will bring us security. As long as we tenaciously hold on to them, we are enslaved. How relevant is the biblical warning, "Do not love the world or the things in the world" (1 John 2:15).—R. W. D.

**YOU CAN'T STORE UP TREASURES IN HEAVEN
IF YOU'RE HOLDING ON TO THE TREASURES OF EARTH.**

These words . . . shall be in your heart. . . .
You shall write them on the doorposts of your house.

DEUTERONOMY 6:6, 9

Shortly after Scottish preacher G. Campbell Morgan's wedding, his father visited the home the newlyweds had just furnished and decorated. After they had shown him the place with pride and satisfaction, he remarked, "Yes, it's very nice, but no one walking through here would know whether you belong to God or the devil!"

Morgan was shocked by his father's gruff but well-meaning comment. But he got the point. From that day forward, he made certain that in every room of his home there was some evidence of their faith in Christ.

Many believers make an effort to include reminders of God's grace and goodness in their homes. Just a Bible verse inscribed on a plaque or a tasteful work of art with a Christian theme may be all that is needed to encourage family members to serve and praise the Lord.—H. G. B.

WHAT'S IN YOUR HOME MIRRORS WHAT'S IN YOUR HEART.

Behold, the tabernacle of God is with men,
and He will dwell with them, and they shall be His people.

REVELATION 21:3

Cartoonists often depict those who have gone to heaven as
white-robed, ghostly forms floating among the clouds or sitting
on golden stairs playing harps. What a far cry from the picture we find in
the Bible!

In 1 Corinthians 15, we read that our resurrection bodies,
although not subject to death, will be real and tangible—not mere
apparitions. And Revelation 21:1–5 tells us that God will bring about "a
new heaven and a new earth." He will bring down "the city of the living
God, the heavenly Jerusalem" (Heb. 12:22), and set it upon the new
earth as the "New Jerusalem." It is described as having streets, walls,
gates, and even a river and trees (Rev. 22:1–5).

Life in that city will be wonderful, free from all the debilitating
effects of sin. There will be no more death, sorrow, mourning, and
pain, for God will make "all things new." But best of all, He Himself
will come to live among us, making possible a new level of intimacy
with Him.—H. V. L.

THE MORE WE LOVE JESUS THE MORE WE'LL LONG FOR HEAVEN.

I have come that they may have life,
and that they may have it more abundantly.

JOHN 10:10

A veteran mountain climber was sharing his experiences with a group of novices preparing for their first major climb. He had conquered many of the world's most difficult peaks, so he was qualified to give them some advice. "Remember this," he said, "your goal is to experience the exhilaration of the climb and the joy of reaching . . . the peak. Each step draws you closer to the top. If your purpose for climbing is just to avoid death, your experience will be minimal."

I see an application to the Christian's experience. Jesus did not call us to live the Christian life just to escape hell. It's not to be a life of minimum joy and fulfillment, but a life that is full and overflowing. Our purpose in following Christ should not be merely to avoid eternal punishment. If that's our primary motivation, we are missing the wonders and joys and victories of climbing higher and higher with Jesus.—D. C. E.

WE GET THE MOST OUT OF LIFE WHEN WE LIVE FOR CHRIST.

He who has begun a good work in you will complete it.

PHILIPPIANS 1:6

In his book *Laugh Again,* Charles Swindoll suggests three common "joy stealers"—worry, stress, and fear. Swindoll says that to resist these "joy stealers" we must embrace the same confidence that Paul expressed in his letter to the Philippians. After giving thanks for the Philippian believers (1:3–5), the apostle assured them "that He who has begun a good work in you will complete it until the day of Jesus Christ" (v. 6).

Whatever causes you worry, stress, and fear cannot ultimately keep God from continuing His work in you. With this confidence we can begin each day knowing that He is in control. We can leave everything in His hands. Resist those "joy stealers" by renewing your confidence in God each morning. Then relax and rejoice.—J. E. Y.

HAPPINESS DEPENDS ON HAPPENINGS; JOY DEPENDS ON JESUS.

*You must continue in the things which you
have learned and been assured of.*

2 TIMOTHY 3:14

*P*art of the training to be a US Secret Service agent includes learning to detect counterfeit money. Agents-in-training make a thorough study of the genuine bills—not the phonies—so that they can spot the fake currency immediately because of its contrast to the real thing.

The child of God can learn a lesson from this. While it is helpful to study false religions and be fully aware of their dangerous dogmas, the best defense against such error is to be so familiar with God's Word that whenever we encounter error, we will spot it at once and won't fall for it.

Let's be diligent in our study of the Word of God. Then, instead of falling into error, we will stand firmly on the truth.—R. W. D.

UNDERSTAND BIBLE DOCTRINE AND YOU WILL DETECT COUNTERFEITS.

Moses brought Israel from the Red Sea;
then they went out into the Wilderness of Shur.

EXODUS 15:22

After God opened the Red Sea for His people, then released the waters to overwhelm Pharaoh's pursuing army, there was a great celebration of praise to the Lord (Exod. 15:1–21). But then it was time to move on in the journey toward the land of promise. "So Moses brought Israel from the Red Sea; then they went out into the Wilderness of Shur" (v. 22). There they traveled for three days without finding water, and they began to complain.

In the divine plan, supernatural intervention is not an end in itself, but it is a means of teaching us that we can always trust and obey the leadership of Almighty God. Will we listen to His voice and obey His Word? If He leads us through the sea, will He not also guide us to a well?

The stunning events recorded in Exodus show that it's possible to experience God's power yet remain spiritually unchanged. To keep that from happening to us, let's use the sweet memory of yesterday's miracle to encourage a bigger step of faith today.—D. C. M.

THE GOD WHO DELIVERED US YESTERDAY
IS WORTHY OF OBEDIENCE TODAY.

We conclude that a man is justified
by faith apart from the deeds of the law.

ROMANS 3:28

A poll for *U.S. News & World Report* asked 1,000 adults their opinion about who would likely make it into heaven. At the top of that list, to no one's surprise, was a well-known religious figure. Several celebrities were also listed. But it was surprising to me that of the people being surveyed, 87 percent thought they themselves were likely to get into heaven.

I can't help but wonder what qualifications for admission into heaven they had in mind. Virtuous character? Giving generous contributions to deserving charities? Following an orthodox creed? Attending church and being involved in religious activities? Commendable as these qualities may be, they miss by an eternity the one thing God requires for entrance into heaven—a personal commitment to Jesus Christ as Savior and Lord (John 1:12; 1 Tim. 2:5).

Are you confident that you're headed for heaven? You can be—but only if you're trusting in Jesus.—V. C. G.

**JESUS TOOK OUR PLACE ON THE CROSS
TO GIVE US A PLACE IN HEAVEN.**

He gives power to the weak.

ISAIAH 40:29

was watching an eagle in flight when for no apparent reason it began spiraling upward. With its powerful wings, the great bird soared ever higher, dissolved into a tiny dot, and then disappeared.

Its flight reminded me of Isaiah's uplifting words: "Even the youths shall faint and be weary, and the young men shall utterly fall, but those who wait on the LORD shall renew their strength; they shall mount up with wings like eagles" (40:30–31).

Life's heartbreaks and tragedies can put an end to our resilience, our endurance, our nerve, and bring us to our knees. But if we put our hope in the Lord and rely on Him, He renews our strength. The key to our endurance lies in the exchange of our limited resources for God's limitless strength. Oh, what an exchange—God's infinite strength for our finite weakness! And it is ours for the asking.—D. H. R.

GOD GIVES STRENGTH IN PROPORTION TO THE STRAIN.

Work out your own salvation with fear and trembling.

PHILIPPIANS 2:12

Every January, health club memberships dramatically increase and exercise rooms become crowded with what some people call "the New Year's resolution crowd." Fitness regulars know that by March many of the newcomers will be gone. "They don't see results as quickly as they think they will," says one club director. "People don't realize it takes a lot of work and perseverance to get in shape."

It's a phenomenon we experience in the spiritual realm as well. Author Eugene Peterson notes that in a culture that loves speed and efficiency, "it is not difficult . . . to get a person interested in the message of the gospel; it is terrifically difficult to sustain the interest." To follow Christ faithfully, Peterson says, requires "a long obedience in the same direction."—D. C. M.

**FAITH IN CHRIST IS NOT JUST A SINGLE STEP
BUT A LIFE OF WALKING WITH HIM.**

O LORD, how manifold are Your works!
In wisdom You have made them all.

PSALM 104:24

The common honey bee organizes a little city inside its hive. It builds 10,000 cells for honey, 12,000 for the larvae, and a special chamber for the queen mother. When temperatures inside the hive become so warm that the honey is in danger of being lost through the softened wax, squads of sentinels automatically take their places at the hive's entrance. Their fast-beating wings create a cooling system that rivals the electric fan.

French scientist René Antoine Ferchault de Réaumur examined a wasp's nest in 1719 and noted that it seemed to be made of a type of crude pasteboard. After further investigation, he discovered that most of the material was obtained from tree fibers. As a result of this study, the first successful production of paper from wood pulp was achieved.

There are millions of similar wonders in our world, more than enough to convince anyone with an open mind and a searching heart that a great, all-wise Creator brought them into being. He deserves our heartfelt worship.—H. G. B.

THE NATURAL WORLD BEARS THE SIGNATURE
OF A SUPERNATURAL CREATOR.

*Blessed be the God and Father of our Lord Jesus Christ,
who has blessed us with every spiritual blessing.*

EPHESIANS 1:3

When disaster strikes, people are exceedingly generous in their outpouring of assistance. After the terrorist attacks in September 2001, New York City was flooded with an estimated $75 million worth of towels, blankets, flashlights, water bottles, canned beans, shovels, toothpaste, stuffed animals, radios, rubber boots, and thousands of other items. There was so much stuff that those affected could not use it all.

This reminds me of what happens when we turn in faith to Christ as our Savior. We were facing a personal disaster. Our sins put us in danger of an eternity of separation from God. The future was dark, hopeless. Then Jesus stepped in and offered rescue. When we trusted Him, our heavenly Father lavished us with spiritual riches. Now we have more blessings than we can possibly use up. We are part of God's family (Eph. 1:5). We have "redemption" and "the forgiveness of sins" (v. 7). We are heirs of the One who owns everything (v. 11). Our inheritance is sealed by the Holy Spirit (vv. 13–14).

What a generous, thoughtful God we serve!—J. D. B.

GOD'S GENEROUS GIVING DESERVES THANKFUL LIVING.

February

He is the head of the body, the church,
. . . that in all things He may have the preeminence.

COLOSSIANS 1:18

John Henry Jowett, the great English preacher, liked to tell about the time he attended the coronation of Edward VII. Westminster Abbey was filled with royalty. Jowett said, "Much bowing and respect was shown as nobility of high rank entered the cathedral." When the king arrived, however, a hush came over the audience. Every eye was on him, and no longer did the dignitaries of lower status receive the gaze and interest of the people. All the subjects fixed their attention on their royal leader.

This is the way it should be in the life of a Christian. Jesus is the King of kings, and He deserves the place of highest prominence. Our devotion is always to be centered on Him. May we never lose sight of King Jesus who deserves our praise and worship. Let us join the heavenly voices and say, "You are worthy, O Lord, to receive glory and honor" (Rev. 4:11). Yes, Christ is the preeminent One!—R. W. D.

FOCUSING ON CHRIST PUTS EVERYTHING ELSE IN PERSPECTIVE.

*"Whoever desires to come after Me, let him deny himself,
and take up his cross, and follow Me."*

MARK 8:34

During World War II, B-17 bombers made long flights from the US mainland to the Pacific island of Saipan. When they landed there, the planes were met by a jeep bearing the sign: "Follow Me!" That little vehicle guided the giant planes to their assigned places in the parking area.

One pilot, who by his own admission was not a religious man, made an insightful comment: "That little jeep with its quaint sign always reminds me of Jesus. He was [a lowly] peasant, but the giant men and women of our time would be lost without His direction."

Centuries after our Savior walked the streets and hills of Israel, the world with all its advances still needs His example and instruction. How do we follow Jesus' ways? First of all, we turn from our sin and entrust our lives to Him as our Savior and Lord. Then, we seek His will in His Word each day and put it into practice by the power of the Holy Spirit within us.—V. C. G.

TO FIND YOUR WAY THROUGH LIFE, FOLLOW JESUS.

How sweet are Your words to my taste,
sweeter than honey to my mouth!

PSALM 119:103

Although his parents were Christians, Cyrus didn't have much use for the Bible. He was more interested in Shakespeare and history. By the time he was twelve, he had charted the entire course of human civilization. But the Bible? He was not interested.

Cyrus grew up to be a respected lawyer. When he was thirty-six, a friend came to his office and confronted him about why he was not a Christian. This conversation led him to faith in Jesus Christ. Realizing he knew almost nothing about the Bible, Cyrus determined to know God's Word better than anything else. Soon it became to him "sweeter than honey" (Ps. 119:103). Thirty years later, in 1909, *The Scofield Reference Bible* was published. The great work of Cyrus Ingerson Scofield was complete.

God's Word is a vital part of our growth as Christians. It's the way we learn what God expects of us, and the way to know God Himself.—J. D. B.

ONE OF THE MARKS OF A WELL-FED SOUL IS A WELL-READ BIBLE.

With joy you will draw water from the wells of salvation.

ISAIAH 12:3

A guide in Israel was preparing to lead a tour into the desert. His instructions to the group were simple and clear: "If you do not have these two items, I will not allow you to accompany us. You must have a broad-brimmed hat and a full bottle of water. These will protect you from the sun, and from the thirst caused by wind and dryness."

Water. It's essential to survival. That's why a woman came to the well in Samaria (John 4:7). She came at noon, when few people were there. Jesus offered her water far better than that from the well. He had "living water," which only He could give (vv. 10, 13–14). I believe she took that water and was spiritually cleansed, for she told everyone what she had experienced: "Come, see a Man who told me all things that I ever did. Could this be the Christ?" (v. 29).

Do you need the cleansing and refreshment Christ offers? He is waiting to satisfy you with the "living water" of salvation and the gift of everlasting life.—D. C. E.

JESUS IS THE ONLY FOUNTAIN WHO CAN SATISFY THE THIRSTY SOUL.

"I and My Father are one."

JOHN 10:30

*I*t is said that Augustine (354–430) was walking on the ocean shore one day and pondering the mystery of the Trinity. He saw a little boy who was playing with a seashell. The youngster scooped a hole in the sand, then went down to the waves and filled his shell with water and poured it into the hole he had made. Augustine asked, "What are you doing?" The boy replied, "I am going to pour the sea into the hole." Then Augustine thought, *That is what I have been trying to do. Standing at the ocean of infinity, I have attempted to grasp it with my finite mind.*

The concept of the Trinity does not fit the framework of common logic. But this is no reason to say it is the invention of theologians. To declare that the one and only God has made Himself known as Father, Son, and Holy Spirit is simply an attempt to define what the Scriptures teach (John 10:29–30; Acts 5:3–4).

To commit our lives to this triune God is to begin to see with the eye of faith His greatness as our Creator, Redeemer, and Sustainer. Doesn't it make sense that the One we worship should be vastly greater than our limited understanding?—D. J. D.

**THE IDEA OF A TRIUNE GOD STAGGERS THE MIND,
BUT TO KNOW HIM SATISFIES THE HEART.**

*"The water that I shall give him will become in him
a fountain of water springing up into everlasting life."*

JOHN 4:14

Clyde Peterson raises beef cattle and Rambouillet sheep on a spread that covers thousands of acres in eastern Wyoming. Clyde told me that the success of a ranch like his, where grass is sparse and high winds blow, depends on two factors: windmills and fences. The fences are essential because they restrict the livestock to certain grazing areas while allowing grass to grow in other sections. And the windmills pump the life-giving water for the animals.

Come to think of it, fences and water are basic to a Christian's spiritual health as well. God's "fences" are the laws and principles of His Word, like God's commandments in Exodus 20 and Matthew 22:37–40, and the exhortations of Galatians 5:16–21. Our "water" comes from Christ, who gives us an ever-present flow of spiritual refreshment "springing up into everlasting life" (John 4:14). We have the privilege to graze in God's "pastures" and to drink freely of the Water of Life.—D. C. E.

IF THE LORD IS YOUR SHEPHERD, YOU HAVE EVERYTHING YOU NEED.

Faithful are the wounds of a friend.

PROVERBS 27:6

Charles Colson, one of President Nixon's closest aides during the Watergate cover-up, became a Christian. In an article titled "The Problem of Power," he wrote, "Christians need to hold one another accountable. Although I know intellectually how vulnerable I am to pride and power, I am the last one to know when I succumb to their seduction. That's why spiritual lone rangers are so dangerous—and why we must depend on trusted brothers and sisters who love us enough to tell us the truth."

Paul confronted Peter face-to-face for his hypocrisy (Gal. 2:11–14). How embarrassing for Peter! But he needed the rebuke. Peter knew from his previous boasting and denial of Christ that he couldn't trust his own estimate of himself.

All of us must come to that realization sooner or later. Don't be a spiritual lone ranger. Turn yourself in.—D. J. D.

TRUE FRIENDS SPEAK THE TRUTH IN LOVE.

FEBRUARY 8

Therefore, having been justified by faith,
we have peace with God.

ROMANS 5:1

I read about a judge who wants to set the record straight. He feels he made a mistake in convicting a young man of a misdemeanor weapons charge fifteen years ago. Since he doesn't know how to reach him, he paid $500 to run an ad in a newspaper. Details relating to the wrong decision were included, along with the judge's name and telephone number. The article also said, "If the man calls, the judge plans to file a writ of *error coram nobis*—admitting that his ruling was faulty and asking another court to erase the conviction."

There is one Judge, however, who never makes mistakes. He is God. He has declared us all guilty of sin and under the sentence of death (Rom. 3:23; 6:23). But even though He is perfectly just, and though we deserve our punishment, He delights in clearing the record of our sins.

How could He do that? Because of His great compassion, He sent His own Son into the world to die for us and pay the penalty we deserved.—R. W. D.

ONLY GOD THE PERFECT JUDGE CAN DECLARE THE GUILTY PERFECT.

"I am the Alpha and the Omega,
the Beginning and the End," says the Lord.

REVELATION 1:8

The meaning of the words *Alpha* and *Omega*—terms that refer to the first and last letters of the Greek alphabet—is fairly easy to understand. Like A and Z, they simply mean "the beginning" and "the end." In life, we understand these concepts. Things begin . . . things end. Jobs start . . . jobs stop. Decades come . . . decades go. Birth . . . death.

But there is something special and unique about the words *Alpha* and *Omega* as they appear in Revelation (1:8, 11; 21:6; 22:13). Jesus Christ used those terms to describe Himself—terms that refer to His deity. Jesus, the *Alpha*, had no beginning. He existed before time, before the creation of the universe (John 1:1). And as the *Omega*, He is not the "end" as we know it. He will continue to exist into the everlasting, never-ending future.

It's mind-boggling and awe-inspiring—this view of our Lord. He's the one "who is and who was and who is to come" (Rev. 1:8). He deserves our praise, our lives, our all!—J. D. B.

FOR TIME AND FOR ETERNITY, JESUS IS ALL WE NEED.

Let every man be swift to hear,
slow to speak, slow to wrath.

JAMES 1:19

The desert jackrabbit has huge ears. They not only improve the animal's hearing, but they also serve as radiators to keep its body temperature regulated. The hare has to rely on this unique cooling system because it doesn't take in enough water in the desert for perspiration to do the cooling.

You may think I'm stretching the point a bit, but there's a sense in which we also need to have "radiator ears." Look again at today's text. To keep from becoming overheated emotionally, we must have ears "large enough" to hear all the facts about a particular situation.

Rather than getting all steamed up over something we hear, we should be very sure we have a good understanding of what is really being said. Only then can we obey God and follow His example. He knows all the facts, and the Scripture says He is "slow to anger, and abounding in mercy" (Ps. 103:8).—M. R. D. II

KEEP A COOL HEAD AND A WARM HEART.

If anyone sins, we have an Advocate with the Father,
Jesus Christ the righteous.

1 JOHN 2:1

Inventor Charles Kettering has suggested that we must learn to fail intelligently. He gave these suggestions for turning failure into success: (1) Honestly face defeat; never fake success. (2) Exploit the failure; don't waste it. Learn all you can from it. (3) Never use failure as an excuse for not trying again.

Kettering's practical wisdom holds a deeper meaning for the Christian. The Holy Spirit is constantly working in us to accomplish "His good pleasure" (Phil. 2:13), so we know that failure is never final. We can't reclaim lost time. And we can't always make things right, although we should try. Some consequences of our sins can never be reversed. But we can make a new start, because Jesus died to pay the penalty for all our sins and is our "Advocate with the Father" (1 John 2:1).

Knowing how to benefit from failure is the key to continued growth in grace.—D. J. D.

FAILURE IS NEVER FINAL FOR THOSE WHO BEGIN AGAIN WITH GOD.

Even so must the Son of Man be lifted up,
that whoever believes in Him should not perish but have eternal life.

JOHN 3:14–15

In April 2002, along with thousands of others in London, I filed past the casket of Britain's Queen Mother as her body lay in state. In the muffled silence of Westminster Hall, I was struck by the sight of the magnificent crown resting on top of the coffin, and the cross standing nearby—symbols of her life and faith. We had come to pay our respects to a much-loved member of the royal family. But on that night it was clear to me that the cross of the Lord Jesus Christ matters far more than any crown.

For all who trust in Christ, the cross symbolizes our hope both in life and in death. No matter what positions of power we may inherit or achieve, none will follow us beyond the grave. But Christ is the giver of abundant life now and forever.

The cross speaks of forgiveness and of peace with God. It points to the merits of Christ and not our own. As we step through the doorway of death, we must lay aside our "earthly crowns." Our only hope is to cling to our Savior, who died so that we could have everlasting life.—D. C. M.

CALVARY'S CROSS IS THE ONLY BRIDGE TO ETERNAL LIFE.

I will go in the strength of the Lord GOD.

PSALM 71:16

In his famous painting titled *A Helping Hand*, Emile Renouf depicted an old fisherman seated in a boat, with a young girl beside him. Both the elderly gentleman and the child have their hands on a huge oar. The fisherman is looking down fondly and admiringly at the girl. Apparently the man has told the child that she may assist him in rowing the boat, and in her desire to help she feels as though she is doing a great share of the task. However, it's obvious that it's his strong, muscular arms that are moving the heavy oar through the water.

I see a parable in this painting. Christ has granted to us the privilege of sharing in His work here on earth. We must never forget, however, that we cannot perform our tasks through our abilities alone, but only as God works in and through us. While He directs us to put our hand on the oar, we must ever be aware of the ultimate source of our power. He is the strength of our life! There can be no true progress spiritually without the power of the Holy Spirit to undergird our life and all that we do.—H. G. B.

**OUR GREATEST WEAKNESS MAY BE
OUR FAILURE TO RELY ON GOD'S STRENGTH.**

*As for man, his days are like grass; as a flower of the field,
so he flourishes. For the wind passes over it, and it is gone.*

PSALM 103:15–16

*Y*ears ago, a young boy wandered from case to case in a
candy store, trying to decide what to buy. His mother, tired of
waiting, called, "Hurry up and spend your money! We must be going."
To this he replied, "But Mom, I only have one penny, so I've got to spend
it carefully."

So too, we have only one life to live, so we must "spend it carefully."

In underscoring the brevity of life, the Bible uses many illustrations,
among them that of a flower. A flower is a thing of loveliness. But what
strikes me most about a flower is that its beauty is so brief.

Because our days on earth are few, we should make the most of
our "flowering time." The nectar of the love of God in our heart should
attract people to the Savior. Your life is brief—make it lovely!—H. G. B.

USING YOUR FEW DAYS WISELY CAN MAKE AN ETERNAL DIFFERENCE.

Become complete. . . .
And the God of love and peace will be with you.

2 CORINTHIANS 13:11

Musician Ken Medema was born blind, but his parents determined to treat him as a normal child. They taught him to play games, ride a bike, and water-ski. They weren't denying his condition; they were affirming his worth as a person. Growing up with that kind of love, Ken developed an inner wholeness that almost made him forget his disability.

One day on campus, he accidentally bumped into another blind student who said, "Hey, watch it. Don't you know I'm blind?" Instead of mentioning his own handicap, Ken apologized. "I'm sorry. I didn't see you."

As Christians, we too bump into tough situations in which our weaknesses are revealed. Unlike Ken, however, we often react immaturely and use our weaknesses as an excuse. "After all, I'm not perfect," we argue. But it's our responsibility to make the needed adjustments. God's part is to keep on affirming His love for us.—D. J. D.

TO GAIN SPIRITUAL STRENGTH,
WE MUST ACKNOWLEDGE OUR WEAKNESS.

*"If anyone desires to come after Me, let him deny himself,
and take up his cross daily, and follow Me."*

LUKE 9:23

he cross in Roman times was designed for death. It had no
other use. So what did Jesus mean when He said that anyone
who wants to follow Him must "take up his cross daily"? He wasn't saying
that we must all be crucified. The "cross" to which He was referring is the
act of putting to death our own heart's desires and quietly submitting to
God's will.

Such dying is denying our need for larger homes, more compliant
children, more accommodating mates. It's putting up with misunderstanding, embarrassment, and loss of esteem. It's accepting our
unchangeable circumstances.

Jesus said we must take up our cross *daily*. We are to rise each
morning and cheerfully, bravely shoulder our load, because there is
something else that is "daily." It is the continuous, sufficient grace of the
One whose strength is made perfect in our weakness.—D. H. R.

IN ACCEPTANCE WE FIND PEACE.

"Woe is me, for I am undone!
. . . My eyes have seen the King, the LORD of hosts."

ISAIAH 6:5

Just a few miles from New Mexico's Carlsbad Caverns is Lechuguilla Cave. Explorers who have descended into its interior describe a wonderland whose beauty is beyond almost anything they have ever seen. One geologist noted, "Everything is alien. . . . I've been in caves that are so beautiful that you just have to leave. You just can't take it." That's an interesting dilemma for explorers, isn't it? To be surrounded by beauty that is overwhelming to the eyes.

Their experience gives us a clue to the problem we have with understanding a holy God. He is so arrayed in splendor, so pure in His goodness, and so beautiful in His character that our sin-darkened eyes cannot bear to look on Him. We cannot endure His glory.

This was the experience of two people in the Old Testament. When Moses asked to see God's glory, the Almighty had to shield him from seeing His face (Exod. 33:18–23). And when Isaiah caught a glimpse of God's majesty, he cried out, "Woe is me, for I am undone!" (Isa. 6:5).—M .R. D. II

GOD'S AWESOME PRESENCE IS BOTH CONVICTING AND COMFORTING.

[The devil] is a liar and the father of it.

JOHN 8:44

It was dusk. My wife and I had just strolled across the famous Charles Bridge in Prague when a man approached us with a wad of money in his hand. "Forty-two Czech korunas for one dollar," he said. The official rate was about 35Ks for one US dollar. So I exchanged 50 dollars for 2,100 Czech korunas.

That evening I told my son about my good fortune. "Dad, I should have told you," he apologized. "Never exchange money on the street." We looked at the bills. The 100K note was a good Czech bill, but the two 1,000K bills were worthless. They looked like Czech money but were Bulgarian notes no longer in circulation. I had been deceived—and robbed!

Satan employs similar tactics (John 8:44). He capitalizes on the deceitfulness of sin, using its "passing pleasures" (Heb. 11:25) to hide the pain that always follows. Our best defense against that deception is to have a growing knowledge of God's Word: "Your Word I have hidden in my heart, that I might not sin against You" (Ps. 119:11). —D. J. D.

GOD'S TRUTH UNCOVERS SATAN'S LIES.

You have need of endurance, so that after you have done the will of God,
you may receive the promise.

HEBREWS 10:36

Scottish physician A. J. Cronin (1896–1981) was forced by illness to take a leave of absence from his medical practice. He then decided to write a novel. But when half done, he became disheartened and threw his manuscript into a garbage can.

Totally discouraged, Cronin was walking the Scottish Highlands and saw a man digging in a bog, trying to drain it for use as a pasture. As Cronin talked with him, the man said, "My father dug at this bog and never made a pasture. But my father knew and I know that it's only by digging you can make a pasture. So I keep on digging."

Rebuked and remotivated, Cronin went home, picked his manuscript out of the garbage can, and finished it. That novel, Hatter's Castle, sold three million copies. Cronin left his medical practice and became a world-famous writer.

At times, you and I may feel trapped by circumstances that demand patience and persistence. Are we willing to keep digging away at whatever "bog" God has assigned to us?—V. C. G.

IN SERVING THE LORD, IT'S ALWAYS TOO SOON TO QUIT.

I am not ashamed of the gospel of Christ,
for it is the power of God to salvation.

ROMANS 1:16

Peter V. Deison, in his book *The Priority of Knowing God*, tells about Ramad, a man in India who was a member of a gang of robbers. On one occasion, while burglarizing a house, Ramad noticed a small black book containing very thin pages just right for making cigarettes. So he took it. Each evening he tore out a page, rolled it around some tobacco, and had a smoke. Noticing that the small words on the pages were in his language, he began to read them before rolling his cigarettes. One evening after reading a page, he knelt on the ground and asked the Lord Jesus to forgive his sins and to save him. He then turned himself in to the police, much to their amazement. Ramad the bandit became a prisoner of Jesus Christ. And in the prison where he served his sentence, he led many others to the Savior.

What was the book he had been reading? It was a Bible. The Holy Spirit took "the gospel of Christ" and it became to Ramad "the power of God to salvation."—R. W. D.

THE POWER OF OUR WITNESS COMES FROM
THE POWER OF THE GOSPEL.

FEBRUARY 21

When they began to sing and to praise, the LORD set
ambushes against the people . . . who had come against Judah.

2 CHRONICLES 20:22

Visitors to the Military Museum in Istanbul, Turkey, can hear
stirring music that dates back to the early years of the Ottoman
Empire. Whenever their troops marched off to war, bands accompanied
them. Centuries earlier, worship singers led the people of Judah into
battle, but there was a big difference. Whereas the Ottomans used music
to instill self-confidence in their soldiers, the Jews used it to express their
confidence in God.

Threatened by huge armies, King Jehoshaphat of Judah knew that
his people were powerless to defend themselves. So he cried out to God
for help (2 Chron. 20:12). The Lord answered, "Do not be afraid nor
dismayed . . . , for the battle is not yours, but God's" (v. 15). Jehoshaphat
responded by worshiping and then by appointing singers to lead the
army (vv. 18, 21). As the people sang, "Praise the LORD, for His mercy
endures forever," God routed their enemies (vv. 22–24).

No matter what battles we may face today, the Lord will help us
when we cry out to Him. Instead of retreating in fear, we can march
ahead with confidence in God's power and sing praise to Him.—J. A. L.

PRAISE IS THE VOICE OF FAITH.

Your Word is a lamp to my feet and a light to my path.

PSALM 119:105

Several years ago I heard about a six-point plan for getting something out of almost any passage of Scripture. It can make your Bible-reading time an opportunity to enjoy God and His message. Read a passage of Scripture and then ask yourself these questions:

- ➢ What did I like?
- ➢ What did I not like?
- ➢ What did I not understand?
- ➢ What did I learn about God?
- ➢ What should I do?
- ➢ What phrase can I take with me today?

This method can help to renew your appreciation for the Bible. Then you, too, will be able to say that God's Word is "the rejoicing of my heart" (Ps. 119:111).—J. D. B.

THE BIBLE ISN'T A DRY BOOK IF YOU KNOW ITS AUTHOR.

*"In the world you will have tribulation;
but be of good cheer, I have overcome the world."*

JOHN 16:33

There's a lake near our home in the mountains that is known for good fishing. To get there, I had to hike two miles up a steep ridge—a hard climb for an old-timer like me. But then I discovered that it's possible to drive within a half-mile of the lake. I spent most of a day driving several mountain roads until I found the one that got me the closest. Then I carefully mapped the road so I could find it again.

Several months later, I drove the road again. I came to a section that was much worse than I remembered—rocky, rutted, and steep. I wondered if I had missed a turn, so I stopped and checked my map. There, penciled alongside the stretch on which I was driving, were the words: "Rough and steep. Hard going." I was on the right road.

Jesus said, "In the world you will have tribulation" (John 16:33). So we shouldn't be surprised if our path becomes difficult, nor should we believe we've taken a wrong turn. We can "be of good cheer" because Jesus also said that in Him we can have peace, for He has "overcome the world" (v. 33).—D. H. R.

FOLLOWING JESUS IS ALWAYS RIGHT—BUT NOT ALWAYS EASY.

Pour out your heart before Him; God is a refuge for us.

PSALM 62:8

Several years ago I had just returned home, weary, alone, and at my wit's end. As I began pouring out my woes before God, I suddenly stopped myself and said, "Father, forgive me. I'm treating You like a counselor!" But the torrent of words flowed on, followed by the same embarrassing apology. Then God's Spirit whispered deep within, "I am your Great Counselor."

But of course! Hadn't He, the Creator of my physical and spiritual makeup, also created the emotional part of me? How reasonable, then, to spread out my ragged feelings before Him. Then came His comforting, corrective counsel, ministered skillfully by the Holy Spirit through His Word. My problems didn't evaporate. But I could rest in God alone. I was at peace again.

Never hesitate to pour out your heart to God. In your day of trouble, you'll find that prayer is the shortest route between your heart and God's.—J. E. Y.

**GOD FILLS OUR HEART WITH PEACE
WHEN WE POUR OUT OUR HEART TO HIM.**

Why are you cast down, O my soul?
. . . Hope in God, for I shall yet praise Him.

PSALM 42:5

In his book *The Good News About Worry*, William Backus recommends "truthful self-talk." He tells about Hester, who wanted to spend time with her grandchildren in another city but was afraid to fly. Finally she began telling herself, "Hester, you are safer in a commercial plane than in a car. If it should crash, it will only land you in heaven. Buy that ticket and get going." Hester eventually boarded a plane and visited her grandchildren.

The writer of Psalm 42 engaged in a similar kind of self-talk. He was in the northern part of the country and could not go to the temple at Jerusalem where he longed to be a part of the worshiping community. The people around him did not share his yearning, and they taunted him. He was deeply despondent. But instead of giving up in despair, he told himself that circumstances would change (vv. 5, 11), and that God would make His presence felt by day and by night even in the north country (v. 8). As he talked to himself about the truths of God's character, he was encouraged and strengthened.—H. V. L.

SELF-TALK IS MOST HELPFUL WHEN YOU
TALK TO YOURSELF ABOUT GOD.

[Wisdom] . . . is a tree of life to those who take hold of her.

PROVERBS 3:18

In a biting comment, one philosopher said of another that he was "the greatest of thinkers and the most petty of men." We admire individuals of high intelligence, but we certainly wouldn't want that statement to be said about us. Better by far to be an ordinary person who by God's grace reflects Christ's character. Better not to be a mental giant who is spiritually petty.

Intelligence and knowledge are God's gifts, and we can admire them. But we must remember that a good heart and godly character are more to be desired than brainpower, and that love is the most praiseworthy of gifts (1 Cor. 13:13).

Even though we may respect friends who are blessed with keen minds, we know that wisdom from the Lord is what we really need.
—V. C. G.

YOU CAN GAIN KNOWLEDGE ON YOUR OWN,
BUT WISDOM COMES FROM GOD.

Keep your heart with all diligence,
for out of it spring the issues of life.

PROVERBS 4:23

I read about a Detroit man who couldn't find his house. He had gone to the right address but all he found was an empty lot. Completely baffled, he asked the *Detroit Free Press* to help him figure out what was going on. A newspaper reporter learned that not only was the house gone, but the deed to the empty lot was in someone else's name.

What had happened? For one thing, a few years had passed since the homeowner had left the city without providing a forwarding address. In addition, he had failed to make arrangements for someone to keep the property in repair. So the house was torn down because a city ordinance called for the removal of neighborhood eyesores.

The homeowner's neglect illustrates the practical truth that neglect leads to loss. This principle also applies to our daily walk with God. If we neglect our times of prayer and fellowship with the Lord, our relationship with Him will deteriorate. We would never want that to happen. We need to establish priorities that honor God.—M .R. D. II

IF YOU SHIRK TODAY'S TASKS, YOU INCREASE TOMORROW'S BURDENS.

Cease to do evil.

ISAIAH 1:16

Three climbers were traversing from Colorado's Brainard Lake across Pawnee Pass when they lost the trail in the snow. The climbers had some critical choices to make. Unfortunately, they did almost everything wrong.

First, they chose to keep on going. When they saw Crater Lake far below, with a gentle slope of snow heading down toward it, they decided to slide down toward the lake. They started slowly, but the slope got steeper and steeper. Soon they were hurtling down. Then they heard water. The slope was heading toward a waterfall! In desperation they dug in their heels, slowing their rapid descent. Fortunately, they stopped their slide and managed to inch their way to a ledge to await rescue.

The progressive nature of sin follows much the same course. First we lose our way and begin a downward slide—slowly at first. Before we realize it, we're hurtling downward, out of control and in great spiritual danger. Like those climbers, we have to do everything we can to stop our slide. Isaiah said it well: "Cease to do evil." Don't keep going. Stop the slide!—D. C. E.

THE TROUBLE WITH A LITTLE SIN IS THAT IT DOESN'T STAY LITTLE.

March

The heavens are Yours, the earth also is Yours.

PSALM 89:11

I am surrounded every day by things that don't belong to me, yet I call them mine. For instance, I refer to the computer I am using to write this article as "my Mac." I talk about "my office," "my desk," and "my phone." But none of this equipment belongs to me. It's mine to use, but not mine to keep.

This kind of situation is not unique to employer-employee relationships. That's the way it is with all of us and all of the things we call our own. When we speak of our family, our house, or our car, we are speaking of people and things God has allowed us to enjoy while here on earth, but they really belong to Him.

Understanding who really holds the title to all we possess should change our thinking. Our time, talents, and possessions are all on loan from God so that we can do His work effectively.—J. D. B.

ALL WE OWN IS REALLY ON LOAN—FROM GOD.

They soon forgot His works; they did not wait for His counsel.

PSALM 106:13

he story is told of a young rich girl, accustomed to servants, who was afraid to climb a dark stairway alone. Her mother suggested that she overcome her fear by asking Jesus to go with her up the stairs. When the child reached the top, she was overheard saying, "Thank You, Jesus. You may go now."

We may smile at that story, but Psalm 106 contains a serious warning against dismissing God from our lives—as if that were possible. Israel took the Lord's mercies for granted, and God called that rebellion (v. 7). They developed malnourished souls because they chose to ignore Him (vv. 13–15). What a lesson for us!

Anticipate great things from God, but don't expect Him to come at your beck and call. Instead, be at His beck and call, eager to fulfill His will.—J. E. Y.

GOD IS NOT A VENDING MACHINE.

What is desired in a man is kindness.

PROVERBS 19:22

I will never forget being in the "big blackout" of November 9, 1965. This widespread power outage darkened eight states in the northeastern United States, and portions of Ontario and Quebec in eastern Canada—covering 80,000 square miles and affecting 30 million people.

With no electric lights, candles were in great demand. An announcer on a New York radio station that stayed on the air because it had auxiliary power reported, "An interesting drama is being unfolded on our streets. The price of candles in many stores has doubled. On the other hand, some good-hearted merchants are offering their candles at half price, or even giving them away."

The very same circumstances produced both self-seeking opportunists and selfless philanthropists. How would we react? Would we have pity on those in need and show kindness to them? (Prov. 19:17, 22). Or would we use it as an opportunity for personal gain?—R. W. D.

OPPORTUNITIES TO BE KIND ARE NEVER HARD TO FIND.

Let your words be few.

ECCLESIASTES 5:2

A senator complained about the length of some of the material published by the Government Printing Office. He pointed out that an explanatory pamphlet on the reduction of the price of cabbage seed required 2,500 words but only 1,821 were used in writing the Declaration of Independence. Yet how much more important is that document!

The Holy Spirit often moved the biblical writers to convey the most significant eternal truths in just a few words. The account of the creation of the world in Genesis contains about 400 words, and about 300 were needed to express the Ten Commandments. And what a world of meaning is bound up in brief statements like "God is love" and "Jesus wept"! Have you ever noticed the concise nature of the recorded sayings of the angels when they delivered God's messages to men? Their utterances were simple and clear, but they were also dynamic and inspiring.—H. G. B.

PEOPLE WHO SPEAK VOLUMES USUALLY END UP ON THE SHELF!

A friend loves at all times.

PROVERBS 17:17

Twenty Chinese couples "tied the knot" in a mass wedding on the Great Wall, according to an official Chinese newspaper. The couples said they chose this site in hopes that their marriages would be like the Great Wall—"able to withstand the winds and rains."

That Chinese ceremony contrasts with another wedding that took place in the aisle of a convenience store. The fun-loving couple said they thought it would be romantic to be married in the place where they met.

Although lasting relationships need the kind of humor and creativity exhibited by the convenience-store wedding, marriages also need the kind of endurance symbolized by the Great Wall. And what is true of marriage is also true of friendships. A faithful companion is always there during times of trouble and adversity (Prov. 17:17). Fair-weather friends aren't friends at all.—M. R. D. II

FAIR-WEATHER FRIENDS ARE USELESS IN A STORMY WORLD.

Stand fast therefore in the liberty
by which Christ has made us free.

GALATIANS 5:1

In 1776, the 13 British colonies in North America protested the limitations placed on them by the king of England and engaged in a struggle that gave birth to a brand-new republic. The infant nation soon adopted that now-famous document known as the Declaration of Independence.

Almost 2,000 years ago, the Lord Jesus cried out on the cross, "It is finished," proclaiming the believer's "declaration of independence." All of humanity was under the tyranny of sin and death. But Christ, the sinless One, took our place on Calvary and died for our sins. Having satisfied God's righteous demands, He now sets free for eternity all who trust in Him.

I thank God for the freedom I enjoy as a United States citizen. But above all, believers everywhere can praise Him for the freedom that is found in Christ!—R. W. D.

OUR GREATEST FREEDOM IS FREEDOM FROM SIN.

I was glad when they said to me,
"Let us go into the house of the LORD."

PSALM 122:1

he *Nashville Banner* reported that 81-year-old Ella Craig had
perfect attendance in Sunday school for 20 years. That's 1,040
Sundays! The article then raised these questions:

1. Doesn't Mrs. Craig ever have company on Sunday to keep
   her away from church?

2. Doesn't she ever have headaches, colds, nervous spells,
   or feel tired?

3. Doesn't she ever take a weekend trip?

4. Doesn't she ever sleep late on Sunday morning?

5. Doesn't it ever rain or snow on Sunday morning?

6. Doesn't she ever get her feelings hurt by someone in the church?

The article concluded by asking, "What's the matter with Mrs.
Craig?" The answer? Nothing at all! But if we are not in church on
Sunday when we can be, there is something wrong with us! We need to
take a lesson from Mrs. Craig.—R. W. D.

WEAK EXCUSES KEEP SOME PEOPLE FROM CHURCH WEEK AFTER WEEK.

Oh, give thanks to the LORD, for He is good!
For His mercy endures forever.

1 CHRONICLES 16:34

"I like to play with the stars," a little girl told her pastor one day when he came to visit her. She was confined to bed because of a severe spinal deformity, and her bed was positioned so that she had a good view of the sky. "I wake up a lot at night and can't get back to sleep," she told the minister, "and that's when I play with the stars."

Her pastor, curious about what she meant by that, asked, "How do you play with the stars?" The child answered, "I pick out one and say, 'That's Mommy.' I see another and say, 'That's Daddy.' And I just keep on naming the stars after people and things I'm thankful for—my brothers and sisters, my doctor, my friends, my dog." And on and on she went, until at last she exclaimed, "But there just aren't enough stars to go around!"

Do you ever feel that way when you think about the many blessings God has showered on you? From time to time, it's good to remember with gratitude His many gifts. As you do, like that little girl, you'll feel like exclaiming, "There just aren't enough stars to go around!"—R. W. D.

THANKFULNESS BEGINS WITH A GOOD MEMORY.

A soft answer turns away wrath.

PROVERBS 15:1

*R*esearchers at Kenyon College conducted a test in cooperation with the US Navy. The purpose was to discover how the tone of the voice affected sailors when they were given orders. The experiments revealed that the way a person was addressed determined to a large extent the kind of response he would make.

For example, when an individual was spoken to in a soft voice, he would answer in a similar manner. But when he was shouted at, his reply came back in the same sharp tone. This was true whether the communication was given face-to-face, over the intercom, or by telephone.

This study reminds me of Proverbs 15:1, which states, "A soft answer turns away wrath, but a harsh word stirs up anger." What we say and how we say it not only makes a difference in the reaction we'll receive, but it also determines whether conflict or peace will result. Many arguments could be avoided and tense situations relaxed if we practiced the truth of this verse.—R. W. D.

TO GET OUT OF A HARD SITUATION, TRY A SOFT ANSWER.

The heavens will pass away with a great noise.

2 PETER 3:10

Several years ago in Florida, I watched the ominously black sky as a howling wind drove the rain in stinging sheets across angrily churning bay-waters. A hurricane was approaching! All day long, radio and TV stations gave urgent instructions on how to guard against the destructive winds and surging tides of the impending storm.

As residents were frantically preparing for the storm, I asked myself, "Why do people take the warnings issued by the weather bureau so seriously, yet stubbornly refuse to hear God's warnings?" In His Word, God has told us that a much greater disaster will come upon the entire world. The Bible says, "The day of the Lord will come as a thief in the night, in which the heavens will pass away with a great noise, and the elements will melt with fervent heat; both the earth and the works that are in it will be burned up" (2 Pet. 3:10).

Yes, that dreadful day is coming. But there is a sure way of escaping God's judgment. Those who have placed their faith in Christ are assured of spending eternity with Him in heaven.—R. W. D.

TO REJECT GOD'S DELIVERANCE IS TO INVITE DESTRUCTION.

You have been grieved by various trials,
that the genuineness of your faith . . . may be found to praise.

1 PETER 1:6–7

The well-known minister and Bible teacher A. T. Pierson (1837–1911) took a tour through a paper mill and was fascinated to see how dirty old rags were being changed into fine quality white bond paper. He wrote, "What a contrast there was between the heap of filthy rags at one end of the process and the pure, spotless, white paper at the other! What a trial the rags go through before they emerge in this new form! Torn to pieces . . . , bleached with chloride of lime till all stains are removed, washed over and over. . . . How like the Divine discipline by which our filthiness is cleansed away."

The Bible is full of stories of God's children who have "gone through the mill": Job on the ash heap, Daniel in a den of lions, John on the lonely Isle of Patmos, Paul with a "thorn in the flesh," and those many unnamed martyrs in Hebrews 11:35–40. Such testing can have a cleansing, transforming, glorifying effect on men and women of faith. —H. G. B.

GOD SOMETIMES PUTS US THROUGH THE MILL
TO PURIFY AND PERFECT US.

MARCH 12

I am the LORD your God . . . ;
open your mouth wide, and I will fill it.

PSALM 81:10

As a boy, I was always thrilled to discover a newly constructed robin's nest. It was fascinating to watch for the eggs and then to wait for those featherless little creatures with bulging eyes and gaping mouths to break out of their shells. Standing at a distance, I could see their heads bobbing unsteadily and their mouths wide open, expecting Mother Robin to give them their dinner.

As I recall those childhood scenes, I think of God's promise: "I am the LORD your God . . . ; open your mouth wide, and I will fill it" (Ps. 81:10). In spite of this gracious offer to ancient Israel, the people ignored God, and He "gave them over to their own stubborn heart, to walk in their own counsels" (v. 12). If they had accepted God's offer, "He would have fed them also with the finest of wheat; and with honey from the rock" (v. 16).

So too, God longs to give us spiritual food. And He will satisfy our spiritual hunger as we study His Word, worship with others, listen to faithful Bible teachers, read literature with good biblical content, and daily depend on Him.—R. W. D.

TO HAVE A FULFILLING LIFE, LET GOD FILL YOU.

MARCH 13

Let us run with endurance the race that is set before us,
looking unto Jesus, the author and finisher of our faith.

HEBREWS 12:1–2

Leslie Dunkin told about a dog he had when he was a boy. His father would occasionally test the dog's obedience. He would place a tempting piece of meat on the floor and give the command, "No!" The dog, who must have had a strong urge to go for the meat, was placed in a most difficult situation—to obey or disobey his master's command.

Dunkin said, "The dog never looked at the meat. He seemed to feel that if he did, the temptation to disobey would be too great. So he looked steadily at my father's face." Dunkin then made this spiritual application: "There is a lesson for us all. Always look up to the Master's face."

Yes, that's good advice. God, of course, will not tempt us to do wrong (James 1:13). We do encounter many temptations, though, and if we keep our eyes fixed on the Lord Jesus we will be able to overcome them. When confronted by enticements that could easily overwhelm us, we need to look to Christ and follow His direction.—R. W. D.

TO MASTER TEMPTATION, KEEP YOUR EYES ON THE MASTER.

Let us consider one another . . . ,
not forsaking the assembling of ourselves together.

HEBREWS 10:24–25

I read an interesting article some time ago that compared a Christian without a church to . . .

> ➤ a student who won't go to school
> ➤ a soldier without an army
> ➤ a citizen who won't vote
> ➤ a sailor without a ship
> ➤ a child without a family
> ➤ a drummer without a band
> ➤ a ballplayer without a team
> ➤ a honeybee without a hive

If you have been neglecting one of God's greatest provisions for your spiritual growth, find a church that believes and teaches God's Word and start attending faithfully. Take time to get to know others and let them get to know you. Ask God to help you find ways to serve others.

Don't be a churchless Christian.—R. W. D.

SEVEN DAYS WITHOUT CHURCH MAKES ONE WEAK.

*Looking for the blessed hope and glorious appearing
of our great God and Savior Jesus Christ.*

TITUS 2:13

PEACE TALKS FALL APART AGAIN. UNEMPLOYMENT RATE RISES. TORNADO RIPS THROUGH TOWN. These newspaper headlines selected at random tend to lead us to despair. There just doesn't seem to be any hope for this world. And yet, according to the Scriptures, the dream of abolishing war is not merely wishful thinking. The idea of prosperity for all is more than a political gimmick. The Bible tells us that the eventual taming of nature is a certainty.

The hope for this world, however, is not to be found in human efforts but in the return of Jesus Christ. He alone can solve the problems that are baffling mankind. The prophet Isaiah said that someday "nation shall not lift up sword against nation, neither shall they learn war anymore" (Isa. 2:4). This glorious prospect will become a reality when the Lord Jesus Himself returns as "King of kings and Lord of lords" (1 Tim. 6:15) to set up His kingdom of peace and righteousness. Because we have this hope, we can be optimistic even in the deepening gloom of this age.—R. W. D.

**THE ONLY HOPE FOR WORLD PEACE
IS THE COMING OF THE PRINCE OF PEACE.**

[Endeavor] to keep the unity of the Spirit in the bond of peace.

EPHESIANS 4:3

Last year I visited a beautiful old church in New Holland, Pennsylvania. Alongside the church is a sprawling old cemetery in which are buried members from three different denominations.

Someday God's trumpet will sound, there will be a shout from heaven, and all the dead in Christ from that cemetery and every burial place in the world will rise as one great company to be with the Lord (1 Thess. 4:16–17). No preferences will be shown to any denominations; but one great church, the body of Christ, will at last be united. Genuine faith in Jesus Christ will be the unifying factor that removes all our denominational distinctions and divisions as we join together in one great anthem of praise to our Lord and Savior.

Father, help us to see other Christians through the eyes of Christ, because one day we will all be one.—D. J. D.

**OUR UNION WITH CHRIST IS THE BASIS
FOR UNITY WITH ONE ANOTHER.**

"Woe is me, for I am undone!
. . . My eyes have seen the King, the LORD of hosts."

ISAIAH 6:5

A little boy announced, "I'm like Goliath. I'm nine feet tall."

"What makes you say that?" asked his mother. The child replied, "Well, I made a ruler and measured myself with it, and I am nine feet tall!"

Many people fail to see their need of salvation because they measure themselves by a faulty standard. By looking at their peers and comparing their behavior with others who have done worse than they have, they come to the conclusion that they are not so bad after all. But such feelings of pride are demolished when people compare themselves with a perfect standard of righteousness.

According to Romans 3:23, we all have sinned and fall short of God's glory. That's why everyone needs to be forgiven. If you're measuring your morality against that of others, you are using the wrong standard of measurement. But if you recognize how far you fall short in the sight of God, reach out in faith to Jesus today and receive His gift of forgiveness.
—R. W. D.

IF WE COULD EARN OUR SALVATION,
CHRIST WOULD NOT HAVE DIED TO PROVIDE IT.

The things which are seen are temporary,
but the things which are not seen are eternal.

2 CORINTHIANS 4:18

I have a friend who was denied a doctorate from a prestigious West Coast university because of his Christian worldview. As he was approaching the conclusion of his studies, his advisor invited him to come into his office and informed him that his dissertation had been rejected.

My friend's first thought was of thousands of dollars and five years of his life taking flight, and his heart sank. But then he thought of the words of the hymn by Rhea Miller: "I'd rather have Jesus than silver or gold, I'd rather be His than have riches untold; . . . I'd rather have Jesus than anything this world affords today." And then my friend laughed— for he realized that nothing of eternal value had been lost.

How we respond to loss is all a matter of perspective. One person is absorbed with the permanent; the other with the passing. One stores up treasure in heaven; the other accumulates it here on earth. Wouldn't you "rather have Jesus"?—D. H. R.

LIVING ONLY FOR TEMPORARY GAIN LEADS TO ETERNAL LOSS.

No good thing will He withhold from those who walk uprightly.

PSALM 84:11

Incredible as it sounds, Alexander Whortley lived in a mini-trailer three feet wide, four feet long, and five feet high until he died at the age of eighty. It was made of wood, had a metal roof, and it housed him and all his meager belongings. No matter where he worked, Whortley chose to spend his life in that cramped space, even though larger quarters were always available.

It isn't likely that any of us have chosen to live in boxes—certainly not if housing with far more elbow room is available. But are we allowing ourselves to be squeezed into narrow boxes of a different sort? Are we hemmed in by an unforgiving spirit, bitterness, or sinful habits? Are we boxed in by unbelief with its coffin-like narrowness of vision, seeing only this little world and this brief lifetime as the hope-suffocating sum total of our existence?

God wants us to live in the expansive joy of His strength, realizing the security of His protection and the blessing of His favor.—V. C. G.

**DON'T LET THE FENCE OF UNBELIEF
KEEP YOU FROM THE FIELD OF GOD'S GRACE.**

Rejoice in the Lord always. Again I will say, rejoice!

PHILIPPIANS 4:4

Beloved hymn writer Fanny Crosby lost her sight when she was only six weeks old. She lived into her nineties, composing thousands of beloved hymns. On her ninety-second birthday she cheerfully said, "If in all the world you can find a happier person than I am, do bring him to me. I should like to shake his hand."

What enabled Fanny Crosby to experience such joy in the face of what many would term a "tragedy"? At an early age she chose to "rejoice in the Lord always" (Phil. 4:4). In fact, Fanny carried out a resolution she made when she was only eight years old: "How many blessings I enjoy that other people don't. To weep and sigh because I'm blind, I cannot and I won't."

Temperament seems to be something that each of us is born with. Some of us have upbeat dispositions, while others play the music of life in a minor key. Yet how we respond to life's trials also affects our overall disposition. When faced with the choice of self-pity or rejoicing, let's respond with rejoicing!—V. C. G.

RATHER THAN REGRET THE THORNS, LET'S REJOICE OVER THE ROSES.

"With everlasting kindness I will have mercy on you,"
says the LORD, your Redeemer.

ISAIAH 54:8

After a round of golf, a British statesman and his friend walked through a field in which cows were grazing. The men were so absorbed in conversation that they forgot to close the gate when they left the fenced area. The statesman happened to notice the open gate, however, and went back to close it. Then he told his friend that this little incident reminded him of a doctor who was dying and was asked by a minister whether there was anything he wanted to say before he slipped away. "No," the doctor replied, "except that through life I think I have always closed the gates behind me." The dying man had learned to put failures and disappointments behind him so they wouldn't rob him of his joy and peace.

As Christians, we should learn that lesson well. When we sin, we can "close the gate" to nagging guilt by confessing our sin to our merciful Lord and accepting His forgiveness (Isa. 54:7-10; 1 John 1:9). Or, if we have a misunderstanding with someone, rather than allowing the irritation to fester, we should go to that person and make things right (Matt. 18:15). Let's close the gate to the failures and disappointments of the past—then move on!—R. W. D.

TO ENJOY THE FUTURE, ACCEPT GOD'S FORGIVENESS FOR THE PAST.

In My Father's house are many mansions. . . .
I go to prepare a place for you.

JOHN 14:2

In America at the turn of the twentieth century, people who were poor and homeless were moved into "poorhouses." These institutions were considered to be just about the worst places a person could live.

A doctor was visiting an elderly woman who was dying in such a home. Because of her surroundings, he was greatly surprised to hear her whisper, "Praise the Lord." So the doctor leaned over and said to her, "How can you possibly praise God here in a poorhouse?" She responded, "That's easy. I just keep thinking about the move into my heavenly mansion."

The assurance that a wonderful home, the "Father's house," awaited her—in contrast to the depressing poorhouse—gave her cause for praise in spite of her poverty.

A wonderful home in heaven awaits every child of God—and the darker earth's pathway, the brighter heaven's prospect.—R. W. D.

**THE RICHES OF HEAVEN WILL MORE THAN COMPENSATE
FOR THE POVERTY OF EARTH.**

When you read, you may understand
my knowledge in the mystery of Christ.

EPHESIANS 3:4

If you have a letter from Mark Twain in your attic, it could be worth a lot of money. A personal, nine-page letter written to his daughter in 1875 sold for $33,000 back in 1991. Ordinary correspondence from the author of *Tom Sawyer* usually brings $1,200 to $1,500 a page. Experts say that even though Twain wrote 50,000 letters during his lifetime, demand is still strong for these personal notes from one of America's favorite authors.

You probably don't have any correspondence from Mark Twain, but chances are you own a priceless collection of letters. Twenty-one of the 27 books in the New Testament are letters written to encourage and instruct Christians. They contain the priceless revelation of Jesus Christ.

To every Christian, the value of the New Testament letters is not their cash value, but the wisdom they bring to an open heart—wisdom from God Himself.—D. C. M.

IF YOU WANT LIFE-CHANGING MAIL,
OPEN YOUR BIBLE AND READ A LETTER FROM GOD.

Behold, your King is coming to you, . . .
lowly and riding on a donkey.

ZECHARIAH 9:9

If Jesus had ridden a spirited horse into Jerusalem, He would have looked more kingly. But as Zechariah had prophesied, He came in a humble way. Why? The answer is that the kings of the East rode donkeys when on errands of peace, while the horse was used as a charger in war. Although Jesus came as Israel's King, He did not come as a political revolutionary.

The multitudes, however, didn't understand. Thinking only in terms of earthly prosperity and freedom from Rome, they enthusiastically welcomed Him. Yet, sad to say, a few days later the crowds were shouting, "Crucify Him!"

Many people today admire Jesus but do not recognize Him as the Savior of sinners. Man's deepest need, though, cannot be met until the sin problem is faced and overcome. For this reason, Christ rode into Jerusalem on a donkey with His face set toward the cross, knowing full well the painful death He would have to suffer there.—H. V. L.

WITHOUT THE CROSS, THERE COULD BE NO CROWN.

The multitudes . . . cried out, saying: "Hosanna to the Son of David!
'Blessed is He who comes in the name of the LORD!'"

MATTHEW 21:9

I have often wondered how many of those people who enthusiastically cried, "Hosanna!" on Palm Sunday shouted, "Crucify Him! Crucify Him!" a few days later. Some may have been keenly disappointed, even angry, that Christ didn't use His miraculous power to establish an earthly kingdom. Hadn't He created a golden opportunity to rally popular support by parading into Jerusalem and offering Himself as King?

Many Jews failed to recognize that before Jesus would openly assert His sovereignty He had to rule in their hearts. Their greatest need was not to be freed from Caesar's rule but to be released from the chains of pride, self-righteousness, and rebellion against God.

The issue is the same today. Christ does not offer immunity from life's hardships, a cure for every disease, or the promise of financial success. What the King offered then is what He offers today—Himself as the sacrifice for our sins, and a challenge to serve Him. If we accept His offer, we will not be disappointed.—D. J. D.

PUTTING CHRIST FIRST BRINGS SATISFACTION THAT LASTS.

He said to Jesus,
"Lord, remember me when You come into Your kingdom."

LUKE 23:42

There were three crosses on Calvary's hill. On one was a man dying *in* sin—he did not accept Jesus. On another was a man dying *to* sin—he trusted Jesus as Savior and Lord (Luke 23:40–43). And on the middle cross was One dying *for* sin. He could die for others because He was God's Son and had no sin of His own. The center cross made all the difference for those two men hanging beside Jesus—the difference between an eternal hell and an eternal heaven.

A man was asked to receive Christ but put it off by saying, "Oh, don't bother me now. There is always the eleventh hour. Remember the dying thief." He was shocked when the persistent Christian said pointedly, "Which thief? Remember, there were two!" The man responded, "That's right. I had forgotten that. I meant the saved one!" That very night he decided to trust Jesus for his salvation.

Look in faith now to that One in heaven who once hung on the middle cross. You too will hear His word of forgiveness and hope.

—H. G. B.

GOD'S JUSTICE AND MERCY MET AT THE CROSS.

He said, "It is finished!"

JOHN 19:30

Author Joseph Conrad had just finished writing a lengthy and intense novel about domination and rescue. Because Conrad's native language was Polish, the task of working out precise English words and phrases was very difficult. When he finally completed the book, he scrawled a single word across the last page. It was not the word *Finished* or *Completed*, but the word *Victory*! And that became the title of the novel.

Early in Jesus' ministry, He told His disciples, "My food is to do the will of Him who sent Me, and to finish His work" (John 4:34). It would be a task more difficult than anyone had ever undertaken. By His sinless life and sacrificial death, He would purchase redemption for the entire human race. On the eve of His death He prayed, "I have finished the work which You have given Me to do" (John 17:4). And on the cross, before committing His Spirit into His Father's hands, He said, "It is finished!" Jesus had won the victory.—D. C. E.

LIFTED UP TO DIE, "IT IS FINISHED!" WAS CHRIST'S CRY.

100

*He also presented Himself alive after His suffering
by many infallible proofs.*

ACTS 1:3

In 1957, Lieutenant David Steeves walked out of California's Sierra Nevada Mountains fifty-four days after his Air Force trainer jet had disappeared. He told an unbelievable tale of how he had lived in a snowy wilderness after parachuting from his disabled plane. By the time he showed up alive, he had already been declared officially dead. When further search failed to turn up the wreckage, a hoax was suspected and Steeves was forced to resign under a cloud of doubt. More than twenty years later, however, his story was confirmed when a troop of Boy Scouts discovered the wreckage of his plane.

Another "survival story" from centuries ago is still controversial. A man by the name of Jesus Christ walked out of the Judean wilderness making claims a lot of people found difficult to believe. He was later executed and pronounced dead. But three days later He showed up alive.

Prophets foretold His coming. Miracles supported His deity. Eyewitnesses verified His resurrection. And today the Holy Spirit confirms to anyone who is seeking to know the truth that Jesus is alive.—M .R. D. II

**THE RESURRECTION OF JESUS IS A FACT OF HISTORY
THAT DEMANDS A RESPONSE OF FAITH.**

*Teach us to number our days,
that we may gain a heart of wisdom.*

PSALM 90:12

The older we get, the shorter life seems. Author Victor Hugo said, "Short as life is, we make it still shorter by the careless waste of time." There's no sadder example of wasted time than a life dominated by fretting. Take, for example, an American woman whose dream of riding a train through the English countryside came true. After boarding the train she kept fretting about the windows and the temperature, complaining about her seat assignment, rearranging her luggage, and so on. To her shock, she suddenly reached her journey's end. With deep regret she said to the person meeting her, "If I'd known I was going to arrive so soon, I wouldn't have wasted my time fretting so much."

It's easy to get sidetracked by problems that won't matter at life's end—difficult neighbors, a tight budget, signs of aging, people who are wealthier than you. Instead of fretting, feed on God's Word and apply it to yourself. Strive to grow in God's wisdom every day. Stay focused on eternal values. Make it your goal to greet your waiting Savior one day with a heart of wisdom, rather than a heart of care.—J. E. Y.

WORRY CASTS A BIG SHADOW BEHIND A SMALL THING.

*"Worthy is the Lamb who was slain to receive
. . . honor and glory and blessing!"*

REVELATION 5:12

Spontaneous celebrations of freedom erupted all across Eastern Europe in the late 1980s as atheistic and tyrannical governments suddenly disintegrated. One of the more unusual displays of liberty took place in Czechoslovakia on November 27, 1989.

Although church bells had not been heard in that freedom-starved nation for 45 years, at noon that day every church bell in the country began to ring. The pigeons were as startled as the people. A sign placed on the front lawn of a church in Prague summed up the joy of the moment. It read simply: The Lamb Wins.

That triumphant message evokes a picture of the meekness and the power of the Lord Jesus Christ. Throughout the pages of Revelation, He is portrayed as the Lamb who redeems us. Yet despite the gentleness represented by a lamb, Jesus is also the mighty Judge who will defeat all who oppose Him. The Lamb will win. Praise the Lamb!—H. W. R.

THE LAMB WHO DIED IS THE LORD WHO LIVES.

I know whom I have believed.

2 TIMOTHY 1:12

Do you know an aglet from a tang? Would you recognize duff if you walked on it? It's not essential to know these terms to make it through life successfully. If you didn't know that an aglet is "the covering on the end of a shoelace," that a tang is "the projecting prong on a tool," or that duff is "the decaying matter found on a forest floor," it's not all that important. You could always look it up.

We can be glad we don't have to know everything to get by in this world. We often can depend on someone else's knowledge. For instance, I don't know how to fix the brakes of my car—but as long as someone else knows and can fix them, I'm okay.

There is a knowledge, however, for which we are individually responsible if we expect to enter heaven. I'm talking about knowing Christ personally. We live in an age of expanding information, and a personal relationship with Christ is the only way to live wisely and be prepared to meet God. Do you know the One who died for you and can forgive your sins? Unless you know Him, all other knowledge is insignificant.—J. D. B.

TO KNOW CHRIST IS THE GREATEST OF ALL KNOWLEDGE.

April

[I pray] that He would grant you . . . to be strengthened
with might through His Spirit in the inner man.

EPHESIANS 3:16

A large company extracts contaminating substances from steel drums by suction. Powerful pumps draw the materials out of the barrels, but the workers must carefully regulate the force of these pumps. If they take out too much air, the drums will collapse like paper cups because the outer pressure will exceed the inner pressure.

Likewise, when adversity and hardship come into our lives, unless God empowers us from within we will be unable to withstand the pressures from without. True, we get solid support from loved ones and Christian friends, but it is our spiritual inner self, strengthened by God's Spirit, that sustains us and keeps us from crumbling.

The Spirit works to strengthen us and renew our minds as we read God's Word and pray. Let's ask the Lord to develop our inner strength so that when life's blows and burdens press upon us we will not cave in.—D. C. E.

THE POWER OF CHRIST IN YOU IS GREATER
THAN THE PRESSURE OF TROUBLES AROUND YOU.

Go therefore and make disciples.

MATTHEW 28:19

A college choir was all set to present its package of music in a large church. The program of sacred song was to be carried live by a local radio station. When everything appeared to be ready, the announcer made his final introduction and waited for the choir director to begin.

But one of the tenors was not ready so the venerable conductor refused to raise his baton. All this time, nothing but silence was being broadcast. Growing very nervous, the announcer, forgetting that his microphone was still on and that he could be heard in the church and on the radio, said in exasperation, "Get on with it, you old goat!"

Later in the week, the radio station got a letter from one of its listeners—a man who had tuned in to listen to the music. When he heard "Get on with it, you old goat!" he took the message personally. He had been doing nothing to further God's work, and this startling message was enough to convict him and get him going again.

Sometimes we need a wakeup call. We need to be reminded that Jesus told us we should go and make disciples. We need to get on with it!—J. D. B.

IT'S WHAT YOU'RE DOING TODAY THAT COUNTS,
NOT WHAT YOU'RE GOING TO DO TOMORROW.

Whoever loses his life for My sake and the gospel's will save it.

MARK 8:35

Martyn, a Cambridge University student, was honored at only twenty years of age for his achievements in mathematics. In fact, he was given the highest recognition possible in that field. And yet he felt an emptiness inside. He said that instead of finding fulfillment in his achievements, he had "only grasped a shadow."

After evaluating his life's goals, Martyn sailed to India as a missionary at the age of twenty-four. When he arrived, he prayed, "Lord, let me burn out for You." In the next seven years that preceded his death, he translated the New Testament into three difficult Eastern languages. These notable achievements were certainly not passing "shadows."

Real fulfillment comes in following Christ. A life lived fully for the Lord is a life that truly satisfies.—R. W. D.

**A FULFILLED LIFE IS A LIFE FULL OF LOVE
FOR THE LORD AND OTHERS.**

Let each one of you speak truth with his neighbor,
for we are members of one another.

EPHESIANS 4:25

A young boy and his stepfather had difficulty communicating
with each other. The man was outgoing; the boy was quiet.
The elder loved to fish; the youngster loved to read. The stepfather,
wanting to get close to the boy, took him on a fishing trip. The boy hated
it but didn't know how to tell his stepfather directly. So he wrote him a
note saying he wanted to go home. The man looked at it and then stuck
it in his pocket.

The fishing trip continued for four more days. When they finally
returned home, the boy shared his frustration with his mother and told
her that his father had paid no attention to his note. His mother said to
him, "Son, your father can't read!"

Good communication occurs not only when we know what we
want to say, but when we know the person to whom we speak. And to
know one another requires a willingness to let others know our weaknesses
and limitations. Paul admonished believers to be "kind to one another,
tenderhearted, forgiving one another" (Eph. 4:32). That's Christlike love,
and it provides the security in which good communication can thrive.
—H. W. R.

WORDS SPOKEN IN LOVE NEED NO INTERPRETER.

All Scripture is given by inspiration of God.

2 TIMOTHY 3:16

The first morning I heard the mockingbird practicing his bagful of imitations outside my window, I was thrilled by the beauty of his songs. Gradually, however, I began to take this early morning songster for granted. One day as I awoke, it dawned on me that I no longer appreciated my regular visitor. It wasn't the mockingbird's fault. He was still there. His beautiful song hadn't changed, but I was no longer listening for it.

As believers in Christ, we may have a similar experience hearing God speak to us in His Word. When we are first saved, the Scriptures, with their soul-stirring instruction and vital spiritual food, are deeply satisfying. As time goes on, however, we routinely read those same portions over and over in a manner that no longer speaks to us. Our spiritual senses grow dull and lethargic, and God's exhilarating Word becomes commonplace to us. But then, what joy we feel when a passage reveals an exciting truth, and once again we "hear" the Lord!

Today, when you read God's Word, listen closely for His voice.

—R. W. D.

WITHOUT A HEART FOR GOD, WE CANNOT HEAR HIS WORD.

Peter answered and said to Jesus,
"Lord, it is good for us to be here."

MATTHEW 17:4

On the back of the pulpit in the church I used to attend were printed these words: "Sir, we would see Jesus!" They were a reminder to the minister that he must never allow anything—no matter how good or interesting—to distract him from focusing on the Savior.

Peter, James, and John needed this reminder too when they witnessed Jesus' transfiguration and the appearance of Moses and Elijah. Commenting on this account, J. B. Nicholson suggests that when Peter said, "Lord, it is good for us," he was focusing on the wonderful experience. Nicholson then says, "Peter was sidetracked, and the Father had to open heaven and speak to him. He said, 'This is My beloved Son, in whom I am well pleased; hear Him.'" God put the focus where it belonged, on Christ.

Let's keep Jesus at the center of our spiritual attention.—H. G. B.

UNLESS CHRIST IS THE CENTER OF INTEREST,
YOUR LIFE WILL BE OUT OF FOCUS.

I will delight myself in Your commandments, which I love.

PSALM 119:47

When Mary Jones was ten years old, she began saving money for something special she wanted to buy. She babysat, tended neighbors' gardens, and sold eggs from her own chickens. By the time she was sixteen, she had accumulated enough money to get what she so desperately wanted.

Was it a new car? A fresh wardrobe? A Nintendo? No, Mary Jones was sixteen in the year 1800, and what she had been saving for was a Bible. But there was no place to buy one in the tiny Welsh village where she lived, so she walked to Bala—twenty-five miles away. There Rev. Thomas Charles had one Bible left to sell, and after some convincing, Mary talked him into selling it to her.

Because of Mary's hunger for the Bible, Rev. Charles and others began discussing the need of making the Scriptures more readily available. The British and Foreign Bible Society was started, and during the next 100 years it distributed more than 200 million copies of God's Word worldwide. To Mary, nothing was more important than the Bible, and her persistence paid huge spiritual dividends.—J. D. B.

MANY PEOPLE STORE THE BIBLE ON A SHELF INSTEAD OF IN THEIR HEART.

The tax collector . . . beat his breast, saying,
"God, be merciful to me a sinner!"

LUKE 18:13

An article in *The Grand Rapids Press* described a woman who overcame her drinking habit—but only after she admitted she had a problem. She said the "emotional moment" came when she brought herself to say, "I'm Betty and I'm an alcoholic."

She had been saying that her slurred speech, drowsiness, and other problems were due to the medication she was taking for a chronic ailment. But the family knew the real cause and confronted her. As a result, she finally faced up to her problem. Before that, she was a hopeless case. But when she said, "I'm an alcoholic," there was hope.

It's much the same way with salvation. As long as a person makes excuses for his sinful behavior, he'll never experience deliverance. It's only when he admits, "I am a sinner and cannot save myself," that the Lord will rescue him from sin and its awful consequences. Remember, salvation is for sinners only.—R. W. D.

JESUS CAN CHANGE THE FOULEST SINNER INTO THE FINEST SAINT.

"Behold, I stand at the door and knock.
If anyone hears My voice and opens the door, I will come in to Him."

REVELATION 3:20

In a conversation with a nine-year-old boy, a youth worker was telling the story of Adam and Eve and how sin entered the world. He told the boy that Jesus died to pay the penalty for his sins, and that if he would ask Him into his heart He would come in. That night the boy invited Jesus to save him.

A few days later the youngster said to the youth worker's wife, "I don't have to talk to God long distance anymore." "Why not?" she asked. Pointing to his heart, he replied, "Because He's only ten inches away."

Amazing! Christ, by whom all things were created (Col. 1:16), comes to live in a sinner's heart so that person senses a close relationship with God. That's the miracle of the new birth. This closeness, however, can be lost if we become lukewarm in our love for Jesus. That's why He portrays Himself as standing outside the door of our heart waiting to be invited in so that this sense of intimacy can be renewed (Rev. 3:20).
—D. J. D.

TO RENEW YOUR LOVE FOR CHRIST, REVIEW CHRIST'S LOVE FOR YOU.

*When he was in affliction, he . . .
humbled himself greatly before the God of his fathers.*

2 CHRONICLES 33:12

A young man was driving an old worn-out car on a desolate road in a downpour when the engine died. As he coasted to the side of the road, another car stopped and the driver got out and asked what was wrong. The stranger opened the hood, tinkered with something, and signaled the driver to turn the ignition key. When the car started, the amazed driver shouted, "Thanks, I was afraid the engine had failed for the last time."

The rescuer replied, "Every car has at least one more start in it if you can get a spark. The same principle applies to people. Someday you will have occasion to apply this knowledge. Remember, as long as a single spark of life remains, it's not too late for anyone to make a fresh start."

Thirty years later, this once-stranded driver is a chaplain in a large prison. He testifies that those words about a fresh start have come back to him again and again. If your life is in disarray, don't despair. Through repentance and faith you can begin again. "As long as a spark remains, it's not too late to make a fresh start."—H. V. L.

IT'S NEVER TOO LATE TO MAKE A FRESH START WITH GOD.

If therefore the light that is in you is darkness,
how great is that darkness!

MATTHEW 6:23

In today's text, Jesus made a seemingly contradictory statement. He called light darkness. We can best understand His words, I believe, by comparing two kinds of light. Consider first the flickering glow of a lightning bug. Two rare chemicals, luciferas and luciferin, produce the lightning bug's light. Both terms are related to the word *lucifer*, which means "light-bearing." (Lucifer is also one of the names for Satan.) Now consider the sun's light. Its brilliance is blinding. By comparison, the lightning bug's light is "darkness."

In Matthew 6, Jesus cautioned His hearers about living for riches and urged them instead to lay up their treasures in heaven. Then He illustrated His warning by referring to "the lamp of the body," the eye. If our focus is on spiritual things, we will be full of light. But if we live for earthly riches, we will become filled with a dark light, which He described as great darkness.

Only Christ can illumine the soul with the light of salvation.
—D. J. D.

SOME PEOPLE HAVE PLENTY TO LIVE ON BUT NOTHING TO LIVE FOR.

No other foundation can anyone lay than that which is laid,
which is Jesus Christ.

1 CORINTHIANS 3:11

*I*n 1992, Hurricane Andrew destroyed thousands of homes in South Florida. Yet in an area where the wreckage looked like a war zone, one house remained standing, still firmly anchored to its foundation.

When a reporter asked the homeowner why his house had not been blown away, he replied, "I built this house myself. I also built it according to the Florida state building code. When the code called for 2" x 6" roof trusses, I used 2" x 6" roof trusses. I was told that a house built according to code could withstand a hurricane—and it did."

Jesus talked about the importance of building our lives on a solid foundation. He said that the person who obeys His Word is like "a wise man who built his house on the rock" (Matt. 7:24). If we build according to His code of obedience, we will not be swept away when crises hit with hurricane-like force. The tempests of temptation and the storms of suffering will not be able to sweep us off a solid foundation of faith and obedience. Adversity may come, yet because we have built according to the code of the unshakable Rock, Jesus Christ, we can emerge with our character strengthened.—V. C. G.

THE STORMS OF OUR LIFE PROVE THE STRENGTH OF OUR ANCHOR.

Do not worry about tomorrow,
for tomorrow will worry about its own things.

MATTHEW 6:34

had never thought of worry as a form of taking on God's responsibility. But the more I thought about it, the more I realized that worry, in its naked form, comes close to doing just that. I thought of this after seeing a sign in a church foyer that read:

Do not feel totally, personally,
irrevocably responsible for
everything. That's My job.
—God

We often feel we must solve all our problems ourselves, and that unless we come up with the right solution all will be lost. Of course, we must take responsibility for our own lives. Yet God wants us to rely on His guidance. When problems arise, our first duty is to bring them to Him in prayer. He may show us that we've created our own difficulty, and may reveal that we must make changes to resolve it. He'll grant forgiveness and give the strength to change. Or He'll assure us that we're doing all we can, and say, "Leave it with Me. Just do your next duty."—D. J. D.

WHEN WORRY WALKS IN, STRENGTH RUNS OUT.

Brethren, if a man is overtaken in any trespass,
you who are spiritual restore such a one.

GALATIANS 6:1

My six-year-old granddaughter was at one of her first ice-skating lessons. Now that Kelsey could glide a little across the ice, Grandpa and Grandma were invited to watch. It was a painful experience! She still took quite a few falls. But Crystal, her instructor, was always right there to pick her up and encourage her. Other skaters stopped to tell her she was doing well. Mom and Dad were watching from the sidelines, cheering her on. Kelsey had plenty of patient instruction and support, so whenever she fell she got right back up and kept trying.

All Christians need that kind of instruction and encouragement, especially new believers. As we set aside old habits and learn new ways of thinking and acting, we may frequently stumble and fall. It's then that we need help from believers who are more mature in their faith. New Christians don't need someone pointing fingers at them and making pious, judgmental pronouncements. And no one should ever laugh at them!

Let's be encouragers who help to bear the burdens of our brothers and sisters in Christ.—D. C. E.

A LITTLE ENCOURAGEMENT CAN MAKE THE DIFFERENCE
BETWEEN GIVING UP OR GOING ON.

I prayed . . . and made confession, and said,
"O LORD, great and awesome God."

DANIEL 9:4

The word *awesome* is freely used these days to describe athletes, coaches, teachers, and even friends. I suppose it's not wrong to use the expression this way. But if you ever stand at the rim of the Grand Canyon, or get a panoramic view from Sandia Peak, a point more than 14,000 feet above sea level, you'll really feel a sense of awe.

That's how I felt last year when I visited those places while on vacation. Although the scenery itself was breathtaking, my feeling of awe had more to do with God than with the spectacular beauties of nature. I had the sense of being in the presence of the One who created these wonders. I found myself saying, "This is only one wonder on one small planet in a universe that includes billions of stars and distances measured in terms of millions of light-years. What an awesome God!"

This sense of awe is healthy and should fill us with fear, gratitude, and love. Fear, because such a God is not to be trifled with. Gratitude, because He reached down in grace to save us from our sins. Love, because by loving us first He enables us to love Him in return.—H. V. L.

IN A WORLD OF MANY SUPERLATIVES, ONLY GOD IS THE GREATEST.

All things come from You,
and of Your own we have given You.

1 CHRONICLES 29:14

John Hauberg and his wife live in a stunning home in Seattle. It is built mostly of glass inside and out. Hundreds of glass artifacts decorate the light-flooded rooms, and even the sinks, shelves, and mantelpieces are made of glass.

You might think that the Haubergs would be in constant fear that something would break. On the contrary, they invite visitors to roam freely throughout their entire home. John is also a connoisseur of Native American crafts, but he has donated his entire collection to the Seattle Art Museum. His motive is not to hoard but to share. "I'm not an owner," he says. "I am a caretaker."

John Hauberg's comment expresses in a simple sentence a basic biblical principle that applies to all our possessions: We aren't owners; we are caretakers. Legally, of course, we own our possessions. But as Christians, we gladly acknowledge with David that "the earth is the LORD's, and all its fullness, the world and those who dwell therein" (Ps. 24:1).
—V. C. G.

THE ONLY THINGS WE REALLY LOSE
ARE THOSE THINGS WE TRY TO KEEP.

"I have finished the work which You have given Me to do."

JOHN 17:4

Miriam Booth, daughter of the founder of the Salvation Army, was a brilliant and cultured woman who began her Christian work with great promise and unusual success. Very soon, however, disease brought her to the point of death. A friend told her it seemed a pity that a woman of her capabilities should be hindered by sickness from doing the Lord's work. With deep insight and gentle grace, Miriam replied, "It's wonderful to do the Lord's work, but it's greater still to do the Lord's will!"

Commenting on John 17:4, blind minister and hymnwriter George Matheson said, "The cup which our Father gives us to drink is a cup of the will. It is easy for the lips to drain it when once the heart has accepted it. . . .The act is easy after the choice."

Yes, that is where the battle lies. If, like Jesus, we delight to do the Father's will, then the work He assigns will be done with grace and without hesitation, no matter what the personal sacrifice may be.—H. G. B.

THE BEST WAY TO DO GOD'S WILL IS TO SAY "I WILL" TO GOD.

Some have strayed concerning the faith.

1 TIMOTHY 6:21

In the early part of this century, an American ship was wrecked off the Scilly Isles near the coast of England. The sea had been calm and the weather clear, but the vessel was caught in a treacherous current that slowly lured it off its course. Before the captain and the crew realized what had happened, the ship had crashed into the rocks.

In life, too, powerful currents of compromise can catch the soul and carry it to shipwreck. Spiritual drifting is usually a slow and imperceptible process. We know it has occurred when we have lost the strong resistance to evil and the passionate desire for truth that we once knew.

For every professing believer who is lost to the Christian cause by a savage assault of evil, a hundred more slowly drift away from God's truth, regular worship, and a life of faith. We must give careful attention to what we know about Christ so that we don't get caught in a drift.—H. W. R.

THE COMPASS OF GOD'S WORD
WILL KEEP YOU FROM SPIRITUAL SHIPWRECK.

He is my refuge and my fortress; my God, in Him I will trust.

PSALM 91:2

Our world is filled with fear. Even in fairly stable and secure countries, people are afraid. According to a *USA Today* article, "We panic over pesticides and cellular phones, ozone holes and mercury fillings."

Science, government, and psychiatry can deal with some of these fears, but there are other fear-producing circumstances that even the world's most powerful military force can't prevent—an earthquake, a tornado, a flood, a fatal disease.

One fear, however, overshadows all others—the fear of our inescapable appointment with death and God's judgment (Heb. 2:14–15). The only antidote for this anxiety, and ultimately all others, is found in gaining confidence that we are in God's protective care. That assurance begins to grow when we put our trust in Jesus as our Savior. Our faith grows as we learn more about the wisdom, love, and power of God, and our fears diminish as we choose to focus on Christ instead.—V. C. G.

THE PERFECT CURE FOR WORRY IS TRUST IN GOD.

One's life does not consist in the abundance of the things he possesses.

LUKE 12:15

*P*hilip Parham tells the story of a rich industrialist who was disturbed to find a fisherman sitting lazily beside his boat. "Why aren't you out there fishing?" he asked.

"Because I've caught enough fish for today," said the fisherman.

"Why don't you catch more fish than you need?" the rich man asked. "What would I do with them?"

"You could earn more money," came the impatient reply, "and buy a better boat so you could go deeper and catch more fish. You could purchase nylon nets, catch even more fish, and make more money. Soon you'd have a fleet of boats and be rich like me."

The fisherman asked, "Then what would I do?" "You could sit down and enjoy life," said the industrialist. "What do you think I'm doing now?" the fisherman replied as he looked placidly out to sea.

Been working all the time? Refusing to take vacations? Life is more than possessions. Learn to trust more fully in the God who has given us all things to enjoy.—D. C. E.

SOME PEOPLE ARE SO BUSY PREPARING FOR A RAINY DAY THAT THEY MISS GOD'S SUNSHINE.

*The sinful passions which were aroused by the law
were at work in our members to bear fruit to death.*

ROMANS 7:5

In Galveston, Texas, a hotel on the shore of the Gulf of Mexico put this notice in each room: **No Fishing From The Balcony.** Yet every day, hotel guests threw in their lines to the waters below. Then the management decided to take down the signs—and the fishing stopped!

In his *Confessions*, Augustine (354–430), reflected on this attraction to the forbidden. He wrote, "There was a pear tree near our vineyard, laden with fruit. One stormy night we rascally youths set out to rob it. . . . We took off a huge load of pears—not to feast upon ourselves, but to throw them to the pigs, though we ate just enough to have the pleasure of the forbidden fruit. They were nice pears, but it was not the pears that my wretched soul coveted, for I had plenty better at home. I picked them simply to become a thief. . . . The desire to steal was awakened simply by the prohibition of stealing."

Human nature is inherently rebellious. Give us a law and we will see it as a challenge to break it. Jesus, however, forgives our lawbreaking and gives us the Holy Spirit. He imparts a new desire and ability so that our greatest pleasure becomes bringing pleasure to God.—H. W. R.

FORBIDDEN FRUIT TASTES SWEET BUT HAS BITTER CONSEQUENCES.

Walk in the Spirit, and you shall not fulfill the lust of the flesh.

GALATIANS 5:16

Our society sends mixed signals. I got a letter from my credit card company, saying, "Mr. Egner, you are one of our most valued customers. We would like to raise your buying power by $3,000." The next day, because I was late in sending a payment of $36.96, I got another letter from the same company. It made me feel like a terrible person. It seemed to be saying that if I didn't pay up immediately, they would take action against me.

Which am I? A valued customer or a terrible person? On one hand, I was urged to go out and spend a lot more money. On the other, I felt threatened because I was late making a payment. It's like the signals our society sends young people. In some ads, movies, and videos they're told to indulge themselves now—with sex or alcohol. Yet at other times they are warned about AIDS and drinking while driving.

Our society sends many conflicting messages; the Bible does not. The Word of God tells us not to listen to our lusts but to follow God's ways, depending fully on the Spirit (Gal. 5:16). If we do that, we will not live with the anxiety that results from following mixed signals.—D. C. E.

**GOD'S SIGNALS ARE MEANT FOR OUR PROTECTION,
CORRECTION, AND DIRECTION.**

Sin shall not have dominion over you,
for you are not under law but under grace.

ROMANS 6:14

When I visit the zoo, I skip the eagles' cage. I can't stand the pain of seeing those majestic birds sit there on their perches day after day, their burnished brown wings draped over them like an ill-fitting old coat. They were created for the heights, to dance among the clouds, not to be prisoners in a cage. Those birds were made to fly.

Many people who profess that they are Christ's men and women are like those caged eagles. They are made to live as free citizens of heaven, but they are imprisoned by their own sin. Their condition must break God's heart. He knows what they could become, but they have put themselves in a cage. And the irony is that it is a cage with open doors.

The apostle Paul said that we who have put our trust in Christ have died with Him to the sin that confined us in our old life. And we are now alive in Him. We are not the person we used to be. Therefore, we must stop facing life as we used to face it. Through Christ, you have been set free! You were never meant to be imprisoned in a cage. Confess your sin and trust God anew. You were made to soar.—H. W. R.

CHRIST IS THE OPEN DOOR OUT OF THE CAGE OF SIN.

With one hand they worked at construction,
and with the other held a weapon.

NEHEMIAH 4:17

*R*emember studying about the Minutemen? During the American Revolution, ordinary citizens banded together to form an effective army. They were farmers and merchants and bankers and blacksmiths. When they heard of trouble, they would drop their work, grab their muskets, and head into battle. No rummaging through the attic looking for that powderhorn. No searching the shed for wadding and shot. No stopping to clean their guns. They were ready in a minute.

We need to be God's minutemen. We should be prepared for action. It may be an opportunity to witness or to encourage a fellow believer facing fierce temptation. Someone in the workplace may be attacking the cause of Christ. Are we ready? We shouldn't have to revive our prayer life or take care of unresolved issues with God. No hunting for dusty Bibles. No forgiveness to seek or offer. No last-minute confession of sin.—D. C. E.

IN GOD'S SERVICE, OUR GREATEST ABILITY IS OUR AVAILABILITY.

Gracious is the LORD, and righteous; yes, our God is merciful.

P S A L M 1 1 6 : 5

Theodore Roosevelt understood the dangers of cynicism when he observed, "The poorest way to face life is to face it with a sneer." Cynicism is a virus that attacks the spirit and breaks down our relationship both to others and to God. The cynic suspects the worst even in the best of people. He can see more evil through a keyhole than others see through an open door.

The psalmist's enemies nearly defeated him, not with knives but through verbal attacks. And the greatest danger came not from the lies told about him but from their effect on his soul and his walk with the Lord.

Beware of cynicism. Avoid making snap judgments about others while under stress. The psalmist did that but eventually realized that his attitude was wrong. God delivered him and replaced his cynicism with vibrant praise. The Lord can do that for you too.—H. W. R.

BLESS GOD IN THE TRIAL AND
YOU WILL BE BLESSED BY GOD THROUGH THE TRIAL.

Through love serve one another.

GALATIANS 5:13

A prominent Christian leader was known for his willingness to help needy individuals with their social and financial problems. When asked why he took time out of his busy schedule to do this, he replied, "When I was a boy, I worked in our family grocery store. I was taught that I should never ask a customer, 'Is that all?' Instead, I was told to say, 'Isn't there anything else?' I have carried this philosophy over into my Christian work."

In Romans 16, the apostle Paul commended many in the church who were like this man. He singled out Priscilla, Aquila, Mary, Persis, and several others who had labored for the Lord with willing hands and loving hearts. They were not content to do minimal service but were always busy ministering to the needs of fellow believers.

When we have experienced the matchless grace of God, our hearts should be filled with compassion for our brothers and sisters in Christ. By extending to them a helping hand and assisting them in whatever way possible, we're actually saying, "God has given me so much. Isn't there anything else I can do for you?"—H. G. B.

YOU CANNOT LOVE GOD WITHOUT SERVING HIM.

Knowing, therefore, the terror of the Lord, we persuade men.

2 CORINTHIANS 5:11

I read a fable about a dog who loved to chase other animals. He bragged about his great running skill and said he could catch anything. Well, it wasn't long until his boastful claims were put to the test by a rabbit. With ease the little creature outran his barking pursuer. The other animals, watching with glee, began to laugh. The dog excused himself, however, by saying, "You forget, folks. I was only running for fun. He was running for his life!"

Motivation makes a difference in almost everything we do. In fact, it determines the way believers serve the Lord. Some people serve Him halfheartedly because they feel obligated. But there are others who serve with urgency and zeal because they recognize the terrible plight of people lost in sin. They are deeply grateful for God's saving grace in their lives, so they go all out for the Lord.

May we be zealous in serving the Lord!—R. W. D.

WHEN CHRISTIANS ARE ON FIRE FOR GOD,
SINNERS WILL BE ATTRACTED TO THE LIGHT.

Even though our outward man is perishing,
yet the inward man is being renewed day by day.

2 CORINTHIANS 4:16

It was a typical summer Sunday evening service. People were scattered throughout the 500-seat auditorium. There was a testimony time, and several people spoke up, sharing from their hearts what God had done.

Then Buddy stood and talked. He was grateful that he could be in church. When he told us that even though he didn't have a ride he was glad he was able to walk the mile or so to church, you could hear the others respond in surprise. On this Sunday night when so many had found reasons to stay away from church, Buddy had come alone, one dark step at a time. Buddy is blind.

We can learn a lot from Buddy. He struggles to do things we can do with little effort, but often neglect. He is more aware perhaps than those of us without physical disabilities that "our outward man is perishing" (2 Cor. 4:16), so he works hard at feeding his "inward man" by meeting with other believers. He knows what the apostle Paul knew: It is only through a strong reliance on the Lord that we can succeed in our Christian life.—J. D. B.

DISCIPLESHIP REQUIRES DISCIPLINE.

He is a double-minded man, unstable in all his ways.

JAMES 1:8

The smooth, shiny lizard known as a skink doesn't ordinarily draw crowds at the zoo. But the little critter discovered by a homeowner in Jacksonville, Florida, created quite a stir because it had two heads, one at each end of its body. What an unusual spectacle! And what an illustration of absolute frustration! When it tried to run, its legs actually moved in opposite directions.

As I studied its picture in a newspaper, I thought, *How incredible!* Yet how typical of many believers in Christ! We all have an innate tendency to sin; but when we are born again by faith in the Lord Jesus, we receive a wonderful new nature. This often creates an intense struggle. We experience a continual conflict between the mind of Christ and our old ways of thinking.

Jesus said, "No one can serve two masters; for either he will hate the one and love the other, or else he will be loyal to the one and despise the other" (Matt. 6:24). Let's yield completely to Christ. It's the only way to avoid the frustration of the double-minded skink.—M. R. D. II

A DOUBLE-MINDED PERSON IS A FRUSTRATED PERSON.

These people . . . honor Me with their lips,
but have removed their hearts far from Me.

ISAIAH 29:13

ourists throughout the centuries have visited the famous
Acropolis, the ancient hilltop religious citadel in Athens. And
thousands of sightseers from all over the world have picked up marble
chunks as souvenirs.

Why hasn't the supply of marble pieces been exhausted long ago?
The answer is very simple. Every few months a truckload of marble
fragments from a quarry miles away is scattered around the whole
Acropolis area. So tourists go home happy with what they think are
authentic pieces of ancient history.

We can be deceived by other kinds of imitations. Religious
language and music, religious objects and services may fool us into
imagining that we are experiencing a firsthand relationship with God
when in reality we are simply going through empty routines. The
possibility of religious deception prompts personal soul-searching.
Our pious practices may be only imitations of the true heartfelt faith
the Lord desires.—V. C. G.

A HYPOCRITE HAS GOD IN HIS MOUTH AND THE WORLD IN HIS HEART.

May

Be doers of the Word, and not hearers only,
deceiving yourselves.

JAMES 1:22

ourses in English composition teach us to avoid the use of the pronoun *I* as much as possible when we write. After all, it's neither good style nor good manners to make ourselves the center of attention. But there are times when the softening of the pronoun *I* can be bad spiritual grammar. For example, the next time you're talking with friends about living for Christ, avoid using *we* or *us* when you point out how Christians can be more effective in serving Christ.

It's easy and vague to say, "We suffer from apathy. We need a new devotion to the Lord." It's tougher to confess, "*I* suffer from apathy. *I* need greater devotion to the Lord." Too often we—oops, excuse me—*I* have said, "We should be doing something about our Sunday school." Or, "We need to get busy about evangelism." What a difference it might make if we were a bit less modest about saying "I."

Changing pronouns may not be the best writing style, but it can lead to a more Christ-honoring lifestyle.—H. W. R.

WHAT WOULD MY CHURCH BE LIKE IF
ALL ITS MEMBERS WERE JUST LIKE ME?

When Israel was a child, I loved him.

HOSEA 11:1

We can spare ourselves pain if we don't let ourselves become emotionally attached to anyone. But we will also miss out on some of the greatest joys in life. The more we love, the more we suffer. That's true. But the path of selfless love is also the path to some of our greatest joys.

In Hosea 11, God spoke of His love for Israel. He compared himself to a father caring for a child (vv. 3–4). But the people who should have brought Him joy caused Him pain instead. They rejected His love and guidance and did not honor Him (vv. 5, 7). God said He would discipline them, yet His sympathy was stirred and He promised He would not destroy the nation (v. 9).

Loving others makes us vulnerable to hurt and disappointment, but the rewards are great when we choose to love in spite of the pain it will bring.—H. V. L.

LOVE OPENS THE DOOR TO BOTH JOY AND PAIN.

At my first defense no one stood with me, but all forsook me.
. . . But the Lord stood with me.

2 TIMOTHY 4:16–17

In her book *Lincoln's Daughters of Mercy*, Marjorie Greenbie tells about Mother Bickerdyke, who worked with General Sherman during the Civil War. She brought relief to thousands of wounded and dying Union soldiers.

Once, when Mother Bickerdyke was giving special attention to a man considered worthless by his comrades, she was asked, "Why do you waste your time on trash like that?" "Because," she replied, "when there's any creature around here so miserable that there's nobody to care for him, he still has two friends in this army. One is God, and the other is me."

Paul certainly wasn't considered worthless by his co-workers, but there were times when he felt alone. Demas had forsaken him; Crescens, Titus, and Tychicus were all away traveling (2 Tim. 4:10, 12). Yet God and one person, Luke, sustained Paul when he stood at his final defense in Rome.

The Lord works through people. With Paul, He used Luke. Some struggling person in your life today may need the Lord—and you!—D. J. D.

ALL AROUND ARE NEEDS TO MEET.
BE GOD'S HEART AND HANDS AND FEET.

The abundance of their joy and their deep poverty
abounded in the riches of their liberality.

2 CORINTHIANS 8:2

*I*n his book *Thinking in the Future Tense*, Edward B. Lindaman refers to "the cafeteria culture of our age." It's the tendency to shy away from life's unpleasant disciplines and seek only what brings immediate pleasure.

Christians are not exempt from this tendency. Some persuasive preachers promote an "abundant life" of success and prosperity through positive thinking, more faith, or giving money to get God's blessing in return. The Bible, of course, teaches us to think positively (Phil. 4:8) and to give liberally (2 Cor. 8:2). But much "prosperity preaching" lacks the nourishing truths of Christ's sacrifice for sin and His demand for godly living. Our God is not only loving, good, and generous; He is also righteous, holy, and demanding. He hates sin and will not compromise with evil.

It's wonderful to hear about the blessings Christ offers, but we also need to experience repentance and self-denial. The picking and choosing of a cafeteria-style Christianity is no substitute for a well-rounded diet, which includes the tough truths of taking up Christ's cross and following Him (Mark 8:34).—D. J. D.

TO BE CONFORMED TO CHRIST, LET GOD'S SPIRIT FORM CHRIST IN YOU.

The wages of sin is death,
but the gift of God is eternal life in Christ Jesus.

ROMANS 6:23

Imagine a debt-free life—an existence without the irritation of those nagging payments hanging over your head every month. It's a prospect that has led financial counselors to create various get-out-of-debt plans that offer relief from financial worry. These are some of the suggestions they make:

➤ Stop all buying on credit.

➤ Cut down on your grocery bill.

➤ Do things yourself instead of paying to have them done.

➤ Quit being an impulse buyer.

Although I can't say I'm debt-free (I'm paying off my house and have other bills due each month), I can testify that in a different and much more important sense, I have no debts. When it comes to the burdensome worry of how to get out from under the weight of my sin, I don't have a care in the world. At one time, I was under the sentence of death because of my sin, but when I put my faith in Jesus Christ my debt was paid off (Rom. 4:7). The penalty of those sins was eliminated, and I am debt-free. It's a great feeling!—J. D. B.

CHRIST PAID A DEBT HE DIDN'T OWE
TO SATISFY A DEBT WE COULDN'T PAY.

In You, O LORD, I put my trust.

PSALM 71:1

An unknown author made this analogy: "Can you imagine the captain of a ship, driven about by rough winds and desiring to drop anchor, trying to find a suitable place to do so right on board his own vessel? Such a thing seems ridiculous, but for the sake of a lesson let's picture the skipper doing that. He hangs the anchor at the bow, but still the boat drives before the wind. He sets it on the deck, but this too fails to hold it steady. At last he puts it down into the hold, but has no better success.

"You see, an anchor resting on the storm-driven craft will never do the job. Only as it is thrown into the deep can it be effective against the wind and tide. In the same way, the person whose confidence is in himself will never experience true peace and safety. His actions are as futile as one who keeps the anchor aboard his own ship. Cast your faith into the great depths of God's eternal love and power. Place your trust in the infinitely faithful One."—R. W. D.

WE'LL BE STEADY IN THE STORM IF WE'RE ANCHORED TO CHRIST.

If anyone is in Christ, he is a new creation;
. . . all things have become new.

2 CORINTHIANS 5:17

A handkerchief made of very valuable material was ruined by an indelible ink blot. The owner could no longer proudly display her prized possession, so she sadly showed it to English art critic and painter John Ruskin. He took it, and with remarkable skill made that ugly ink blot the center of a beautiful design. The woman's handkerchief was then far more valuable than before.

God our Maker faced a similar situation, except the problem was immeasurably greater. Adam was God's supreme creation, but he had ruined himself by sin. With his original perfection stained and disfigured, he was fit only to be eternally discarded. But by the amazing strategy of the cross, our gracious God, the Supreme Artist, took ruined sinners and recreated them to reflect the beauty of Christ's holiness.

When we put our faith in the crucified Savior, we are not only completely forgiven, but God's Holy Spirit transforms us, making us into the Creator's prized possession. As the apostle Paul wrote in his letter to the Ephesians, we will be displaying throughout eternity "the exceeding riches of His grace in His kindness toward us in Christ Jesus" (2 Cor. 2:7). —V. C. G.

GOD CAN TRANSFORM A SIN-STAINED SOUL INTO A MASTERPIECE OF GRACE.

My son, . . . do not forsake the law of your mother.

PROVERBS 6:20

As I read Proverbs 6:20, which refers to "the law of your mother," I recall some of my mother's unique "laws" that have helped me many times. The first I call "the law of the warm kitchen." When we got home from school on a cold winter's day or when the holidays rolled around, the kitchen was always so warm from baking and cooking that the windows were steamed. It was also warm with a mother's love.

A second law I call "the law of a mother's perspective." When I would come to her all upset over some childish matter, she would often say, "Pay no attention." Or, "Ten years from now you'll have forgotten all about it." That helped me put things into perspective.

But above all was my mother's "law of faith." She had an unswerving trust in God that kept her strong and gentle amid the fears, pressures, and sacrifices of the war years and of the 1950s.

Mom's been with the Lord now for many years. Yet I'm still grateful for her "laws," because they have helped me through many difficult days. Christian mother, remember you, too, are writing "laws" for your children.
—D. C. E.

NO ONE IS POOR WHO HAS A GODLY MOTHER.

Having been born again . . . through the Word of God.

1 PETER 1:23

Chocolate lovers around the world know the name Cadbury, whose delectables have been produced near Birmingham, England, for more than 100 years. Millions of people have enjoyed them, but few know the unusual story of Helen Cadbury, daughter of the founder.

At age twelve, Helen Cadbury received Jesus Christ as her personal Savior. She immediately became interested in witnessing and growing spiritually, so she began carrying her huge Victorian Bible to school. Because it was so cumbersome, her father gave her a small New Testament she could put in her pocket. Helen's Christian friends admired it and acquired one of their own so they could carry it with them and read it every day. Soon they were calling themselves the Pocket Testament League and began giving New Testaments to people who promised to read them.

The Pocket Testament League has become a worldwide ministry with millions of members. And the basic idea of sharing God's Word with others is good for all of us. Carry a Bible or New Testament with you; read it and give it away!—D. C. E.

A MEASURE OF OUR LOVE FOR GOD IS OUR DESIRE TO SHARE HIS WORD.

Do not forget to do good and to share.

HEBREWS 13:16

The story is told of a young boy living in a poverty-stricken section of a big city who found his way into a gospel meeting and was converted. Not long afterward, someone tried to shake his faith by asking him several puzzling questions: "If God really loves you, why doesn't someone take better care of you? Why doesn't He tell somebody to send you a new pair of shoes?" The boy thought for a moment and then said, as tears filled his eyes, "I guess He does tell somebody, but somebody forgets!"

While it's true that the believer's primary obligation is to lead people to Christ, we sometimes use that as an excuse to escape our responsibility to also "do good and to share" (Heb. 13:16). We need to keep our spiritual balance and not forget to "do good to all, especially to those who are of the household of faith" (Gal. 6:10). If unbelievers who don't even know the Lord are conscious of the needs of other people, how much more should we, who have experienced the love of God personally, seek to relieve the suffering and lift the burdens of those who are less fortunate.
—R. W. D.

THE MORE CHRIST'S LOVE GROWS IN US,
THE MORE HIS LOVE FLOWS FROM US.

I can do all things through Christ who strengthens me.

PHILIPPIANS 4:13

Swedish hymnist Lina Sandell Berg served with her father in an evangelistic ministry. As they were traveling by ship, he accidentally fell overboard and drowned. In need of the comfort that only God can supply, she wrote the following words that are still sung by Christians around the world:

> *Day by day and with each passing moment,*
> *strength I find to meet my trials here;*
> *trusting in My Father's wise bestowment,*
> *I've no cause for worry or for fear.*

Secular counselors advise us to draw strength from our own inner resources. But that's hopelessly unrealistic. The simple fact is that in and of ourselves we don't have what it takes to deal with all of life's pressures and problems. Even the strongest among us have weaknesses. We're susceptible to vacillating moods, sinful temptations, and enslaving habits.

In times of conflict and defeat, we are forced to confess that we need a source of strength beyond ourselves, an always-available source on which we can draw—the inexhaustible grace of God.—V. C. G.

WHEN GOD GIVES A BURDEN, HE ALSO GIVES THE GRACE TO BEAR IT.

Whoever calls on the name of the LORD shall be saved.

ROMANS 10:13

Bible teacher Gary Burge stood at one end of a long, empty Gaza street. He was in Israel to do research for a book about Palestinian believers, and he wanted to talk to a Dr. Hassan at the Ali Arab hospital. The hospital was at the other end of the street, so he started walking. He soon discovered why the street was empty. On one side was the Israeli militia; on the other were Palestinian youths.

Halfway up the street, the calm was shattered by angry shouts, the chaotic clatter of rocks bouncing off plastic military shields, and the pop of rifles firing rubber bullets. Burge broke into a run. As he reached the hospital, he shouted desperately, "Dr. Hassan! I have come to see Dr. Hassan!" The door opened slightly, and a hand pulled him inside. Burge had called the name of the one who could save his life.

For sinners, "there is no other name under heaven given among men by which we must be saved" (Acts 4:12). Jesus is that name, "the name which is above every name" (Phil. 2:9). Our situation is desperate. The only way of escape is to call on Jesus, who promises to save us from all our sin. But we must ask Him.—D. C. E.

TO GET INTO HEAVEN, IT'S WHO YOU KNOW THAT COUNTS.

Be strong and of good courage;
. . . for the LORD your God is with you wherever you go.

JOSHUA 1:9

I was in England during World War II working as a surgical technician in an army hospital when I heard the shocking radio announcement: "Franklin Delano Roosevelt is dead!" I was saddened and troubled. Was Vice President Harry Truman qualified to be President? I was relieved when I heard him say that he felt as if an enormous weight had fallen on his shoulders and that he desired people everywhere to pray for him. This reassured me that he humbly recognized his inadequacies and his need for God's help.

Few of us will ever be thrust into a position of leadership with duties of that magnitude, but most of us know the feeling of inadequacy in the face of great responsibilities. When we face a new challenge, we can take courage from God's words to Joshua (1:9). We can accept our opportunity as from Him and believe that He will give us all we need to do it well. If we meditate on His Word, obey it, prayerfully rely on Him, and work diligently, He will do the rest. He will equip us for the task.—H. V. L.

GOD'S CALL TO A TASK INCLUDES HIS STRENGTH TO COMPLETE IT.

You shall not take the name of the LORD your God in vain.

EXODUS 20:7

The third commandment was taken so seriously by Israel that at one time the scribes wouldn't even write the name Yahweh (Jehovah) until they had first taken a bath and changed their clothes. Then after they had written it, they would take another bath and change their clothes again. Their focus on the word itself, however, often overlooked the broader implications of the commandment.

J. I. Packer says, "What is forbidden is any use or involvement of God's name that is empty, frivolous, or insincere." This includes any kind of irreverence, because it fails to take seriously God's character and reputation, which is represented by His name. Nor are we to use the name God or Jesus Christ as profanity, because this expresses neither praise, worship, nor faith. The commandment also relates to breaking a promise when God's name is used to back one's word.

Thank God for the name Jesus, which means Savior. He provides the forgiveness and help we need to keep the third commandment and become men and women known for being true to their word.—D. J. D.

IF YOU CARE ABOUT GOD, HANDLE HIS NAME WITH CARE.

You shall not covet your neighbor's house . . .
nor anything that is your neighbor's.

EXODUS 20:17

A store owner in Maine stubbornly refused to carry a new product. "You must remember, young feller," said the storekeeper to the salesman, "that in this part of the country every want ain't a need."

Confusing our wants with our needs goes to the heart of coveting and explains why we are so often driven by the desire for more and more. We fail to see that life's greatest fulfillment is not found in accumulating things but in knowing God.

The tenth commandment may seem like an add-on compared to such big-ticket items as murder, stealing, lying, and adultery, but it is foundational to all the other commandments and ensures peace and contentment. It is the only command that zeroes in on a forbidden attitude rather than an action. Yet it is a safeguard against the temptation to break the other nine commandments.—D. J. D.

**CONTENTMENT IS WANTING WHAT YOU HAVE,
NOT HAVING EVERYTHING YOU WANT.**

When he saw him, he had compassion.

LUKE 10:33

In her book *Kindness: Reaching Out to Others*, Phyllis J. Le Peau relates this story: "Some seminary students were asked to preach on the story of the Good Samaritan. When the hour arrived for their sermon, each one was deliberately delayed en route to class. As the students raced across campus, they encountered a person who pretended to be in need. Ironically, not one of the students stopped to help." Le Peau commented, "After all, they had an important sermon to preach."

What about us? Every time we meet someone in need, we live the parable of the Good Samaritan. Do we take the time and trouble to get involved? Perhaps we can assist a neighbor who is in material need, or lend a sympathetic ear to a troubled person. Maybe we can share the gospel with someone the Lord brings into our lives today. Or will we be like the religious leaders who quickly passed by on the other side and offered no help?

Let's honor our Lord by responding to the needs of others as He would.—D. C. E.

KINDNESS IS NEVER OUT OF SEASON.

You have not passed this way before.

JOSHUA 3:4

When our son Stephen was eight, he was invited to stay overnight at a cousin's house. It was his first time away from home and it all sounded like an exciting adventure. But when we got ready to leave, he started getting that homesick feeling! With tears glistening in his eyes and his voice quavering, he cried, "Mommy, I don't feel so good. I'd better go home with you."

My wife responded, "It's up to you, but I know you'd have a good time."

"But Mommy," Stephen whimpered, "they said they were going to climb a big hill tomorrow, and I've never been there before!"

Perhaps right now you are anxious about some new and untried pathway on which the Lord is leading you. Then listen to God's Word and take courage: "I will never leave you nor forsake you" (Heb. 13:5). "I will instruct you and teach you in the way you should go; I will guide you with My eye" (Ps. 32:8). Place your hand by faith in your heavenly Father's hand, and let Him lead the way.—R. W. D.

GOD DOES NOT ASK US TO GO WHERE HE DOES NOT LEAD.

Show me your faith without your works,
and I will show you my faith by my works.

JAMES 2:18

*W*hen Dave Thomas died in early 2002, he left behind more than just thousands of Wendy's restaurants. He also left a legacy of being a practical, hard-working man who was respected for his down-to-earth values. In his book *Well Done*, Thomas said, "Roll-up-your-shirtsleeves Christians see Christianity as faith and action. They still make the time to talk with God through prayer, study Scripture with devotion, be superactive in their church, and take their ministry to others to spread the Good Word." He went on to say they are "anonymous people who may be doing even more good than all the well-known Christians in the world."

That statement has more meat in it than a Wendy's triple burger. Thomas knew that faith must be accompanied by works or it is dead. Let's roll up our sleeves and get to work. There's plenty to do.—J. D. B.

A LIVING FAITH IS A WORKING FAITH.

The LORD God formed man of the dust of the ground.

GENESIS 2:7

Man has always wondered about the origin of life. The ancient Egyptians believed that frogs and toads originated in the silt of the Nile. Aristotle believed that worms came from dew and slime, and that mice sprang into life out of dank soil. Modern science is also interested in origins. A *Time* magazine cover story, "How Did Life Begin?" speculated that life began when certain molecules encountered any one of three "ideal" conditions. They proposed that life could have begun in a "warm little pond" (Darwin's original idea), near hydrothermal vents (underwater geysers on the ocean floor), or in bubbles floating on the warm ocean surface.

These evolutionary theories are pointless because we already know how life began. The Bible says that life began when God created it (Gen. 1–3). We did not evolve from primitive life forms. Our existence isn't based on a molecular accident. We were designed and created by a Master Designer who has a plan and a purpose for our lives.

Scientific theories have their place, but they're wrong when they contradict what the Bible says. Let's give honor and praise to our mighty Creator.—D. C. E.

THE DESIGN OF CREATION POINTS TO THE MASTER DESIGNER.

I will sanctify My great name,
which has been profaned among the nations.

EZEKIEL 36:23

In a *New York Times* interview, a widely recognized man voiced his displeasure with a fast-food chain in whose TV commercials he had appeared. He felt that the quality of some of the items he advertised had been diminishing. Since people associated his name with the product, he didn't want the corporation's lowered standards to damage his own name.

The Lord is also jealous for His name. In Ezekiel 36, He declared that He had been disgraced by the rebellious practices of His chosen people Israel. They had "profaned" His name among the nations (v. 21). The same thing happens today when we as Christians live in disobedience to the Lord. Our sinful actions reflect poorly on Him. We're not just hurting our own reputation when we fail to live up to God's holy standards —we're giving unbelievers an excuse for their low opinion of Him.

During His earthly ministry, Jesus carefully protected the name of His heavenly Father. If we fall short of His example, we can be sure that the Lord will keep His promise to discipline His people for His "holy name's sake" (v. 22). God's jealousy for His character should motivate us to live more faithfully for Him.—M. R. D. II

WE HONOR GOD'S NAME WHEN WE LIVE AS OBEDIENT CHILDREN.

If they cannot exercise self-control, let them marry.

1 CORINTHIANS 7:9

According to the *National & International Religion Report*, before the majority of American marriages take place, the man and woman have already been living together. The report goes on to point out that this practice has devastating effects. "Marriages that are preceded by living together have 50 percent higher disruption (divorce or separation) rates than marriages without premarital cohabitation."

The temptations were similar in the first century. That's why Paul had to make it clear to the believers at Corinth that they had no business being involved in sexual immorality. He said that if they found their passions becoming so strong that they could not control their sexual desires, there was an answer. It was not found in an immoral relationship; it was found in marriage.

In a day when immorality continues to devour people, let's do all we can to promote the joys and privileges of love that is honoring to God—the love that is shared in marriage. There is no substitute for pure love.—J. D. B.

SAVING YOURSELF FOR MARRIAGE WILL HELP TO SAVE YOUR MARRIAGE.

*Choose for yourselves this day whom you will serve.
. . . But as for me and my house, we will serve the LORD.*

JOSHUA 24:15

Abe Lincoln told the story of a blacksmith who heated a piece of iron in the forge, not knowing what he was going to make. At first he thought of shaping it into a horseshoe but changed his mind. After hammering on the iron for a while, he decided to try to make it into something else. By this time the metal was no longer malleable. Holding it up with his tongs and looking at it with disgust, the blacksmith tossed it into a vat of water. "Well," he shrugged, "at least I can make a fizzle out of it!"

Joshua would have seen an important lesson in that story. He knew that a meaningful life must have a clear purpose. "Choose!" he urged his followers. If you're not going to live for God, then decide against Him. If you are going to live for God, then let your life reflect that decision. But whatever you do, decide! Joshua made it clear that he and his family had made their choice to serve the Lord (24:15). For him, life was not an amusement park but an arena where important decisions had to be made.—H. W. R.

**IF YOU DECIDE NOT TO CHOOSE,
YOU'VE ALREADY MADE THE WRONG CHOICE.**

God will wipe away every tear from their eyes.

REVELATION 21:4

Many years ago a doctor made a house call on a dying patient, who asked, "Doctor, what will heaven be like?" The physician paused, trying to think of a helpful reply. Just then they heard the sound of scratching on the closed door of the patient's bedroom. "Do you hear that?" the doctor asked. "It's my dog. I left him downstairs, but he got impatient and came up here looking for me. He doesn't know what's in this room, but he knows his master is here. I believe that's how it is with heaven. We don't know what it's like, but we know that Jesus will be there. And really, nothing else matters."

The Bible gives us a few faith-strengthening glimpses of what life will be like beyond the closed door of death. We know that heaven will be a place of radiant splendor (Rev. 21:23). We know that it will be a place of reunion as we meet again those whom we have loved and from whom we have been parted for a little while (1 Thess. 4:17). We know that there will be "no more death, nor sorrow, nor crying" (Rev. 21:4). But above all, when we get to the other side, we will rejoice because Jesus is there, and we will be with Him forever.—V. C. G.

TO BE WITH JESUS FOREVER IS THE SUM OF ALL HAPPINESS.

As for me, I will walk in my integrity.

PSALM 26:11

He was a politician noted for his integrity. Although this description might be viewed by some as a contradiction in terms, it certainly was used often and correctly to describe US Congressman Paul Henry. After the three-term member of the House of Representatives lost a battle with brain cancer in 1993, political commentator David Broder said, "He was a model of what a public servant should be."

There was good reason for Paul Henry's integrity. He was a Christian who devoted his life and service to the Lord. In many ways his life mirrored the characteristics mentioned in Psalm 26. The psalmist David said that he (1) walked in God's truth, (2) avoided sinful entanglements, and (3) enjoyed worshiping God. In a similar way, Paul Henry (1) sought to live by biblical principles, (2) was on guard against the influence of those who were ungodly, and (3) regularly worshiped at his local church.

As we grow more and more like the One we worship, our lives will be marked by truth and right thinking. Each day we should ask God to help us to live a life of integrity.—J. D. B.

INTEGRITY IS THE MARK OF TRUE CHARACTER.

We also glory in tribulations,
knowing that tribulation produces perseverance.

ROMANS 5:3

A tourist in Maine was watching a farmer build a stone wall. After a few moments, he inquired about the wall's strange dimensions. It was four feet high and five feet wide. The farmer explained, "I'm building it like this so that if it ever blows over, it will be taller than it was before."

No doubt the industrious fence-maker said this with tongue in cheek, yet there is a good lesson to be drawn from this story. Even though the storms of trial may seem to blow us over, the Lord uses such experiences to make us "taller" than we were before.

Sometimes in the midst of great trials, it may seem as if the Lord has abandoned us. But we can "glory in tribulations, knowing that tribulation produces perseverance" (Rom. 5:3). Yes, we can grow taller through trial.—H. G. B.

FAITH NEEDS EXERCISE TO GROW.

*Grow in the grace and knowledge
of our Lord and Savior Jesus Christ.*

2 PETER 3:18

When Thomas Naylor was teaching business management at Duke University, he asked his students to draft a personal strategic plan. He reports that "with few exceptions, what they wanted fell into three categories: money, power, and things—very big things, including vacation homes, expensive foreign automobiles, yachts, and even airplanes." This was their request of the faculty: "Teach me how to be a money-making machine."

That's not exactly an exalted ambition! No thought of humanitarian service, and no thought of spiritual values! Yet, what those students wanted was what many people want—maybe what most people want.

The apostle Paul's overriding ambition was totally different. His consuming desire was to know Jesus and become increasingly conformed to His holy example (Phil. 3:10). He wanted to serve Him by proclaiming the life-changing good news of God's grace.—V. C. G.

A WISE PERSON SETS HIS EARTHLY GOALS ON HEAVENLY GAINS.

God is my strength and power, and He makes my way perfect.

2 SAMUEL 22:33

*P*eople who live without hope can become suicidal. So it was with an Italian prisoner of war being held on a military base in the United States during World War II. He had become despondent after learning that his wife had died in Italy. The camp commander, knowing that the man had been a stonemason, asked him if he could design a chapel for the base. The POW accepted the assignment and even supervised its construction.

Today a unique chapel stands at the Letterkenny Army Depot in Chambersburg, Pennsylvania. The formerly despondent prisoner found renewed hope by using his God-given talents to bless others.

When you are in despair, the first step on the pathway to new hope is to take care of your physical needs. Then listen to God's voice through the Scriptures. The Lord will show you your spiritual condition and tell you what He would have you do to bless others.—D. J. D.

GOD GIVES HOPE TO US AS WE GIVE HELP TO OTHERS.

The wicked man . . . is caught in the cords of his sin.

PROVERBS 5:22

ible teacher Henrietta Mears once told her students, "A bird is free in the air. Place a bird in the water and he has lost his liberty. A fish is free in the water, but leave him on the sand and he perishes. . . . The Christian is free when he does the will of God and is obedient to God's command. This is as natural a realm for God's child as the water is for the fish, or the air for the bird."

Although King Solomon didn't use the word *freedom* in Proverbs 16, he understood that it comes only within the sphere of honoring God and His Word. By contrast, bondage comes to those who ignore God's truth. Liberty results from practicing humility, trust, careful conversation, and self-control (vv. 19–24). But bondage inevitably enslaves those who are governed by willful rebellion, pride, arrogance, strife, and malicious trouble-making (vv. 18, 27–30).

Do you want to be free? Jesus said, "If you abide in My word, you are My disciples indeed. And you shall know the truth, and the truth shall make you free" (John 8:31–32). Jesus is the ultimate source of true freedom.—M. R. D. II

FREEDOM IS NOT HAVING YOUR WAY, BUT YIELDING TO GOD'S WAY.

There will be false teachers among you, who will secretly
bring in destructive heresies, even denying the Lord.

2 PETER 2:1

A New York City couple received through the mail two tickets to a smash Broadway hit. Oddly, the gift arrived without a note, and they wondered who had sent it. But they still attended the show and enjoyed it immensely. Returning to their apartment, they discovered that their bedroom had been ransacked. Valuable furs and jewels were missing. On the pillow was this simple note: "Now you know."

Like that nameless thief, a false teacher knows what people want and appeals to their desires (2 Pet. 2). He doesn't wear a lapel pin to warn of his lies, but he comes disguised as a representative of the truth. He claims he will enrich lives, but those who follow him often learn at a high cost that they have been deceived.

Jesus, however, is a teacher we can trust completely. He offers us the gift of eternal life because He truly loves us. Accepting His gift of salvation is the first step in protecting ourselves from the deceptive gifts that false teachers offer.—H. W. R.

WISE ARE THOSE LAMBS WHO GRAZE CLOSE BY THEIR SHEPHERD.

The memory of the righteous is blessed,
but the name of the wicked will rot.

PROVERBS 10:7

On Memorial Day in the United States, thousands of people visit cemeteries and monuments to remember and honor their loved ones. They ponder a name carved in stone and recall the person for whom it stands.

This kind of reflection on the lives of those who have gone before us can encourage us to evaluate the way we are living today. When people hear our name, do they think of someone who is faithfully living for Christ?

King Solomon observed: "The memory of the righteous is blessed" (Prov. 10:7). "A good name is to be chosen rather than great riches" (Prov. 22:1). "A good name is better than precious ointment" (Eccles. 7:1).

By our attitudes and actions, we are creating the memories that will be associated with our names in life and in death.—D. C. M.

THE MEMORY OF A FAITHFUL LIFE
SPEAKS MORE ELOQUENTLY THAN WORDS.

First cleanse the inside of the cup and dish,
that the outside of them may be clean also.

MATTHEW 23:26

Have you heard about the man who took his old car to a dealer and asked him to sell it for him? When the dealer asked how many miles were on it, the man replied, "It's got 230,000." The salesman replied, "It'll never sell unless you turn back the mileage." So the man left.

When the car salesman hadn't heard from the man for several weeks, he called him. "I thought you were going to sell that old car."

"I don't have to anymore," came the reply. "It's only got 77,000 miles on it now. Why should I sell it?"

The old car still had a sick engine, bad rings, and a transmission that slipped. Turning back its odometer had not changed that! In the same way, people who try to please God by living a good life without first trusting in Christ are like the Pharisees who were clean on the outside but still filthy on the inside (Matt. 23:25).—D. C. E.

WE'RE SAVED BY GOD'S WORK, NOT BY GOOD WORKS.

June

Count it all joy when you fall into various trials.

JAMES 1:2

Author Leo Buscaglia's father came home one evening and sadly told the family that his business partner had stolen the assets of the firm. Bankruptcy was unavoidable. Instead of despairing, Leo's mother went out, pawned some jewelry, and prepared a delectable dinner. When family members protested, she replied, "The time for joy is now when we need it most, not next week."

Have you run into difficult circumstances recently? Has some calamity gripped your heart with fear and sorrow? God doesn't want you to wear a hypocritical, smiling face. But He does want you to trust Him through all your circumstances—including calamities! He wants you to accept failure, sickness, and loss as opportunities for growth in faith and obedience.

Our wise and loving heavenly Father longs for us to submit to His sovereign control. Only as we do that can we agree with James and rejoice even in calamity.—V. C. G.

LIFE'S TRIALS SHOULD MAKE US BETTER—NOT BITTER.

Let each one of you speak truth with his neighbor.

EPHESIANS 4:25

*I*f television commercials are telling the truth, glamorous movie stars and athletes use products that everyone ought to buy. But, as *Time* magazine reports (and most viewers suspect), many celebrities don't use the products they endorse.

And what about autobiographies? According to the same article, they are not always written by the individuals whose names they bear but by writers who aren't mentioned. This dishonesty, *Time* suggests, is a symptom of the deception that is creeping into our society. What will civilized life become as people increasingly ignore God's commands against lying? (Exod. 20:16; Lev. 19:11).

God's Word urges us to tell the truth (Prov. 12:17–22). Only as we obey Him can we hope to prevent our society from being consumed by suspicion and mistrust. We are to be truth-tellers like Jesus, of whom Scripture says, "Nor was deceit found in His mouth" (1 Pet. 2:22). Let's strive for that holy standard today.—V. C. G.

ALL THE TROUBLE IN THE WORLD BEGAN WITH ONE LIE.

*Above all, [take] the shield of faith with which you will be able
to quench all the fiery darts of the wicked one.*

EPHESIANS 6:16

United States Army and Pentagon officials are developing a
sophisticated armor system to protect tanks against enemy fire.
According to the *Army Times*, this new system will protect armored
vehicles against the latest kinetic energy rockets, which are long, thin,
sharp-pointed projectiles that pierce armor when they hit head-on. The
Smart Armor System (SAS) will keep these missiles from penetrating the
armor of tanks because special reactive tiles will deflect them.

As followers of Jesus Christ, we need protection from the "fiery
darts" being hurled at us by Satan. He has some powerful missiles that
can stir up within us doubt, fear, disappointment, impurity, lust, greed,
selfishness, covetousness, and pride. And he attacks us when we are most
vulnerable in these areas. But God has given us the shield of faith for our
protection to deflect Satan's most powerful missiles. When we trust God,
believing what He tells us in His Word, the enemy's most deadly attacks
will be futile.—D. C. E.

GOD'S WORD IS A SURE DEFENSE AGAINST TEMPTATION.

You have been my defense and refuge in the day of my trouble.

PSALM 59:16

The nineteenth-century hymnwriter Ira D. Sankey was walking with his young son on a cold winter day. As they came to an icy spot, Mr. Sankey said, "My boy, you'd better let me take your hand."

The youngster didn't want to take his hand from his warm pocket, so he disregarded his father's suggestion. Just then he lost his footing and took a nasty fall. "All right, Daddy," he said, "let me hold on to your coat."

But the boy's weak grip was not enough to hold him up when his feet went out from under him again. Getting up, he said, "Daddy, you'd better hold my hand!" He didn't fall again.

Put your hand in God's hand. It's your best guarantee against falling in life's slippery places.—D. J. D.

GOD WILL KEEP YOU FROM FALLING IF YOU PUT YOUR HAND IN HIS.

Death and life are in the power of the tongue.

PROVERBS 18:21

Words of encouragement can be "life words," bringing new motivation to our lives. Mark Twain said that he could live for a whole month on one good compliment!

As a youth, Larry Crabb had developed a stutter that humiliated him in a school assembly. A short time later when praying aloud in a church service, his stutter caused him to get both his words and his theology mixed up in his prayer. Expecting stern correction, Larry slipped out of the service, resolving never to speak in public again. On his way out he was stopped by an older man who said, "Larry, there's one thing I want you to know. Whatever you do for the Lord, I'm behind you one thousand percent." Larry's resolve never again to speak publicly weakened instantly. Now, many years later, he addresses large crowds without stuttering.

Paul told us to season our speech "with grace" so that we may know how to answer others (Col. 4:6). Then we will speak "life words" that bring encouragement.—J. E. Y.

**CORRECTION MAY MOLD US,
BUT ENCOURAGEMENT WILL MOTIVATE US.**

Do not lay up for yourselves treasures on earth.

MATTHEW 6:19

The trouble with storing up treasures on earth is that they are so temporary. Some of them, such as buildings or jewelry or certificates of deposit, can be so easily destroyed. A little spark, a theft, an economic downturn, and they are gone.

I heard a missions speaker compare the value of US dollars with the currency of a central African nation. He said that one American dollar would purchase 1,700,000 units of that country's currency. Wow! We could take $1,000 over there, convert it, and ship back billions! But we wouldn't be rich because that nation's money is worthless in the United States.

The same is true of the treasures of earth. They may be of value down here, but they have no worth in heaven. How much better it is to accumulate the treasures of heaven through service to Christ, obedience to Him, moral purity, faith, love, and investing our lives in helping others! It's worthless to treasure the treasures of earth.—D. C. E.

**WE LAY UP TREASURES IN HEAVEN
AS WE LAY DOWN TREASURES ON EARTH.**

He who has the Son has life;
he who does not have the Son of God does not have life.

1 JOHN 5:12

Hikers in California's Sierra Mountains are surprised to encounter ten-foot-high fences with barbed wire stretched around the top. What do they see inside the fence-surrounded enclosures? Some vital communication equipment like a radio tower? No, they see only a few gnarled trees, maybe just a twisted stump with a few needles. A sign reads: DO NOT ENTER. BRISTLECONE PINE PROTECTION ZONE. PLEASE PROTECT THESE TREES. They are the oldest living things on earth.

Pamphlets explain that these bristlecone pines were flourishing when Jesus walked on earth, and that the oldest were seedlings at the time of the Exodus from Egypt. Eventually, though, regardless how carefully they are protected, those trees will die. They are not destined to live forever. But Christians have the certainty of everlasting life. To be sure, our bodies will die. Yet by God's grace and power, our souls will never perish. Our bodies will be raised up and, as Paul said, be changed from mortal to immortal (1 Cor. 15:53). We who believe in Christ will live forever!—V. C. G.

WANT TO LIVE FOREVER? LET JESUS LIVE IN YOU NOW.

Untaught and unstable people twist
to their own destruction . . . the Scriptures.

2 PETER 3:16

An art enthusiast displayed on the walls of his office a collection of etchings, including one of the Leaning Tower of Pisa. Every morning he noticed it was crooked, so he straightened it. Finally one evening he asked the cleaning woman if she was responsible for moving the picture each night. "Why, yes," she said, "I have to hang it crooked to make the tower straight!"

In a similar way, some people have the habit of twisting the Scriptures to make their imperfect lives look better or to justify their own opinions. The apostle Peter warned his readers about the kind of people who do not approach God's Word with honest motives and respect for its authority, and who distort its message. They will incur God's judgment (2 Pet. 3:16–17).

Unless we review the Bible prayerfully and humbly, we may get a wrong message and be drawn away from our steadfastness in Christ. God gave us His Word as a light to guide our steps. If we obey it each day, we will find it to be an unfailing source of strength and truth.—H. G. B.

WE MUST ALIGN OURSELVES WITH THE BIBLE,
NEVER THE BIBLE WITH OURSELVES.

If God so loved us, we also ought to love one another.

1 JOHN 4:11

What gives us the power to love as Christ loved? Only the indwelling Holy Spirit can motivate us to Christlike deeds of compassion, forgiveness, and self-sacrifice.

The apostle John wrote, "If we love one another, God abides in us, and His love has been perfected in us. By this we know that we abide in Him, and He in us, because He has given us His Spirit" (1 John 4:12–13).

A mother asked her young son to clean her shoes. He worked on them diligently until they were spotless and shiny. To show her appreciation, his mother gave him a dollar. When she went to put the shoes on, she found something wadded up in the toe of one of them. It was her dollar wrapped in a note that read: "Here's yer dallar, Mom. I dun it fer luv."

Fueled by the Holy Spirit, we too can serve others, motivated by Christ's love.—D. C. E.

WE DO NOT FUNCTION WELL ON ANYTHING BUT LOVE.

The fool has said in his heart, "There is no God."

PSALM 14:1

An unbelieving lawyer had a plaque on his office wall that read: GOD IS NOWHERE. His small daughter, while waiting for him one day, passed the time by copying that motto over and over on a piece of paper. Unintentionally she spaced the letters in a way that completely changed their meaning. Adding a space between the letters W and H, she wrote GOD IS NOW HERE.

The letters on the sign in the attorney's office may be read two different ways, but only one meaning is true. Many people look at God's mighty handiwork in the universe and think that it simply says "wild chance." But others see it as saying "wise Creator." The Bible gives us the right interpretation. Those who see God as NOW HERE instead of NOWHERE are the ones who know how to read the sign.—R. W. D.

GOD IS NOT SIMPLY HERE. HE IS EVERYWHERE.

Those who do not obey the gospel . . .
shall be punished with everlasting destruction.

2 THESSALONIANS 1:8–9

During the Franco-German war of 1870–71, a homeowner found two unexploded shells near his house. He cleaned them up and put them on display near his fireplace. A few weeks later he showed them to a visitor. His friend, an expert in munitions, had a horrible thought, "What if they're still loaded?" After examining the shells, he exclaimed, "Get them away from the fire immediately! They're as deadly as the day they were made!" Without realizing it, the homeowner had been living in peril.

Likewise, many people unknowingly live in constant jeopardy of something far worse—a Christless eternity in hell. Failing to recognize the consequences of unbelief, they risk sealing their doom at any moment. We cannot exaggerate the danger of rejecting Christ and living in unbelief, for what we do with Him and His offer of salvation determines where we will spend eternity.—H. G. B.

OUR MAIN BUSINESS IN THIS WORLD
MUST BE TO SECURE OUR PLACE IN THE NEXT.

Because you have rejected the word of the LORD,
He also has rejected you.

1 SAMUEL 15:23

According to *The Blunder Book* by M. Hirsh Goldberg, the company that won the bid to construct the 100 miles of track for the Washington, D.C., subway system projected the cost to be $793 million. When it was completed, however, it cost $6.6 billion. Goldberg said the same company that built the subway system received a contract to build the Saudi Arabian city of Jubail. The initial estimate was $9 billion. But when the project was finished, the bill came to $45 billion. That's a cost overrun of $36 billion!

These unexpected construction expenses are of little significance, however, compared with the unexpected costs of our sins against God. The life of King Saul shows us the enormous price of disobedience. He never figured that his continued willfulness and stubborn pride would eventually cost him his honor, his family, his friends, his influence for good, and his fellowship with God. He lost it all.

Father, help us to count the costs of our sin. First, help us to see the enormous cost paid by Your Son on the cross for us. Then, help us to see the inevitable cost of failing to trust You today.—M. R. D. II

SIN ADDS TO YOUR TROUBLE AND MULTIPLIES YOUR DIFFICULTIES.

Lay up for yourselves treasures in heaven.

MATTHEW 6:20

There's an old legend about three men who were crossing a desert on horseback during the night. As they approached a dried-up creek bed, they heard a voice commanding them to stop and dismount, pick up some pebbles, put them in their pockets, and not look at them until the next morning. The men were also promised that if they obeyed they would be both glad and sad. After they did as they were told, the three mounted their horses and went on their way.

As the first gray streaks of dawn began to spread across the eastern sky, the men reached into their pockets to pull out the pebbles. To their great surprise, they had been transformed into diamonds, rubies, and other precious gems. It was then that they realized the significance of the promise that they would be both glad and sad. They were happy that they had picked up as many pebbles as they did, but sorry—so sorry— that they had not collected more.

We will no doubt feel something like that when we get to heaven. We will be happy for the treasure we laid up in heaven while on earth and joyful for the rewards Christ will give us. But we will also experience regret for not having done more to serve Him.—R. W. D.

THE CROWNS WE WEAR IN HEAVEN MUST BE WON ON EARTH.

*Oh, the depth of the riches both of
the wisdom and knowledge of God!*

ROMANS 11:33

*B*ible teacher E. S. English told of a visit to the Orient by
Eugene Ormandy and the Philadelphia Orchestra. In one city,
the local orchestra performed Beethoven's Fifth Symphony for the visiting
musicians. According to reports, it was not done very well. Then at the
end of the first movement, the host conductor passed the baton to
Eugene Ormandy. What a transformation! You would have thought he
had been conducting the local orchestra for years. As the members of the
Philadelphia Orchestra listened, they were impressed in a new way with
Ormandy's talent and genius. They realized they had begun to take him
for granted and had lost sight of his greatness.

As believers in Christ, we often fall into a similar pattern in our
relationship to God. We take Him and His marvelous attributes for
granted. Because we are carried along daily by His unending stream of
love and mercy, we begin to accept His goodness as an ordinary part of
life. We might even forget what a great God we have. Together, let's exalt
our great God!—P. R. V.

NEVER LET GOD'S GOOD GIFTS CAUSE YOU TO FORGET THE GIVER.

He who covers his sins will not prosper,
but whoever confesses and forsakes them will have mercy.

PROVERBS 28:13

In 1945, just months after World War II had ended, American newspapers reported that occupation forces in Japan had arbitrarily destroyed five atomic cyclotrons. Enraged scientists and public officials called the action "a crime against mankind." They likened the destruction of this valuable research equipment to the burning of a library.

An investigation revealed that the cyclotrons had been destroyed by mistake. What is most interesting, however, is the way the error was handled by the military. According to author M. Hirsh Goldberg, some officials called for a cover-up. But General Leslie R. Groves, the officer in charge, issued a statement admitting that the War Department had made an error. The press was surprised by such honesty and soon lost interest in the story. Later, after the dust had cleared, General Groves concluded, "Honest errors, openly admitted, are sooner forgiven."

That sounds like Proverbs 28:13. If we cover our sin, God will remove His blessing from our lives. But if we confess it, the Lord will forgive us and show us mercy. Facing up to our sin is the best way to put it behind us.—M. R. D. II

SIN BRINGS FEAR; CONFESSION BRINGS FREEDOM.

In [Christ] you also are being built together
for a dwelling place of God.

EPHESIANS 2:22

The explorers who first entered Peru found huge, impressive buildings that may have been standing for as long as 2,000 years. These ancient Inca structures were built of hand-hewn rocks of different sizes and shapes. Some were three-sided, some four-sided, and some seven-sided. Without the use of mortar, they were fitted together so perfectly that they stood for many centuries, even through earthquakes.

God builds His church in much the same way. The Bible pictures the church of Jesus Christ as a building, and each believer is a block in that building. Peter said that we, "as living stones, are being built up a spiritual house" (1 Pet. 2:5). Because we are all different, that's not an easy process. People with a variety of backgrounds, abilities, interests, and needs make up Christ's true church. Yet when we let the Lord Jesus do His work among us, shaping us and assigning our place in the structure, we become part of a strong, solid edifice.—D. C. E.

THE PERMANENCE OF THE CHURCH IS BASED ON
THE CHARACTER OF ITS BUILDER.

Love one another fervently with a pure heart.

1 PETER 1:22

When our forefathers came to America, the land had to be cleared before it could be cultivated. They soon discovered that cutting down the trees was but a small part of their task. A far more difficult job was clearing out the roots. If they were not removed, the area would soon be covered with a second growth, and the farmers would have to start all over again.

Our hearts are like that ground. Every bit of hidden anger and every trace of an unforgiving attitude must be thoroughly rooted out before we can "love one another fervently with a pure heart." When a dispute is only superficially resolved, the arguing may stop, but the resentment and distrust continue. There has been no genuine reconciliation. We must go beyond an outward truce and show love for others even when we disagree with them.

Don't just smooth out quarrels on the surface! Go deeper. Ask God to reveal any hidden bitterness in your heart and to help you forgive the one who has wronged you.—H. G. B.

RESENTMENT MUST BE UPROOTED IF FORGIVENESS IS TO FLOWER.

"This sickness is . . . for the glory of God."

JOHN 11:4

F. B. Meyer wrote, "The child of God is often called to suffer because there is nothing that will convince onlookers of the reality and power of true religion as suffering will do, when it is borne with Christian fortitude." Notice that the important thing is how we respond to suffering.

Have you ever heard the legend of the mignonette and the gravel walk? (The mignonette is a plant that has greenish yellow spikes of perfumed flowers.) "How fragrant you are this morning!" said the gravel walk. "Yes," said the mignonette, "I have recently been trodden upon and bruised, and it has brought forth all my sweetness." "But," said the gravel walk, "I am trodden on every day, and I only grow harder."

The commentary on life is obvious. Some who suffer send forth a sweetness that blesses all who come in contact with them, while others become hard and bitter under adverse circumstances. How do you respond to suffering?—H. G. B.

GOD CHOOSES WHAT WE GO THROUGH.
WE CHOOSE HOW WE GO THROUGH IT.

Therefore what God has joined together,
let not man separate.

MATTHEW 19:6

It is the custom in one area of the Netherlands for newlywed couples to enter their house through a special door. The door is never used again until one dies and the body is carried out through that same door.

God designed marriage like that house. It has one door that is locked tightly. That lock, which keeps the marriage bond secure, is loving commitment for life, which includes a commitment to being reconciled if the relationship should break.

Commitment provides the foundation for achieving security and intimacy in Christ based on forgiveness and the rebuilding of trustworthiness. Theodore Bovet put it like this: "I have bound myself for life; I have made my choice; from now on my aim will not be to choose a woman who will please me, but to please the woman I have chosen." Every marriage needs commitment like that.—D. J. D.

A GOOD MARRIAGE REQUIRES DETERMINATION
TO BE MARRIED FOR GOOD.

*Their joy and their deep poverty abounded
in the riches of their liberality.*

2 CORINTHIANS 8:2

After the war in Korea, a Westerner traveling through the countryside noticed an old man and a young boy struggling to pull a plow through the soil to prepare a small field for planting. When the foreigner greeted them, they stopped and straightened up with a groan. They showed no self-pity but flashed a friendly smile.

The Westerner, who was a Christian, learned their story. They were believers too. Their little chapel had been destroyed in the war. The Christians who had survived agreed to rebuild their place of worship, and each member gave what he could.

The old man and the boy were so destitute, however, that they had no money to contribute. They had lost their family and their home in the fighting, and the only thing that remained was their ox. After earnestly praying, they had decided to sell it and give the money to help rebuild the chapel. Now they had to pull the plow themselves. The Westerner reported, "To them, the gift was not a sacrifice but a delight."—H. G. B.

SACRIFICE IS THE TRUE MEASURE OF GENEROSITY.

"The LORD is my portion," says my soul,
"therefore I hope in Him!"

LAMENTATIONS 3:24

A mother wrote me that she had prayed daily for the safety of her son, but one day he was killed in an accident on the job. "For the past four years," she said, "I have been searching for the answer to why."

In another family, a sudden heart attack snatched Ray from Sylvia's side, leaving her to face life alone. When my wife and I visited her at the funeral home, we were met by a woman who was grieving but not asking God for an explanation.

What made the difference? Was it wrong for that mother to question God? Not at all! Sylvia too must have wondered about God's purpose in this tragedy. But from past experience she had come to know Him to be completely trustworthy. She could suspend judgment. "I don't need to ask why," she told us.

To suspend judgment when God is silent honors Him because it refuses to charge Him with being unjust. Those who express such faith are strengthened by God's Spirit and come to see how strong and good God really is.—D. J. D.

WHEN WE BLESS GOD IN OUR TRIALS
WE ARE BLESSED BY GOD THROUGH OUR TRIALS.

He also predestined [us] to be conformed
to the image of His Son.

ROMANS 8:29

had a friend who was a professional photographer. He told me that the hours he spent in the darkroom made the difference between a mediocre picture and a superior one. The pictures were taken in his studio where the subject was indelibly impressed on the sensitive film. But that was just the beginning. The film then had to undergo the careful process of development, which required darkness, the right temperatures, special chemicals, and time. Only through this procedure could the impression on the film be "brought out" and printed.

Similarly, at the moment of salvation, a permanent "impression" of the Savior is made in our heart. But it takes a lifetime with many trials and testings for His image to be developed in us.

Let's thank God for the "darkroom" that He uses to make us "perfect and complete, lacking nothing" (James 1:4).—P. R. V.

CONVERSION IS THE MIRACLE OF A MOMENT;
MATURING TAKES A LIFETIME.

They shall see His face.

REVELATION 22:4

When John W. Peterson first started writing gospel melodies and lyrics, some were rejected by publishers. One such occurrence was especially disturbing. Peterson had just written "Over the Sunset Mountains" after meditating on that glorious day when we will enter the joys of heaven and see the Savior. The music editor he approached seemed pleased with his song but made this small suggestion: "Take out the name Jesus, and enlarge a little more on heaven." Peterson thought, Heaven without Jesus? That is unthinkable! So he picked up his manuscript and left.

Soon another song came into his mind that expressed his heartfelt reaction: "I have no song to sing but that of Christ my King, to Him my praise I'll bring forevermore! His love beyond degree, His death, that ransomed me, now and eternally I'll sing it o'er."

God honored John Peterson for not compromising the truth. Eventually both songs were published, and over the years they have brought comfort to many.—H. G. B.

**THE MORE YOU LOVE JESUS,
THE MORE YOU'LL LOOK FORWARD TO HEAVEN.**

JUNE 24

Put on the Lord Jesus Christ,
and make no provision for the flesh, to fulfill its lusts.

ROMANS 13:14

he full-page ad in the *National Geographic* magazine was
simple, direct, and unmistakably clear. Those who read it had
to know that its sponsor cared about their welfare. The page looked
like this:

A complete set of instructions

for the first-time smoker.

Don't.

American Heart Association

We're fighting for your life.

God runs "ads" too. Romans 13:9 is one example. It contains
several commands that are meant to keep us spiritually strong and
healthy. There is one vital difference, however, about God's advertising.
His instructions come with the offer of forgiveness through Jesus'
death on the cross, and the guarantee of His Spirit's power to fulfill the
righteous requirements of the law (Rom. 8:4). Our part is to trust
Jesus. These additions to God's ads make them truly effective.—D. J. D.

GOD'S LAW SHOWS US A NEED THAT ONLY GOD'S GRACE CAN SUPPLY.

Lying lips are an abomination to the LORD,
but those who deal truthfully are His delight.

PROVERBS 12:22

The first governor-general of Australia was a man by the name of Lord Hopetoun. One of his most cherished possessions was a four-hundred-year-old ledger he had inherited from John Hope, one of his ancestors. Hope had owned a business in Edinburgh, where he first used this old ledger. When Lord Hopetoun received it, he noticed that it had inscribed on its front page this prayer, "O Lord, keep me and this book honest!" John Hope knew that he needed God's help to maintain his integrity.

Honesty is an extremely important quality for the Christian. Shading the truth, withholding the facts, juggling the figures, or failing to give our employer a full day's work for a full day's pay—these are all dishonest activities, and they displease God.

An acquaintance of mine said of a mutual Christian friend, "He's true-blue, all wool, and a yard wide." He meant that our friend was genuine, truthful, and trustworthy—honest in motive as well as in action. May it be so with you and me.—P. R. V.

IT TAKES COURAGE TO BE HONEST AND TRUE IN ALL YOU SAY AND DO.

It is good for me that I have been afflicted,
that I may learn Your statutes.

PSALM 119:71

Shortly before Scottish missionary John G. Paton died, a friend said to him, "I am sorry to see you lying on your back." Smiling, Paton asked, "Do you know why God puts us on our backs?" After his friend answered no, the missionary replied, "In order that we may look upward."

Another Christian who viewed suffering from the right perspective was songwriter Eugene Clark. Afflicted with severe rheumatoid arthritis and glaucoma, Clark spent the last ten years of his life bedridden. Yet he continued composing songs and writing articles to the glory of God— enriching the lives of thousands through his ministry. Though down physically, he learned to keep looking up.

Sunny skies, worry-free days, and calm nights are not always the best environment for developing spiritual stamina. It is often in the hour of affliction that we draw close to our loving heavenly Father. Being down teaches us to look up.—P. R. V.

WHEN YOU LOOK OUT, IT MAY BE NIGHT;
BUT WHEN YOU LOOK UP, IT'S ALWAYS LIGHT.

Their conscience also bearing witness, and . . .
their thoughts accusing or else excusing them.

ROMANS 2:15

Some people need a little help to know how to act in public. So taxicab drivers in Paris came up with an idea to help their riders behave themselves. It's an electric cushion rigged to a powerful battery. If the driver notices that his passenger is about to do something unacceptable (like robbing or assaulting him), he pushes a button and zaps the rider with 52,000 volts of low-tension electricity.

That may seem like a drastic way to alert someone who is out of line, but it is a little like the right/wrong monitor God has put in all of us. Each of us is equipped to receive signals to warn us when we have done wrong. It's called conscience, and it works in everyone—religious or not.

In Romans 2, Paul defined the role of the conscience in people who were not believers, but the same applies to Christians. He called it the law of God written in our hearts (v. 15). It lets us know when we have done good or evil. It either accuses us (as it did for David in 2 Sam. 24:10) or excuses us (as it did for Paul in Rom. 9:1).—J. D. B.

CONSCIENCE IS A SAFE GUIDE ONLY WHEN GUIDED BY GOD.

*"My food is to do the will of Him who sent Me,
and to finish His work."*

JOHN 4:34

To a child in Botswana, being sent on an errand by an elder is his greatest honor. This idea is captured in the Botswana proverb, "The fat [or delight] of a child is to be sent." The word fat refers to the choicest part of the meat and the fat, which are always served first to the elders at the family meal. After the rest of the men and the women have eaten, there is usually very little meat left for the children—only gravy. Thus, the "fat" came to refer to the most choice or delightful part of anything.

Jesus said His "food" was to do the will of the One who sent Him, and to finish His work (John 4:34). As children of God, we too should be eager to please our heavenly Father. Stop and think about it a moment. We have all been commissioned by Christ. He has commanded us to go. For us, the "fat" ought to be the blessing of doing the will of God. We can apply to ourselves the truth of the Botswana proverb, "The fat of a child is to be sent."—D. C. E.

DUTY ALONE IS DRUDGERY; DUTY WITH LOVE IS DELIGHT.

The path of the just is like the shining sun,
that shines ever brighter unto the perfect day.

PROVERBS 4:18

Looking at a picture of the great scholar Bertrand Russell in his later years made me feel sad. Although his face reflected courage, it was grim and showed no sign of joy or hope. He was born into a Christian home and taught to believe in God, but he rejected his training and became an outspoken atheist. His daughter, Katherine Tait, said of him, "Somewhere at the bottom of his heart, in the depths of his soul, there was an empty space that once had been filled by God, and he never found anything else to put in it."

A picture of my Grandpa Vander Lugt, taken in his old age, presents a striking contrast. It reflects a beautiful serenity born of a deep faith in God nurtured for many years. When he was in his late eighties, he still played pranks and joked with us. And I remember how peacefully he talked with us as he lay dying.

Grandpa's life is an illustration of Proverbs 4:18, "The path of the just is like the shining sun, that shines ever brighter unto the perfect day." On what path are you walking? Your choice will make all the difference in the world.—H. V. L.

THOSE WHO LIVE FOR ETERNITY CAN DIE WITH SERENITY.

JUNE 30

God is faithful,
by whom you were called into the fellowship of His Son.

1 CORINTHIANS 1:9

John Gilmour, a godly Britisher who loved to witness for Christ, always carried gospel books to give to people as he had opportunity. One day he was walking in a little village when he came across an old Irishman selling lids, kettles, and saucepans. Gilmour greeted the man, "Good morning, how is business today?" "Oh," said the Irishman, "I cannot complain."

Then Gilmour said, "What a grand thing it is to be saved!" The old man looked intently at him and replied, "I know something better than that." "Better than being saved? I would like to know what that is." With a warm smile, the man responded, "The companionship of the Man who saved me, sir."

The Christian life does not consist only of being forgiven and going to heaven when we die. Christ wants us to enjoy fellowship with Him every day. That's how we get to "know Him and the power of His resurrection, and the fellowship of His sufferings, being conformed to His death" (Phil. 3:10).—P. R. V.

WHEN HUMAN FRIENDSHIP FAILS,
CHRIST'S FRIENDSHIP STILL PREVAILS.

By faith the walls of Jericho fell down
after they were encircled for seven days.

HEBREWS 11:30

I was delighted to see this headline on the front page of the newspaper: "New Study Backs Biblical Version of Jericho's Demise." The Associated Press article began, "The walls of Jericho did come tumbling down as recounted in the Bible, according to an archaeological study." Archaeologist Bryant G. Wood of the University of Toronto said, "When we compare the archaeological evidence at Jericho with the biblical narrative describing the Israelite destruction of Jericho, we find remarkable agreement." Wood noted that the Bible places the event after spring harvest and indicates that the Israelites burned the city—both factors confirmed by the archaeological remains.

Once again, archaeology bears testimony to the truthfulness of Scripture. But we don't believe the Bible just because its authenticity is attested to by man's word. We believe it because it is God's Word. As 2 Timothy 3:16 tells us, "All Scripture is given by inspiration of God." We can therefore have complete confidence in what it says. It's a fact— the walls of Jericho did fall. The Bible stands!—R. W. D.

TO THE WISE, GOD'S WORD IS SUFFICIENT.

I will come again and receive you to Myself;
that where I am, there you may be also.

JOHN 14:3

The nineteenth-century lecturer Wendell Phillips was deeply devoted to his invalid wife. His speaking engagements, however, often required him to be away from her. At the close of a lecture one night in a town many miles from his home in Boston, Phillips' friends urged him not to attempt to return home until morning. "The last train has left," they said, "and you will have to hire special transportation into the city. It is cold and sleeting, and you face miles of rough riding before you get home." He replied, "But at the other end of those miles I shall find my beloved Anne."

We who love Christ can press on through life's trials because at journey's end we know Jesus is waiting for us. Someday we will see the face of the One who gave Himself for our salvation. We will see our Savior, and we will be like Him.—P. R. V.

WE MAY WALK A DESERT PATHWAY,
BUT IT LEADS TO THE GARDEN OF GOD.

Those who were scattered went everywhere preaching the word.

ACTS 8:4

If a starfish is cut up, any pieces that contain a part of the central disc will develop into a new starfish. Some oyster fishermen found that out, much to their dismay, when their oyster beds became infested with starfish. The fishermen cut up the starfish they caught and tossed the pieces back into the water. Rather than destroying them, however, they were actually helping them multiply.

Throughout the centuries, Christians have been hated and viciously opposed in many nations. But persecution did not destroy Christianity. Even under the most dire circumstances, it has not only survived but thrived. Jesus said of His church that "the gates of Hades shall not prevail against it" (Matt. 16:18).

The church of the Lord Jesus Christ, no matter how severely persecuted, continues to grow. Even the forces of hell itself cannot overcome it!—R. W. D.

THE CHURCH—ROOTED IN GOD—CAN NEVER BE UPROOTED BY MAN.

The LORD is in His holy temple.
Let all the earth keep silence before Him.

HABAKKUK 2:20

In 1861, during the US Civil War, author and lecturer Julia Ward Howe visited Washington, D. C. One day she went outside the city and saw a large number of soldiers marching. Early the next morning she awoke with words for a song in her mind.

She was aware of all the ugliness of the war, but her faith led her to write: "Mine eyes have seen the glory of the coming of the Lord." She saw, I believe, that in spite of and through all the ugliness, God was "marching on" toward the day when He will right the wrongs of the ages.

If we believe that God is "marching on," in spite of all the brutal conflicts that mark our day, we will not despair. We can quietly await the final verdict from our Lord, who rules the universe from "His holy temple" (v. 20).—H. V. L.

SOMEDAY THE SCALES OF JUSTICE WILL BE PERFECTLY BALANCED.

They surrounded me like bees.

PSALM 118:12

*S*ome beekeepers have the skill of tending hives without getting stung. They seldom put veils over their faces or wear protective clothing, yet they can go from hive to hive and still escape harm. The explanation for this is simple. They remain calm and deliberate in their movements. Even though a bee comes directly toward them or settles on their exposed skin, they make no effort to protect themselves.

Likewise, how one faces difficulties in life is extremely important. The writer of Psalm 118 said his enemies surrounded him like a swarm of bees, but he knew that in the Lord's strength he could successfully meet the challenge.

Many of us have been in similar situations, for troubles seldom come one at a time. Instead, they buzz around and threaten us from all sides. If we fret and rebel under testing, we aggravate our problems and are sure to feel the pain of defeat. On the other hand, calmly expressing our faith in God through praise and prayer will bring us the sweetness of new grace and power.—H. G. B.

FAITH IS THE BEST ANTIDOTE FOR FEAR.

The Word became flesh and dwelt among us.

JOHN 1:14

Corrie Ten Boom was not looking forward to her turn to speak. She and the others in her ministry team had gone to a prison to talk to the inmates about Christ. They had set up their equipment at one end of a long corridor lined with cells. The men peered through the bars to see the visitors.

First, a woman sang, and the prisoners tried to drown her out. Then, when a young man stood to pray, the noise grew worse. Finally, it was Corrie's turn. Shouting to be heard, she said, "When I was alone in a cell for four months ——" Suddenly, the corridor grew quiet. With those few words, Corrie established a bond with the prisoners. They realized that she knew what they were going through. Her time in a World War II prison camp made her one of them.

This incident reminds us of something important about Jesus' coming to this earth. When He "became flesh and dwelt among us," He became one of us. Therefore, He understands our suffering. He knows what we are going through.—J. D. B.

JESUS KNOWS YOUR NEED. HE'S BEEN THERE.

Follow Me, and I will make you fishers of men.

MATTHEW 4:19

I'm amused by the story of the boy who was fishing in a stream when a group of teenagers arrived on the scene with their rods and reels and fancy flies. They thrashed the water as they joked and laughed, casting and reeling in repeatedly but catching nothing. The boy sat intently watching the tip of his tree-branch pole. Every so often he pulled up a fish. Finally one of the fellows shouted, "How do you do it? We've got special flies but we're not catching anything!" The boy looked up long enough to reply, "I'm fishing for fish. You're fishing for fun."

At least four of Christ's disciples were fishermen. They knew that it took their full attention and energies to catch fish. Therefore, when Christ commanded them to leave their nets and "catch men," they realized it would demand their all. That's how we should view our part in fulfilling the Great Commission. Making Christ known is not an optional pastime for the excitement it may bring or the stories we can tell of souls won. It is serious business, requiring prayer, courage, sacrifice, perseverance, and singleminded purpose.—P. R. V.

MEND YOUR NETS WITH PRAYER, CAST THEM IN FAITH, AND DRAW THEM WITH LOVE.

As the elect of God, holy and beloved, put on tender mercies.

COLOSSIANS 3:12

There is a lot at stake when NASA launches a space shuttle. That's why the experts make sure everything relating to the liftoff is in order—the rockets, the crew, the weather, the tracking stations. Although no blastoff can ever be guaranteed safe, a clean pre-launch checklist is NASA's best hope of avoiding a tragedy in space.

Just as NASA won't let the shuttle go without first checking out all systems, so also we as Christians should never enter a new day without making a careful check of our lives. A good place to start is Paul's list of Christian character traits. Ask yourself:

- Have I put on compassion and kindness?
- Have I put on humility, gentleness, patience?
- Have I put on love?
- Does the peace of God rule in my heart?
- Am I thankful?
- Does the word of Christ dwell in me?
- Will I do everything in Jesus' name?—J. D. B.

AN HONEST SELF-EXAMINATION IS A TEST CHRIST ALWAYS HELPS US PASS.

The woman whom You gave to be with me,
she gave me of the tree, and I ate.

GENESIS 3:12

*T*read a funny anecdote about a businessman from Europe who moved to the United States and taught himself English. One day a salesman called on him to sell him a dictating machine. The man asked if he could try it out before deciding whether to buy it. The salesman agreed. When he returned several days later, he asked the businessman what he thought of the recording device. "Vell," said the prospective customer, "I'll tell you, it ain't so bad, bott it toks vith an havul haxent!"

This story reminds me of the tendency we all have to avoid responsibility for our own faults. This problem began in the Garden of Eden. When God confronted Adam about eating the forbidden fruit, he blamed Eve. She in turn blamed the serpent. But they were both guilty. They were individually responsible for their own actions.

Let's be careful about blaming people for failures that may actually be our own. When the fault is ours, we must confess it to the Lord and not "pass the buck."—R. W. D.

ALL WHO HUMBLY CONFESS, THE SAVIOR WILL BLESS.

Elisha the son of Shaphat is here,
who poured water on the hands of Elijah.

2 KINGS 3:11

A park in Manila commemorates the men and women of the U. S. Armed Forces who gave their lives there during World War II. Their names are inscribed on marble pillars. Those who won the Congressional Medal of Honor have a star by their names.

One entry is unusual. These words are engraved by the star: Walter Peterson, Chief Water Bearer. I don't know who he was or what his duties were. But he served the troops, and he did his duty well enough to receive our country's highest award.

What about your job in the Lord's service? Does it seem insignificant, with no public attention? No matter. Do it well. Someday the Lord Himself will award you His "Medal of Honor."—D. C. E.

ALL SERVICE RENDERED TO THE LORD
IS SURE TO GAIN HIS RICH REWARD.

O Lord, how manifold are Your works!
In wisdom You have made them all.

PSALM 104:24

an we learn anything about God from a watermelon? According to William Jennings Bryan, famous American lawyer and creationist, a watermelon speaks volumes about God. Bryan wrote, "Recently someone planted just one little seed in the ground. Under the influence of sunshine and shower, it took off its coat and went to work gathering about 200,000 times its own weight. It forced all that material through a tiny stem and built a watermelon. On the outside it had a covering of green; within that, a rind of white; and within that, a core of red. Scattered on the inside were more seeds—each capable of doing the same work all over again. What architect drew the plan? Where did that little watermelon seed get its tremendous strength? Where did it find its flavoring extract and its coloring matter?"

Bryan then pointed out that until we can comprehend the amazing watermelon, we dare not underestimate the power of the Almighty. In showing us these wonders, the Lord has demonstrated His infinite wisdom and power. As we contemplate God's marvelous creation, we are amazed at His handiwork.—H. G. B.

THE WEALTH OF GOD'S CREATIVE SKILL
FILLS THE EARTH AND SEA AND SKY.

I also count all things loss for the excellence
of the knowledge of Christ Jesus my Lord.

PHILIPPIANS 3:8

Pastor Ray Stedman told of a little boy who was asked by his mother how his Sunday school class had gone that morning. The boy said, "Oh, we had a new teacher. Guess who she was." "Who?" she replied. "It was Jesus' grandmother," he informed her. Amused, she asked, "What made you think that?" The boy answered, "Well, all she did was show us pictures of Jesus and tell us stories about Him."

That youngster probably had loving, picture-toting grandparents. He saw that Jesus was all-important to his teacher, so he concluded that she must be His grandmother. His logic may have been faulty, but his response makes a strong point: We talk most about what or who is most important to us.

Is Jesus the focus of our life? Do others sense how important He is to us? If not, maybe we need to take more time getting to know Him.—P. R. V.

**THE MORE YOU THINK ABOUT CHRIST,
THE MORE YOU'LL WANT TO TALK ABOUT CHRIST.**

The kingdom of God is not in word but in power.

1 CORINTHIANS 4:20

Some people have the idea that when their life has run its course and they take their last breath, they will no longer exist. But more—much more—lies ahead! Frank W. Boreham (1871–1959) illustrates this in his book *Wisps of Wildfire*. "A few weeks ago, in a small boat, I was making my way up one of the most picturesque of our Australian rivers. The forestry on both banks was magnificent beyond description. . . . A canoe glided ahead of us. Presently, the waters seemed to come to an end. . . . We watched the canoe, and to our astonishment, it simply vanished! . . . When we came to the point at which the canoe had so mysteriously disappeared, we beheld a sudden twist in the river artfully concealed by the tangle of bush. The blind alley was no blind alley after all!"

Then, making reference to believers who had died, Boreham observed, "[They] have gone on—like the canoe. It had turned a bend in the river; they have turned a bend in the road." Life may seem to end at death. At that "bend in the road," however, the Christian is introduced into a new world where life at its best is enjoyed throughout the eternal ages.—R. W. D.

WHEN A CHRISTIAN DIES, HE HAS JUST BEGUN TO LIVE.

If you show partiality, you commit sin.

JAMES 2:9

C lothing companies try to offer garments that match the public's perception of what a successful person wears. To determine this, a clothing analyst performed an experiment with raincoats. An actor wearing a tan raincoat approached people at a subway station. He explained that he had left his wallet home and asked to borrow train fare. People were surprisingly generous with this supposedly unfortunate executive. Then the actor wore a dark raincoat and approached people in the same way with the same story. This time he was treated differently. Not only would no one give him money, but he was physically threatened. The opposite reaction was linked to the color of the coat. People saw the dark garment as threatening and judged the man with suspicion.

Aren't we also guilty of judging by appearances? Don't we let externals determine how we respond to people? Whenever we discriminate according to race, age, gender, or income level, we are sinning (James 2:9). God is impartial, and when we accept all people equally we are reflecting His character.—D. C. E.

PREJUDICE LETS YOU FORM OPINIONS WITHOUT GETTING THE FACTS.

JULY 15

Discretion will preserve you . . .
from the man who speaks perverse things.

PROVERBS 2:11–12

A nobleman went to see how Josiah Wedgwood made his superb pottery. A young apprentice was told to give the guest a tour of the factory. As they walked through the plant, the visitor began to use foul language, ridicule the Bible, and make light of sacred things. At first the young man was shocked, but after a while he began to laugh at the man's remarks. Wedgwood, who had joined them, was greatly disturbed by what he saw happening to his apprentice.

At the end of the tour, the nobleman asked if he could purchase a particular vase that he admired. Wedgwood told him that it had taken many hours to produce its exquisite shape and color. As he handed the beautiful vase to his visitor, he deliberately let it crash to the floor. Cursing angrily, the nobleman said, "That's the one I really wanted, and now it's shattered because of your carelessness." "Sir," said Wedgwood, "there are things more precious than any vase. I can make another vase, but you can never give back to my helper the innocent heart you've degraded by your profanity!" Let's stay alert to the subtle and destructive influences all around us.—H. G. B.

IF YOU'RE NOT ON GUARD AGAINST EVIL,
YOU'LL BE INFLUENCED BY EVIL.

216

Blessed is the nation whose God is the LORD.

PSALM 33:12

John Wycliffe, John Knox, David Livingstone, Hudson Taylor, Charles Haddon Spurgeon, G. Campbell Morgan—what a notable list of Christian leaders from Great Britain! They established vital churches, publishing houses, and mission societies. In spite of this godly heritage, a recent edition of the *London Times* stated, "Britain emerges as one of the most irreligious countries in the Western world from the latest survey by the British Social Attitudes team."

What happened? The emotional scars of two World Wars, the loss of a world empire, and the weakening effects of liberal clergy could all be cited as causes. But there is a deeper, spiritual reason for the decline of any nation. Its citizens lose interest in God. They don't believe He makes any difference in their lives, so they make gods out of their own accomplishments.

May we as citizens humble ourselves and honor God and His Son Jesus Christ. It's the only way any nation can become, and remain, great.—D. L. B.

THE HIGHWAYS OF HISTORY ARE STREWN WITH THE WRECKAGE OF NATIONS THAT FORGOT GOD.

These words which I command . . .
you shall teach them diligently to your children.

DEUTERONOMY 6:6–7

Al Menconi thinks he knows why Christian young people turn to secular rock music. In his publication *Media Update*, Menconi observed that rock music meets three of their most basic needs: (1) The rock star (via tapes, CDs, and videos) spends huge amounts of time with the young person. (2) The rock star accepts the young person as he or she is. (3) The rock star relates to the young person's problems.

Of course, rock musicians do not actually love your son or daughter, Menconi points out. They are in it for the money. But they do meet the three basic needs of companionship, acceptance, and identification. Fulfilling these needs is the primary domain of parents. When they fail, young people somehow fill that void with something, or someone, else.

Are you spending time with your children, loving them unconditionally, and trying to be understanding? If not, you may be causing them to run into the open arms of those who might meet their needs, but who care nothing about them.—J. D. B.

TIME SPENT WITH YOUR CHILDREN IS TIME WISELY INVESTED.

Behold, God is my salvation, I will trust and not be afraid.

ISAIAH 12:2

Two friends met one day on a city street and walked together for several blocks. In the course of conversation, one said to the other, "I found a wonderful verse when I read the Bible today." "Oh," said his friend, "what is it?" "Psalm 56:3," he replied. "It says, 'Whenever I am afraid, I will trust in You.'" "That's very good," said the other, with a smile on his face. "But I found an even better verse in my reading today. It's Isaiah 12:2, 'I will trust and not be afraid.'"

Are we doomed to respond in fear every time troubles arise? No. Jesus said, "Let not your heart be troubled; you believe in God, believe also in Me" (John 14:1). Continual reliance on the Lord puts up a shield against the fears that haunt us. So whether we turn to God in an emergency or confidently accept each circumstance as coming from His hand, our ever-present Savior is more than sufficient to give us peace. Either way works! The key to conquering fear is immediately putting our trust in God.—P. R. V.

KEEP YOUR EYES ON GOD AND YOUR FEARS WILL VANISH.

Now by this we know that we know Him,
if we keep His commandments.

1 JOHN 2:3

At an art auction, Van Gogh's painting *Portrait of Dr. Gachet* sold for the high bid of $82.5 million. And Renoir's beautiful *Au Moulin de la Galette* was auctioned for $78.1 million. Now, admittedly, these are wonderful paintings. But only a few people in the world can afford to hang one of these on their living room wall. Both of these paintings are available as reproductions, and you can buy a Renoir or Van Gogh for your home. Nobody invests in them, however, because they are only copies. They have very little value.

I see a parallel in the spiritual realm. Our world is filled with religion, and much of it appears to be Christian. Many people talk about Jesus, insist on clean living, carry Bibles, and go to church. But they aren't the real thing. They are only pretenders.

In the second chapter of his first epistle, the apostle John gives three marks of a true believer in Jesus: obedience to Christ (v. 3), genuine love for fellow Christians (v. 10), love for God and not for the world (vv. 15–17). Let's be sure we are true followers of Jesus, not mere imitations.—D. C. E.

DON'T PRETEND TO BE WHAT YOU DON'T INTEND TO BE.

Jesus said to him, "Today salvation has come to this house."

LUKE 19:9

A woman was contacting her high school classmates about their 35th reunion. Many were excited about seeing their old friends. One man wrote back to the woman, "I have the five Bs—baldness, bifocals, bridgework, bulges, and bunions." A woman quipped, "I wasn't half the woman then that I am today" (referring to her weight). But another woman said, "I can't wait to see everyone. I've changed completely. In high school I was the class 'tramp.' I had no standards and everybody knew it. But a few years after high school I received the Lord Jesus as my Savior. My life was transformed. Because of Christ, I'm not the person I was, and I want my classmates to know about it."

Receiving Christ marks the beginning of a brand-new life. Then as we grow in the grace and knowledge of the Lord, sinful attitudes are replaced with godly traits. Selfishness gives way to caring, greed to generosity, lust to purity. Has Christ transformed your life? Can you truly say, "I'm not the person I was"?—D. C. E.

GOD FORMED US; SIN DEFORMED US; CHRIST CAN TRANSFORM US.

If children, then heirs—
heirs of God and joint heirs with Christ.

ROMANS 8:17

Milton Petrie is a modern millionaire and a generous one at that. According to a *New York Times* article, Mr. Petrie, once worth more than a billion dollars, reads the New York papers "for stories of people life has kicked in the face. He then reaches for his checkbook." The wealthy benefactor often requires anonymity as a condition for his generosity. But sometimes he tells enough to make his unusual story interesting. For instance, the *Times* article ended with what he had said about his chauffeur. "This guy's in my will for $1 million and he doesn't know it." Then the article concluded, "Surprise!"

We may feel a bit envious of this chauffeur, who probably discovered his good fortune after reading Petrie's comment in the *New York Times* article. But when we are born again, we come into enormous spiritual wealth. Read Ephesians 1. Think of what it means to be named an heir of Christ!—M. R. D. II

IF YOU HAVE CHRIST, YOU ARE TRULY WEALTHY.

He will gather the lambs with His arm,
and carry them in His bosom.

ISAIAH 40:11

*D*uring the early years of missionary activity in China, four members of one family accepted Christ as Savior, but the youngest, a little boy, did not. Later, he came to his father and said he wanted to receive the Savior and live for Him. The father felt he was not old enough to understand what he was doing, so he explained what it meant to make a commitment to Jesus. He told him that following Christ would not always be easy. The boy gave this touching reply: "God has promised to carry the lambs in His arms. I am only a little boy. It will be easier for Jesus to carry me."

The simplicity and genuineness of that boy's faith made a profound impression on the father, who quickly sensed that his son knew what he was doing. Soon the youngster publicly declared his faith in Christ.

How comforting to the children of God, young or old, that the mighty arms of our Redeemer have drawn us near to His heart! There is no place of greater security than the Shepherd's arms.—P. R. V.

WITH GOD'S ARMS UNDERNEATH, YOU CAN FACE WHATEVER IS AHEAD.

Because you were faithful in a very little,
have authority over ten cities.

LUKE 19:17

American botanist George Washington Carver (1864–1943) said that he once asked God to tell him about the universe. According to Carver, the Lord replied, "George, the universe is just too big for you to understand. Suppose you let Me take care of that."

Humbled, Carver asked, "Lord, how about a peanut?" The Lord said, "Now, George, that's something your own size. Go to work on it and I'll help you." When Carver was done studying the peanut, he had discovered more than 300 products that could be made with that tiny bit of God's world.

God appoints us to places of service best suited to the talents He has given us. We are to develop our abilities and diligently use our God-given opportunities, no matter how small they may seem. If God wants to promote us, He'll do it in His own way and time.—D. J. D.

IT'S A BIG THING TO DO A LITTLE THING WELL.

Walk in the Spirit,
and you shall not fulfill the lust of the flesh.

GALATIANS 5:16

An elderly man who grew an amazing amount of food in a small garden said, "I have little trouble with weeds because I leave them no room. I fill the ground with healthy vegetables."

I tried his formula a few years ago when I found the weeds outgrowing my impatiens in a 5x5 area. After pulling out the weeds, I added another box of flowers and watered them well. I had to uproot a few weeds, but the flowers soon took over, leaving no room for unsightly vegetation.

This formula works not only in horticulture but is also effective in keeping sins of the flesh out of our lives. Paul put it like this: "Walk in the Spirit, and you shall not fulfill the lust of the flesh" (Gal. 5:16). Are spiritual weeds getting you down? If so, pull them out. Confess your sins. Trust God to forgive you. Become accountable. Then fill your life with good things. You'll soon find your garden fruitful and productive, with no room for weeds.—H. V. L.

SIN CANNOT FLOURISH WHERE GODLINESS IS CULTIVATED.

Do not lay up for yourselves treasures on earth,
where moth and rust destroy.

MATTHEW 6:19

"Buried Life Savings Just a Rotten Idea." That headline drew my attention to an Associated Press article in our local newspaper. It told about a man in Beijing, China, who, at eighty-two years of age, suffered a devastating financial loss. Mistrustful of banks, he had dug a hole in the ground five years earlier and deposited his life savings in it. When the man needed some cash, he dug up the money. To his dismay, he discovered that it was moldy almost beyond recognition. He was able to salvage only about one-third of his savings.

Our Lord said, "Do not lay up for yourselves treasures on earth, where moth and rust destroy and where thieves break in and steal; but lay up for yourselves treasures in heaven" (Matt. 6:19–20). Investing in the lives of others and growing in our relationship with God are spiritual treasures. They are not subject to destruction or thievery. They are fully protected. Their value never diminishes.—R. W. D.

THE BEST INVESTMENTS PAY ETERNAL DIVIDENDS.

You have kept me alive. . . . Sing praise to the LORD.

PSALM 30:3–4

As a deadly tornado ripped through Will County, Illinois, a young father sat cradling his infant child, born just three weeks before. When the fierce, howling winds finally subsided and calm had returned, the man's house was gone—and so was his baby. But, according to the news report, the father found his child in a field near his house—alive and well! And so was the rest of his family.

When asked by a reporter if he was angry that he had lost everything he owned, he replied, "No, I just thank God I have my baby and my family. Some people don't have that. Nothing else is important."

When things are going well, we can easily get preoccupied with what we own. We become tied to so many nonessential, unimportant things. We tend to grow overly concerned about cars, houses, furniture, appliances, clothes, and countless other trappings of modern life. But when life is reduced to the essentials, as it was in the Illinois tornado, we recall again that life itself is enough reason to praise God.—J. D. B.

PRAISE GOD FOR LIFE AND FOR PEOPLE TO SHARE IT WITH.

Let a man so consider us, as servants of Christ.

1 CORINTHIANS 4:1

It was the final rehearsal for the coronation of Queen Elizabeth. The orchestra had concluded its last piece. The archbishop stood proudly at the altar. Nearby stood the officers of state. All at once a spine-tingling fanfare of trumpets burst forth. This was the signal for the entrance of the Queen. At that exact moment, the massive doors opened and in walked four servant girls pushing carpet sweepers. They had come to do the final cleaning before the ceremony.

Just as no one would have crowned one of those cleaning girls as queen, so also we should not give to servants of the Lord the kind of adoration that belongs only to Christ, our King. Great Christian statesmen, well-known evangelists, popular gospel recording artists, Christian authors, pastors of large congregations—all are but servants of the King of kings. We must never grant to them hero status. Nor should we argue about who's best. We are all God's servants. Let's reserve our highest praise for Christ the King.—D. C. E.

GODLY PEOPLE ARE BUT SERVANTS OF THE MOST HIGH GOD.

Where envy and self-seeking exist,
confusion and every evil thing will be there.

JAMES 3:16

There's a legend about a Burmese potter who had become envious of the prosperity of a cleaning man. Determined to put this man out of business, the potter convinced the king to issue an order requiring the man to wash one of the emperor's black elephants and make it white. The cleaning man replied that according to the rules of his vocation he would need a vessel large enough to hold the elephant, whereupon the king commanded the potter to provide one. So the potter constructed a giant bowl and had it carefully delivered to the cleaning man. But when the elephant stepped into it, it crumbled to pieces beneath the weight of the enormous beast. Many more vessels were made, but each was crushed in the same way. Eventually it was the potter who was put out of business by the very scheme he had devised to ruin the man he envied.

The Old Testament word for envy means "to burn, or to inflame." That's an apt description of what goes on inside an envious person's heart. At first those feelings seem harmless enough, but as they continue to smolder they eventually create a fire that destroys the envious person himself. Remember, envy always backfires!—P. R. V.

AS A MOTH DESTROYS A GARMENT, SO ENVY DESTROYS A MAN.

With great power the apostles gave witness . . .
and great grace was upon them all.

ACTS 4:33

A musician was walking down the street with a friend when they heard an organ grinder playing a familiar tune. They stopped to listen for a moment, but then the musician hurried away, saying, "That sound drives me crazy."

A few weeks later, these same men went to hear a great orchestra. At the close of a certain piece, the musician stood to his feet, cheering wildly and waving his program. The friend smiled. The tune was the same one that was played by the organ grinder on the street.

There's a world of difference between the grand symphony of the Christian faith lived out prayerfully in the energy of the Holy Spirit and a profession of faith lived out meekly in the energy of the flesh. When people can see the touch of God in a person's life, they are attracted to the Christian faith. That's why the first-century believers had such an influence on their world. We represent the same Savior, but do our lives have the same impact?—H. V. L.

**IF WE HIDE OUR SHINING LIGHT,
HOW WILL OTHERS BE GUIDED IN SIN'S NIGHT?**

I press toward the goal for the prize of
the upward call of God in Christ Jesus.

PHILIPPIANS 3:14

In World War I, the American 308th regiment was surrounded by enemy forces. Casualties were heavy and supplies were short. The unbearable situation intensified when American artillery began shelling the sector where the 308th had dug in. The only communication was by carrier pigeon. In desperation, a sergeant released the last bird with a note pleading for the Americans to hold their fire.

As soon as the pigeon lifted off, a stray bullet grazed the side of his head and tore out his left eye. Then a piece of shrapnel hit his chest, shattering his breastbone. But his homing instinct was strong and he struggled onward. Somewhere in the flight another piece of shrapnel tore off his left leg, leaving the message cannister dangling from torn ligaments. The pigeon made it to his loft, however, and the order went out immediately to stop shelling. The 308th survived.

Facing incredible, life-threatening obstacles, the apostle Paul carried the gospel to a dying world. But he was able to continue because he kept the goal of "the upward call of God" ever before him.—D. C. E.

THE GAINS OF HEAVEN WILL MORE THAN COMPENSATE
FOR THE LOSSES OF EARTH.

231

You will cast all our sins into the depths of the sea.

MICAH 7:19

George Woodall was a missionary to London's inner city. One day a young woman he had led to the Lord came to him and said, "I keep getting worried. Has God really forgiven my past?"

Mr. Woodall replied, "If this is troubling you, I think I know what He would say to you. He would tell you to mind your own business." "What do you mean?" she inquired with a puzzled look. He told her that Jesus had made her sins His business. When He took them away, He put them behind His back, dropped them into the depths of the sea, and posted a notice that reads, "No fishing!"

Although the Bible doesn't put it in those terms, the principle is certainly accurate. When our sins are covered by the blood of Christ, they are blotted out completely and forever (Isa. 43:25).—H. G. B.

WHEN GOD FORGIVES, HE FORGETS.

August

To Him who is able to do exceedingly abundantly . . . be glory.

EPHESIANS 3:20–21

As four Christian women made their way through the dense Thailand jungles to visit some new converts, they were ambushed at gunpoint by three communist rebels. When the men found that the women had no money, they angrily told them they were going to kill them. The women pleaded with their captors not to shoot, but the men were adamant. Then one of the workers asked them if they could tell them about God's love before they were shot. Surprisingly, the gunmen agreed! So Kleun Anuyet explained that Jesus had died on the cross because He loved them.

The men did an astonishing thing—they dropped their guns, and tears began to flow. The ringleader said, "If Jesus has that much love, then I want it too." Soon all three accepted Christ as Savior. Today they are serving God as fulltime Christian workers.

When Paul prayed for the Ephesians, he referred to "the power that works in us" (3:20). It was that indwelling strength that allowed those brave women to witness of God's love while staring down the barrel of a gun.—J. D. B.

OUR NEEDS CAN NEVER EXHAUST GOD'S SUPPLY.

I saw the LORD. . . . Then I said, "Here am I! Send me."

ISAIAH 6:1, 8

In his book *A Bunch of Everlastings*, Frank W. Boreham writes about William Carey, the shoemaker who became a famous missionary to India. He says, "There he sits . . . , the Bible spread out before him, and a homemade map of the world on the wall! In the Bible he saw the King in His beauty; on the map he caught glimpses of the far horizons. To him the two were inseparable; and, moved by the vision of the Lord which he caught in the one, and by the vision of the limitless landscape which he caught in the other, he left his shop and made history."

For many of us, the extent of our caring reaches only to our immediate family or to a small group of friends. What will it take to enlarge our perspective so that we become concerned about the lost in other lands? We need the same experience that motivated William Carey and the prophet Isaiah! Once they caught a glimpse of God's holiness, they recognized their own desperate condition and the terrible plight of those about them. Isaiah put it this way: "I saw the Lord." Then, when his sin was purged, he prayed, "Here am I! Send me."—P. R. V.

OPEN YOUR HEART TO GOD AND
HE WILL OPEN YOUR EYES TO THE LOST.

When we were still without strength, . . .
Christ died for the ungodly.

ROMANS 5:6

Winston Churchill was honoring members of the Royal Air Force who had guarded England during World War II. Recounting their brave service, he declared, "Never in the history of mankind have so many owed so much to so few." A similar sentiment appears on a memorial plaque in Bastogne, Belgium, where raged the famous Battle of the Bulge, one of the bloodiest conflicts of World War II. The inscription, in honor of the U.S. 101st Airborne Division, reads: "Seldom has so much American blood been shed in the course of a single action. Oh, Lord, help us to remember!"

These are fitting and well-deserved tributes to the courageous men and women who sacrificed so much in battle. But there is One whose selfless sacrifice resulted in even greater benefits for mankind. Jesus Christ, the eternal Son of God, became a man. As the sinless One, He died on a cross and shed His blood to pay for the sins of the entire world. In so doing, He guaranteed our freedom—freedom from the penalty, power, and someday even the presence of sin. Of Christ it can be said: Never in the history of mankind have so many owed so much to one Man.—R. W. D.

SALVATION IS FREE BECAUSE CHRIST PAID THE ENORMOUS PRICE.

Having food and clothing, with these we shall be content.

1 TIMOTHY 6:8

A little girl walking in a garden noticed a particularly beautiful flower. She admired its beauty and enjoyed its fragrance. "It's so pretty!" she exclaimed. As she gazed on it, her eyes followed the stem down to the soil in which it grew. "This flower is too pretty to be planted in such dirt!" she cried. So she pulled it up by its roots and ran to the water faucet to wash away the soil. It wasn't long until the flower wilted and died.

When the gardener saw what the little girl had done, he exclaimed, "You have destroyed my finest plant!" "I'm sorry, but I didn't like it in that dirt," she said. The gardener replied, "I chose that spot and mixed the soil because I knew that only there could it grow to be a beautiful flower."

Often we murmur because of the circumstances into which God has sovereignly placed us. We fail to realize that He is using our pressures, trials, and difficulties to bring us to a new degree of spiritual beauty. Contentment comes when we accept what God is doing and thank Him for it. Let's trust Him and allow Him to bring us to maturity.—P. R. V.

CONTENTMENT ENABLES YOU TO GROW WHERE GOD HAS PLANTED YOU.

I am the way, the truth, and the life.
No one comes to the Father except through Me.

JOHN 14:6

The first missionary to the Kiowa Indians was a woman named Miss Reside. After living with the Indians long enough for them to know what it meant to be a Christian, they began calling her "Aim Day Co." Explaining the significance of this name, Chief Bigtree said, "When we Kiowas see anyone on the wrong trail, we call out, 'Aim day co,' which means 'Turn this way.' Our sister came to us from a far land and found us on the wrong path and in great danger. She stood and called to us and said, 'Turn this way,' and then she showed us the Jesus road. God bless Miss Aim Day Co."

The Lord Jesus declared that there are only two paths to take in life. One is the narrow way that ascends to life eternal. The other is the broad way that descends to the pit of destruction (Matt. 7:13–14). And He said that He is "the way" (John 14:6).—H. G. B.

THERE IS NO OTHER ROAD TO GOD THAN JESUS, THE "LIVING WAY."

I am among you as the One who serves.

LUKE 22:27

*S*amuel L. Brengle, a brilliant orator and highly successful pastor, was so burdened by the plight of the inner city poor that he resigned his church and joined the Salvation Army in London. Soon after being inducted, he was given the task of cleaning a pile of muddy boots. This was too much! Inwardly he rebelled. But then he thought about how Jesus washed the feet of His disciples. He asked the Lord for a servant spirit, cleaned the boots, and went on to a fruitful ministry among the disadvantaged. He learned to be a servant.

This attitude does wonders! It frees us from the hurt feelings, animosities, jealousies, and resentment that cause us so much misery and cripple us spiritually.

Ask Jesus to help you have a servant spirit. It will change your life.—H. V. L.

IF YOU'RE TOO BIG TO DO LITTLE THINGS,
YOU'RE TOO LITTLE TO DO BIG THINGS.

I call to remembrance the genuine faith . . .
which dwelt first in your grandmother Lois and your mother.

2 TIMOTHY 1:5

"My great-grandfather owned this rifle," the man said proudly. In his hand was a mint-condition rifle from the days when the pioneers were moving across the American West. I admired its beautiful walnut stock and shiny brass fittings. "It came down to my grandfather, who passed it on to my father, who gave it to me. It's been in the family more than one hundred years. I'm going to give it to my son when he turns twenty-five."

We give a lot of thought to what we pass on to our children. My wife Shirley cherishes the crystal and chinaware that belonged to her grandmother. It may be something different in your home: a rolltop desk, a handmade quilt, or an old family Bible. Heirlooms are important to us.

But there are other things we can pass on to our children that are even more important, things like honorable character or a good name. And don't forget the example of your faith in the Lord Jesus. It is the most valuable "heirloom" of all.—D. C. E.

WHAT'S LEFT IN OUR CHILDREN IS MORE IMPORTANT
THAN WHAT'S LEFT TO THEM.

*Lying lips are an abomination to the LORD,
but those who deal truthfully are His delight.*

PROVERBS 12:22

If things weren't already strange enough in today's society, now some people want to abolish honesty. One noted physician, for example, appeared on a network news-and-talk show and proclaimed, "Lying is an important part of social life, and children who are unable to do it are children who may have developmental problems."

I wonder, is the saying "Honesty is the best policy" becoming obsolete? Two surveys taken recently may indicate that many people think it is. A *USA Today* poll found that only 56 percent of Americans teach honesty to their children. And a Louis Harris poll turned up the distressing fact that 65 percent of high school students would cheat on an important exam.

It looks like it's time for those of us who live by God's standard to recommit ourselves to honesty. In a society that treats honesty like an artifact from an ancient world, let's "deal truthfully" in everything. It's a sure way to bring "delight" to our heavenly Father.—J. D. B.

IF YOU ALWAYS TELL THE TRUTH, YOU'LL NEVER BE TRAPPED BY A LIE.

O LORD, You have searched me and known me. . . .
Such knowledge is too wonderful for me.

PSALM 139:1, 6

Two couples vacationing in England were driving along the shore of a large body of water. As they were discussing whether it was the English Channel or the Falmouth Estuary, they saw two women walking along the sidewalk.

"John, pull over there and I'll ask those ladies if this is the English Channel," said Max. He rolled down the window and said to one of the women, "Excuse me, ma'am, is that the English Channel?" She glanced over her shoulder and said, "Well, that's part of it."

That woman's answer also applies to people. Like the English Channel, a large part of who we are lies unseen by others and even ourselves. When we realize this, we can more lovingly and honestly relate to people and to God. Although the actions of others may be annoying and even unkind, if we knew all the reasons behind them we might be more tolerant and merciful.—D. J. D.

YOUR LIFE'S AN OPEN BOOK TO GOD—WHAT DOES HE READ IN YOU?

My voice You shall hear in the morning, O Lᴏʀᴅ;
in the morning I will direct it to You.

Psᴀʟᴍ 5:3

I heard about a little boy who didn't want to get out of bed one day. He told his parents, "I won't get up until I see Jesus." At first they didn't know what he meant. But when he pointed to a picture on the wall, which was a painting of Christ, they understood. He wouldn't get out of bed until it was light enough to see the face of Jesus.

That boy's remark reminds me that our first thoughts when we wake up to a new day should be directed to our Lord in heaven. English preacher Joseph Parker said, "The morning is the time for meeting the Lord, for then we are at our best, having a new supply of energy. Blessed is the day that is opened with prayer! Holy is the dawn that finds us on 'top of the mount' with God!"—H. G. B.

Gᴇᴛ ʏᴏᴜʀ sᴏᴜʟ ɪɴ ᴛᴜɴᴇ ᴡɪᴛʜ Gᴏᴅ
ʙᴇғᴏʀᴇ ᴛʜᴇ ᴄᴏɴᴄᴇʀᴛ ᴏғ ᴛʜᴇ ᴅᴀʏ ʙᴇɢɪɴs.

He gives power to the weak, and to those who have no might
He increases strength.

ISAIAH 40:29

A South American company purchased a fine printing press from a firm in the United States. After it had been shipped and completely assembled, the workmen could not get it to operate properly. The most knowledgeable personnel tried to adjust it, but to no avail.

The company finally sent a wire to the manufacturer, asking for a representative to come and fix it. Sensing the urgency of the request, the U.S. firm sent the designer of the press. When he arrived on the scene, the company officials were skeptical because he was young. After discussing the situation, they sent this cable to the manufacturer: "Your man is too young. Send a more experienced person." The reply came back, "He made the machine. Let him fix it!"

Mankind is in a similar situation. Every area of life seems to be in chaos. People don't know how to "put it all together." If this describes your situation, there is an answer. You will find forgiveness, cleansing, peace, and order when Jesus, who has made you, is invited to come in and take control of your life.—P. R. V.

TO MAKE YOUR LIFE COMPLETE, LET THE CREATOR TAKE CONTROL.

Though He was rich, yet for your sakes He became poor.

2 CORINTHIANS 8:9

As the Cadillac owner walked to his car, he saw a boy about ten years old staring intently through the windows. Wondering what he was up to, the man put his hands on the youngster's shoulders, pulled gently, and asked him what he was doing. The boy said he was interested in cars and had read a lot about different models. He then told him many details about this particular year and body style.

After a bit, the boy asked, "Mister, how much did you pay for this car?" The man replied, "Nothing. My brother gave it to me." The boy responded, "I wish . . ." but stopped in mid-sentence. The man chuckled, "You were going to say, 'I wish I had a brother like that.'" "No, I was going to say, 'I wish I could be a brother like that.' You see, sir, I have a brother who is crippled and I'd like to do a lot of things for him."

What an unusual boy! What an unselfish attitude! Lord, help us to be that kind of giver.—H. V. L.

SACRIFICE IS THE TRUE MEASURE OF GENEROSITY.

Whatever things you ask when you pray,
believe that you receive them, and you will have them.

MARK 11:24

When Hudson Taylor went to China, he made the voyage on a sailing ship. As it neared the channel between the southern Malay Peninsula and the island of Sumatra, the missionary heard an urgent knock on his stateroom door. He opened it, and there stood the captain of the ship. "Mr. Taylor," he said, "we have no wind. We are drifting toward an island where the people are heathen, and I fear they are cannibals."

"What can I do?" asked Taylor. The captain explained. "I understand that you believe in God. I want you to pray for wind." "All right, Captain," Taylor said, "I will, but you must set the sail."

"Why, that's ridiculous! There's not even the slightest breeze. The sailors will think I'm crazy." Nevertheless, the captain finally agreed. Forty-five minutes later he returned and found the missionary still on his knees. "You can stop praying now," said the captain. "We've got more wind than we know what to do with!"

Hudson Taylor believed that God answers prayer. What about you? Do you really expect Him to respond? Pray and then "set the sail."—P. R. V.

WHEN YOU PRAY FOR RAIN, CARRY AN UMBRELLA.

He said to them,
"Come aside by yourselves to a deserted place and rest a while."

MARK 6:31

A band of explorers in Africa hired some villagers to help them on their journey through the jungle. The group set out and pushed on relentlessly for several days. Finally the tribesmen sat down and would go no farther. When asked the reason, their leader answered, "We've been going too fast. We must pause and wait for our souls to catch up with our bodies!"

Many Christians who have overextended themselves in a flurry of church activities or other worthwhile pursuits have experienced a similar feeling. Being so preoccupied with helping others, they suddenly feel as if they have left behind the most important part of themselves—their soul. They have lost intimate contact with the Lord.

If our schedule leaves no time for rest and nurturing our spiritual life, we are just too busy! God does not ask us to be constantly on the go, rushing here and there. Sometimes He wants us to "rest a while" so that our souls can "catch up" and be refreshed for the challenges that lie ahead.—H. G. B.

SET ALL ELSE ASIDE AND WITH GOD ABIDE.

The fruit of the Spirit is . . . self-control.

GALATIANS 5:22–23

During his term as President of the United States, Lyndon Johnson was somewhat overweight. One day his wife challenged him with this blunt assertion: "You can't run the country if you can't run yourself." Respecting Mrs. Johnson's wise observation, the President lost 23 pounds.

As believers in Christ, we are challenged by the author of Hebrews to rid ourselves of "every weight, and the sin which so easily ensnares us" (Heb. 12:1). This includes anything that encumbers our spiritual effectiveness. By discipline and self-control, we must shed any habit, practice, or attitude that is hindering our service for the Lord. Such self-discipline is necessary if we are to "run with endurance the race that is set before us" (v. 1).

The way to achieve this self-control is to place ourselves under the Holy Spirit's control. In Galatians 5:16, the apostle Paul admonished, "Walk in the Spirit, and you shall not fulfill the lust of the flesh." And according to verse 23, the "fruit of the Spirit" includes self-control.—R. W. D.

THE BEST WAY TO EXERCISE SELF-CONTROL IS TO SUBMIT TO THE SPIRIT'S CONTROL.

*We have the prophetic word confirmed,
which you do well to heed.*

2 PETER 1:19

A man who lived on Long Island, New York, bought a high quality barometer. When it was delivered to his home, the arrow appeared to be stuck, pointing to the section marked "Hurricane." According to the noted Bible teacher and author E. Schuyler English, who told this story, the man shook the barometer, but the indicator stayed the same. So the man sat down and wrote a scorching letter to the store where he had bought it. The following morning on the way to his office in New York City, he mailed the letter. Later that day a hurricane struck the East Coast. That evening the man returned to Long Island to find that his barometer was missing—and so was his house.

That man's skepticism may seem ridiculous. But there is a clear indicator of the future that is more certain and dependable than any barometer, and all too often we do not take it seriously. It is God's eternal Word, the Bible. And it's never wrong! If you ignore the truth of God's Word, you invite the disaster of inescapable judgment.—P. R. V.

TO IGNORE THE BIBLE IS TO INVITE DISASTER.

The sheep follow him, for they know his voice.

JOHN 10:4

A man in Australia was arrested and charged with stealing a sheep. But he claimed emphatically that it was one of his own that had been missing for many days. When the case went to court, the judge was puzzled, not knowing how to decide the matter. At last he asked that the sheep be brought into the courtroom. Then he ordered the plaintiff to step outside and call the animal. The sheep made no response except to raise its head and look frightened. The judge then instructed the defendant to go to the courtyard and call the sheep. When the accused man began to make his distinctive call, the sheep bounded toward the door. It was obvious that he recognized the familiar voice of his master. "His sheep knows him," said the judge. "Case dismissed!"

As you think about Jesus and all He's done for you, is your heart drawn to Him? Do you enjoy reading the Bible and communing with God in prayer? Do you have a deep longing to learn all you can about the Lord so that you can become more like Him? Those who belong to Christ know and respond to His voice.—H. G. B.

THE LAMB WHO SAVES US IS ALSO THE SHEPHERD WHO LEADS US.

The eyes of the LORD run to and fro throughout the whole earth.

2 CHRONICLES 16:9

We are living in a time of tremendous advances in technology. For example, the United States now has "eyes in the skies"—orbiting satellites with highly sophisticated equipment that make it possible to monitor the military activities of any nation on earth. Objects only two feet long can be detected and identified from an altitude of 100 miles. Satellites are continually scanning the entire world, noting any suspicious movement of planes, ships, or tanks.

Another kind of world surveillance has been going on since creation. Second Chronicles 16:9 says that "the eyes of the LORD run to and fro throughout the whole earth." Knowing that our heavenly Father sees everything we do should motivate us to live in a way that pleases Him. And it should be a source of comfort to us because the God who sees also cares for His own.—R. W. D.

TO KNOW THAT GOD SEES US BRINGS
BOTH CONVICTION AND COMFORT.

Watch therefore, and pray always.

LUKE 21:36

In 1857 a money panic hit the United States. Although the entire nation was in a state of perplexity, the main force of the blow was felt in New York City, the center of finance. The now-famous Fulton Street noonday prayer meeting had been organized there a short time before the panic hit. As the uncertainty increased, this gathering grew in size and spiritual intensity. Similar groups began springing up all over the city. The movement spread across the country, and a great wave of petitions ascended to heaven. Thousands of Americans turned their hearts toward God. This spiritual awakening became known as the "Prayer Meeting Revival," and it is credited with sustaining the nation in an hour of great crisis.

Imagine what great things could happen if believers from all walks of life would gather to plead for God's mercy! If our concerns were channeled into prayer, the tide could be turned. Yes, prayer is today's imperative. Are we doing our part?—P. R. V.

PRAYING IS WORKING WITH GOD.

If anyone sins, we have an Advocate with the Father,
Jesus Christ the righteous.

1 JOHN 2:1

The great inventor Charles Kettering suggested that we must learn to fail intelligently. He said, "Once you've failed, analyze the problem and find out why, because each failure is one more step leading up to the cathedral of success. The only time you don't want to fail is the last time you try."

Kettering gave these suggestions for turning failure into success: (1) Honestly face defeat; never fake success. (2) Exploit the failure; don't waste it. Learn all you can from it. (3) Never use failure as an excuse for not trying again.

The inventor's practical wisdom holds double meaning for the Christian. Because the Holy Spirit is constantly working in us to accomplish His good purposes (Phil. 2:13), we know that failure is never final. We cannot reclaim lost time; nor can we always make things right, although we should try. Some of the consequences of our sins can never be reversed. But we can make a new start because we have an Advocate before God—Jesus, whose death fully paid for all our sins even before we were born.—D. J. D.

SUCCESS IS FAILURE TURNED INSIDE OUT.

He has put a new song in my mouth—praise to our God.

PSALM 40:3

Pastor and lecturer Thomas DeWitt Talmage (1832–1902) told the story of an accident that occurred on a ferry on one of the Great Lakes. A little child standing by the rail suddenly lost her balance and fell overboard. "Save my child!" cried the frantic mother. Lying on the deck was a great Newfoundland dog, which plunged into the water at the command of his master. Swimming to the girl, he took hold of her clothing with his teeth and brought her to the side of the boat, where both were lifted to safety. Although still frightened, the little girl threw her arms around that big shaggy dog and kissed him again and again. It seemed a most natural and appropriate thing to do.

Likewise, a response of love and gratitude should flow from every person who has been rescued by the Savior through His self-sacrificing death on the cross. He came from heaven's glory to suffer and die that we might have eternal life.—P. R. V.

PRAISE IS THE SONG OF A SOUL SET FREE.

Let each one of you in particular so love his own wife as himself.

EPHESIANS 5:33

Douglas MacArthur II, nephew of the famous World War II general, served in the state department when John Foster Dulles was Secretary of State. One evening Mr. Dulles called MacArthur at his home. His wife answered the phone and explained that her husband was not there. Not recognizing who the caller was, she angrily complained, "MacArthur is where MacArthur always is, weekdays, Saturdays, Sundays, and nights—in that office!"

Within minutes Dulles had MacArthur on the phone. He gave him this terse order: "Go home at once, Boy. Your home front is crumbling!"

Those same words might well be directed to many husbands and fathers today. Spending their time in pursuit of other interests, they neglect their wives and children. Providing a comfortable house, nutritious food, and adequate clothing is commendable. But a family also needs the presence, love, and influence of a God-fearing, Christ-honoring head of the house.—R. W. D.

CHRISTIAN HOMES DON'T JUST HAPPEN—THEY'RE BUILT.

It is God who avenges me.

PSALM 18:47

*S*omeone once wrote: "When you are quick to fight your own battles, Jesus steps aside and gives you the job." But if we refuse to retaliate, God will intervene on our behalf.

When a Hindu woman became a follower of Christ, her unsaved relatives tried to make her life miserable. One day a missionary asked her, "When your husband is angry and persecutes you, what do you do?" She replied, "I just cook the food better and sweep the floor a little cleaner. When he speaks unkindly, I answer him mildly, trying to show him in every way that when I became a Christian I also became a better wife."

That husband resisted all the sermons of the missionary, but he could not withstand the practical preaching of his wife. The Holy Spirit used that woman's gracious testimony, and eventually the man received Christ. If we let God fight our battles, we can't lose.—H. G. B.

THE POWER OF LOVE CAN TURN AN ENEMY INTO A FRIEND.

*Pray to your Father who is in the secret place;
and your Father . . . will reward you openly.*

MATTHEW 6:6

reat public performances require persistent private preparation. Take the game of baseball, for example. A batter hits a ground ball to the right of the pitcher. The shortstop goes to his left, fields the ball, and in one motion throws it to first base. He is so fluid in his movement that we praise his athletic ability. Yes, he has talent, but he has spent many hours with a coach who helped him to perfect his fielding technique.

The same is true with the person in the thirty-second television commercial. She looks so relaxed and natural. But what we don't see is the time she spent with the director during rehearsal.

The Scottish preacher Alexander Whyte met a person one Sunday who said to him, "Dr. Whyte, you preached today as if you had come straight from the presence of God." Whyte replied, "Perhaps I did."

We who believe on Jesus have an invisible means of support. Let's take advantage of this privilege. Our public life will be transformed if we spend private time with God.—H. V. L.

WHEN YOU HAVE BEEN ALONE WITH JESUS, PEOPLE WILL KNOW IT.

*Beloved, now we are children of God;
and it has not yet been revealed what we shall be.*

1 JOHN 3:2

A man visited a piano manufacturing plant. The guide took him first to a large workroom where men were cutting and shaping wood and steel. Nothing there bore any resemblance to a piano. Next they visited another department where parts were being fitted into frames, but still there were no strings or keys. In a third room, more pieces were being assembled—but still no music. Last of all, the guide took his guest to the showroom, where a skilled musician was playing the music of the masters on a beautiful piano. The visitor, who had just become aware of all the steps involved in the development of this marvelous musical instrument, was now able to appreciate its beauty more fully.

The apostle John said, "It has not yet been revealed what we shall be." God has saved us, and is now changing us into the image of Christ "from glory to glory" (2 Cor. 3:18). One day that work will be completed, because we were "predestined to be conformed to the image of His Son" (Rom. 8:29). But for now, we are in an ongoing process.

God is not finished with you yet. Someday He will be, and the glory of the showroom will be worth all the time spent in the workroom.—P. R.V.

**THE CONVERSION OF A SOUL TAKES A MOMENT;
GROWTH OF A SAINT TAKES A LIFETIME.**

We know that all things work together
for good to those who love God.

ROMANS 8:28

Professor E. C. Caldwell ended his lecture. "Tomorrow," he said to his class of seminary students, "I will be teaching on Romans 8. So tonight, as you study, pay special attention to verse 28. Notice what this verse truly says, and what it doesn't say." Then he added, "One final word before I dismiss you—whatever happens in all the years to come, remember: Romans 8:28 will always hold true."

That same day Dr. Caldwell and his wife met with a tragic car-train accident. She was killed instantly and he was crippled permanently. Months later, Professor Caldwell returned to his students, who clearly remembered his last words. The room was hushed as he began his lecture. "Romans 8:28," he said, "still holds true. One day we shall see God's good, even in this."—D. J. D.

ADVERSITY MAY BE GOD'S BLESSING IN DISGUISE.

*When she could no longer hide him, she took an ark of
bulrushes for him, daubed it with asphalt and pitch. . . .*

EXODUS 2:3

It is generally known that the Standard Oil Company has
operating wells in Egypt, but the reason for their going to that
ancient land is probably not so familiar. Some years ago one of their
directors, reading the third verse of Exodus 2, recognized in it a clue
of importance. It states that the ark of bulrushes which the mother of
Moses made for her child was "daubed with asphalt and pitch."
The gentleman reasoned that this was almost a certain indication of a
productive oilfield underneath. So the company sent out Charles
Witshott, its expert geologist, to investigate. The results were pleasingly
positive! "In checking with a regional office of the company I find that at
present they have twenty-six splendid wells in that area that are now
averaging 139,500 barrels of crude petroleum each day!"

Yes, the Bible is an up-to-date Book. Its facts are accurate and its
precepts are true. It helped Standard Oil Company accrue its assets, but
far more important, it can give to all who heed its admonitions the riches
of God's grace and the eternal treasures of heaven! It is a mine of spiritual
wealth in which the true searcher never fails to unearth golden nuggets of
truth!—H. G. B.

THE BIBLE IS THE WORD OF GOD, INERRANT AND ALL-WISE.

The blood of Jesus Christ . . . cleanses us from all sin.

1 JOHN 1:7

The much maligned skunk is really an intelligent creature. Note, for instance, the ingenious way he rids himself of fleas. First he gathers a mouthful of grass or straw and then slowly wades into a stream until only his muzzle is visible. At this time the straw gives him the appearance of having a large, bushy mustache. As the skunk submerges, the fleas are kept busy moving upward to get out of the water until finally the dry stalks he holds in his mouth are black with hundreds of the tiny insects. Our striped friend then opens his mouth, releasing the grass, and his unwelcome guests go floating down the stream. He has freed himself of the itch-producing pests by placing them in an environment which is unfavorable to them.

The believer—who though saved still has to contend with his "old nature"—should hate his sins and desire freedom from them as much as the skunk wants to be rid of his pesky fleas. Communion with God by means of Bible study and prayer, accompanied with humble confession of sins, will give the believer freedom from the accusations of a guilty conscience and provide the daily cleansing he needs.—H. V. L.

**ONLY AS YOU WALK IN THE LIGHT CAN YOU
ENJOY A LIFE OF SPIRITUAL VICTORY.**

He was wounded for our transgressions.

ISAIAH 53:5

H. A. Ironside told the story of a group of pioneers who were traveling westward by covered wagon. One day they were horrified to see in the distance a long line of smoke and flame stretching for miles across the prairie. The dry grass was on fire, and the inferno was advancing upon them rapidly. The river they had crossed the day before would be of no help as they would not be able to return to it in time. One man, however, knew what to do. He gave the command to set fire to the grass behind them. Then, when the ground had cooled, the whole company moved back upon it. The people watched apprehensively as the blaze roared toward them. A little girl cried out in terror, "Are you sure we won't be burned up?" The leader replied, "My child, we are absolutely safe, nothing can harm us here, for we are standing on the scorched area where the flames have already done their work."

Christian friend, do not be afraid of death and the judgment that will follow. You are now safely seated "in the heavenly places in Christ Jesus" (Eph. 2:6), because by faith you have taken refuge in the "burned-over place" of Calvary. Let this be your comfort: you are standing in safety "where the fire has been."—H. V. L.

TO ESCAPE GOD'S JUSTICE, FLEE TO HIS LOVE!

The heavens declare the glory of God;
and the firmament shows His handiwork.

PSALM 19:1

The trip to the moon on July 20, 1969, was one of the most carefully planned scientific projects ever undertaken. The entire world held its breath as the "Eagle" made its descent to the moon's surface, and Neil Armstrong placed his foot where man had never walked before. Many questions filled the minds of people everywhere. What was the surface like? Would there be signs of life? Of what elements is that shining satellite composed? To help unravel these mysteries, the astronauts were to bring back soil samples. When they returned with this "treasure trove," scientists in Houston could hardly wait to get their hands on it. Any intelligent person would have immediately assumed that there must be a "mind" or a "designer" behind such work. Yet many today, looking out upon the starry skies that "declare the glory of God" and at the intricacies of life here upon earth that bear the imprint of their Maker, tell us that all these things are the chance products of blind evolution!

"If one footprint on the sand convinced Robinson Crusoe that a person was on his island," writes Fred Meldau, "then by the same logic we know that the Creator made the world because He left, as it were, countless footprints of His activities."—R. W. D.

NATURE IS BUT A NAME FOR AN EFFECT WHOSE CAUSE IS GOD!

It pleased the Father that in Him all the fullness should dwell.

C OLOSSIANS 1:19

The Rosetta Stone, discovered in 1799, is a stone bearing inscriptions in three languages, one of which is ancient Egyptian hieroglyphics. The scholar Thomas Young surmised that the names of the king and other royalty were the key to deciphering the inscriptions. He was correct.

Likewise, when German scholar Georg Fredrick Grotefend deciphered cuneiform, the ancient near-eastern writing system, he guessed that a certain sequence of signs referred to King Darius. He too was right. In both cases, the king's name became the key to unlocking the language.

There's another King whose name is the answer to some of life's most troubling questions. He is Jesus Christ. If we are rightly related to Him, we have the key to the issues of sin and guilt and heaven and hell. He gives eternal significance to our trials and the weaknesses of body and mind that we all face as members of a fallen human race. Yield to His lordship. Christ is the answer.—P. R. V.

IN CHRIST ALL THINGS HOLD TOGETHER.

September

Do not present your members as instruments
of unrighteousness to sin.

ROMANS 6:13

You've probably heard the story of the man who walked into the office of a country doctor, clutching his arm and in great pain. "Doc, you gotta help me," he moaned. "I broke my arm in two places. What should I do?" "Well," responded the doctor, "there's only one thing for you to do. Stay outa them places!"

That may have been useless advice for that patient, but in the spiritual realm there is great protection in avoiding situations that tempt us to sin. It may be that the conversation during lunch with one of our co-workers always turns into complaining about our boss. Perhaps when we play golf with John we use his bad language after a poor shot.

Breaking sinful habits is difficult. The patterns may be deeply established. Our bodies and minds crave the release some things seem to bring. Sinful patterns can be broken only as we live by the power of God and depend on the Holy Spirit to warn us and help us "stay outa them places" where we are sure to fall.—D. C. E.

KEEP OUT OF YOUR LIFE
ALL THAT WOULD CROWD CHRIST OUT OF YOUR HEART.

Do not worry about tomorrow,
for tomorrow will worry about its own things.

MATTHEW 6:34

A church bulletin carried a story of a frail little woman who suffered a fall that resulted in a bad hip fracture. The doctor set the bones as best he could, but a concerned look on his face revealed the seriousness of her condition.

The next day when he visited his patient in the hospital, she was in great anxiety. "Oh, Doctor," she begged, "how long am I going to have to stay in bed?" With great wisdom and tenderness he replied, "Only one day—one day at a time!" That was good psychology; it was also good biblical counsel.

Jesus taught the same important lesson when He said, "Do not worry about tomorrow, for tomorrow will worry about its own things. Sufficient for the day is its own trouble" (Matt. 6:34). God's help and guidance are given like manna in the wilderness—one day's supply at a time.—H. G. B.

DON'T TRY TO BEAR TOMORROW'S BURDENS WITH TODAY'S GRACE.

The wisdom that is from above is first pure,
then peaceable, . . . without partiality.

JAMES 3:17

General Robert E. Lee was a devout follower of Jesus Christ. It is said that soon after the end of the American Civil War, he visited a church in Washington, D. C. During the communion service, he knelt beside a black man. An onlooker said to him later, "How could you do that?" Lee replied, "My friend, all ground is level beneath the cross."

The uprooting of prejudice begins at the cross of Calvary. Like little children, Christians should be the least prejudiced people in the world. We have come to know God in Christ, who died for us "while we were still sinners" (Rom. 5:8). The Lord offers His salvation to everyone—to people of all nations, of all social and economic classes. We should see all people as God sees them—people whom He loves and for whom Jesus died. God's love, like the warm rays of the sun, will drive away the mist of prejudging others.—D. J. D.

SOME CONVICTIONS ARE NOTHING MORE THAN PREJUDICES.

Others have labored, and you have entered into their labors.

JOHN 4:38

In the Lord's kingdom there are sowers and there are reapers. Some do the unrewarding work of plowing and scattering the precious seed of God's Word, and some reap the benefits of other people's labors and are privileged to gather the abundant harvest. Yet both are vitally needed because no one can do alone the extensive work that Christ commands.

In eastern countries, professional weavers are sometimes unable to complete in a lifetime the large tapestries assigned to them. When one artisan dies, however, another picks up the threads and weaves according to the original pattern.

The same is true with evangelists, missionaries, and everyone who engages in the Lord's work. They labor faithfully until death. Then others build on the work they began. Jesus said, "One sows and another reaps" (John 4:37). How beautiful is the thought that all Christians are working together in one great task that will bring to completion God's eternal plan!—H. G. B.

NO CHRISTIAN HAS NOTHING TO DO!

Believe in the LORD your God, and you shall be established.

2 CHRONICLES 20:20

Some snowflakes (scientists call them crystals) glitter like diamond tiaras; others resemble delicate lace doilies. Although all snowflakes are different from each other, they have remarkable similarities. Every snowflake has six points. They are made of molecules of hydrogen and oxygen. All snowflakes are symmetrical.

Interestingly, snowflakes come into existence because at the center of each one is a tiny bit of foreign matter. The water vapor that turns into a snowflake always collects around a particle of dust floating in the atmosphere. The tiny particle may be as small as one one-hundred-thousandth of a millimeter in size. Yet it must be there for a snowflake to form.

Now liken this to life. Obstacles, like those dirt particles, can provide the catalyst for something wonderful. Sometimes illness, accident, or heartbreak intrudes into our lives. But its presence gives the Christian the opportunity to let God make something beautiful out of it.—D. C. E.

GOD TRANSFORMS TRIALS INTO BLESSINGS
BY WRAPPING THEM IN HIS GRACE.

"I must work the works of Him who sent Me while it is day."

JOHN 9:4

In his book *Lest Ye Faint*, Franklin Logsdon tells of the president of a Christian college who entered the chapel service one morning with a solemn expression on his face. Following the hymn, he stood up to speak to the student body. He said, "I have just received a telephone message bearing sad news. A fine young man who graduated from this school three years ago has died suddenly."

A hush fell over the audience. Scanning slowly the students, the president asked, "If all you desire to do, if all you hope to do, had to be crowded into three short years, what would you do differently today?"

Time is a priceless gift from God. How we should guard it with care and use it to the fullest!—P. R. V.

**HE WHO HAS NO VISION OF ETERNITY
DOESN'T KNOW THE VALUE OF TIME.**

He who keeps you will not slumber.

PSALM 121:3

During World War II, a young navy pilot made an air strike against the Japanese-held Chichi Jima Island. His plane was struck by anti-aircraft fire, and he had to bail out over the Pacific. Another pilot spotted his chute just as it hit the water and radioed his position. Within minutes, the submarine USS Finback surfaced and rescued the flyer. Safely on board, he silently thanked God for sparing his life. That young pilot was George Bush, the man who became the 41st President of the United States.

In Psalm 121, God is portrayed as a guardian who never sleeps. The Hebrew root word for guard appears six times in eight verses. It is translated "keeps" and "preserve." Every imaginable danger is covered, from our foot slipping (v. 3) to the sun's scorching heat (vv. 5, 6) to our life being taken (v. 7). From morning until night, God guards us (vv. 3–8). As children of God, we are more adequately cared for than any president or government official. He who saves us from sin is our bodyguard now and forevermore.—D. J. D.

**NO DANGER CAN COME SO NEAR THE CHRISTIAN
THAT GOD IS NOT NEARER.**

Behold, now is the accepted time; behold,
now is the day of salvation.

2 CORINTHIANS 6:2

*I*magine yourself as a writer, typing away on a personal computer. You're in the middle of creating a multi-page article. The words are flowing, and you're beginning to think about your acceptance speech for the Pulitzer Prize. Suddenly and without warning, the lights dim and your computer screen blinks. From an adjoining office you hear someone yell, "Hit the save button!" But it's too late. You were so intent on getting your ideas down that you failed to save any of it. When the electricity went off, your document vanished. It's gone forever because it wasn't saved.

What's true of computer documents is true of people. Every person who rejects Christ will realize when death comes, which sometimes strikes more suddenly than an electrical outage, that it's too late to "hit the save button." According to the Bible, our destiny is sealed for eternity when we die. That's why we are urged to believe on the Lord Jesus Christ today (Acts 16:31; 2 Cor. 6:2). Imagine the horror of realizing it's too late. You will have lost everything—forever.—J. D. B.

IT'S NEVER TOO EARLY TO RECEIVE CHRIST,
BUT AT ANY MOMENT IT COULD BE TOO LATE.

Whenever I am afraid, I will trust in You.

PSALM 56:3

A young woman was waiting for a bus in a crime-ridden area when a rookie policeman approached her and asked, "Want me to wait with you?" "That's not necessary," she replied. "I'm not afraid." "Well, I am," he grinned. "Would you mind waiting with me?"

Christians need that kind of honesty. Like that policeman, we must admit that sometimes we become fearful—fearful about dying, about getting cancer, about losing our mind, about losing our job, about our children getting into trouble. We don't like to admit this, so we may ignore, deny, or repress our fears. But to overcome fear, we must first acknowledge it.

The apostle Paul wasn't ashamed to admit being afraid. "I was with you in weakness, in fear, and in much trembling," he said in 1 Corinthians 2:3. The verse that immediately follows his admission of fear tells how he overcame it. He faced up to his fear and then he relied on God.—D. J. D.

TO ADMIT WE ARE AFRAID IS TO ADMIT WE ARE HUMAN.

All the things you may desire cannot compare with [wisdom].

PROVERBS 3:15

Advertisers are increasingly targeting their messages to children between the ages of nine and fifteen. Because of the strong influence of this age group on the purchasing habits of parents, millions of dollars are being spent to get their attention. The ad people know that a young, satisfied consumer could become a lifelong customer —eager to buy their products far into the future.

In a similar way, we need to be influencing our young people to "buy into" the good things God has in store for them throughout all of life. According to Proverbs 3, some fantastic things lie ahead for the young person who chooses God's way: long life and peace (v. 2), favor in the sight of God and man (v. 4), direction from God (v. 6), health and strength (v. 8), abundance (v. 10), happiness (v. 13).

The world spends millions convincing our children they can't be happy without a certain kind of shoe. How much more important they learn that happiness comes through walking with God!—J. D. B.

**TELL YOUR CHILDREN OF ONE WHO
LOVES THEM EVEN MORE THAN YOU.**

Freely you have received, freely give.

MATTHEW 10:8

I read about a man in Santiago, Chile, named Muñoz who was arrested for drunkenness. As the police were taking him to jail, two Christians stopped them and asked if they could take care of him. The officers agreed. Faithful to Christ's commands, the believers fed the man, cared for him, found him a job, and told him about Jesus.

The gospel brought new life to Muñoz. He became sober, employed, and industrious. He began to repair shoes and was able to make a simple living for his family. He started to talk to his neighbors about the love of God that was changing his life. Soon he was leading a group of neighbors in worship. Before long he became pastor of a congregation of 70 with a Sunday school attendance of 150 children. Muñoz' life was changed because two Christian men gave him the gift of love.

If you believe in Christ and have experienced for yourself the wonderful love of God, don't keep it for yourself alone. Be a giver of love.—D. C. E.

A HEART FULL OF LOVE ALWAYS HAS SOMETHING TO GIVE.

God so loved the world that He gave His only begotten Son.

JOHN 3:16

From *Leadership* magazine comes the story of an old Japanese farmer who had just harvested a rice crop that would make him rich. His farm was on a high plain overlooking the village at the ocean's edge. A mild earthquake had shaken the ground, but the villagers were used to that, so they took little notice. But the farmer, looking out to sea, saw that the water on the horizon appeared dark and foreboding. He knew at once what it meant—a tidal wave. "Bring me a torch, quick," he shouted to his grandson. Then he raced to his stacks of rice and set them ablaze. When the bell in the temple below rang the alarm, the people scrambled up the steep slopes to help save their neighbor's crop. But the farmer met them at the edge of the plain, shouting, "Look! Look!" They saw a great swell of water racing toward them. As it crashed ashore, the tiny village below was torn to pieces. But because that farmer willingly sacrificed his harvest, more than 400 people were spared.

God the Father also gave up something he held dear, His only Son. As a result, millions have experienced salvation through faith in Him. How thankful we should be for Jesus Christ—God's sacrifice!—D. C. E.

SALVATION IS FREE, BUT SOMEONE PAID AN ENORMOUS PRICE.

Whoever drinks of the water
that I shall give to him will never thirst.

JOHN 4:14

In an article for *Christianity Today* titled "A Tale of Two Kittens," Margaret Clarkson draws a spiritual lesson from two cats she had as pets. The first, Mehitable, was a plain calico cat born in a shed down by the river behind Clarkson's home. This cat never forgot her early upbringing. She hunted, fished, and survived on her own. When thirsty, she drank from the river.

Figaro, her handsome black successor, was different. He too loved life by the river. But he didn't hunt except for occasional sport. And he refused to drink from the river. If Clarkson forgot to fill his water bowl, especially in summer, he'd soon become listless. Clarkson commented, "To live at the edge of a great, flowing river and to suffer thirst—how sad!"

We who are God's children sometimes act like Figaro. We know that Jesus is the Living Water. He satisfied our spiritual thirst when He saved us. Yet many of us who came to Him in desperation for our salvation don't return to Him again and again to help us grow.—D. C. E.

JESUS IS THE LIVING WATER—JUST ONE DRINK WILL MAKE US WHOLE.

SEPTEMBER 14

There shall be no more death, nor sorrow.

REVELATION 21:4

A hospital ship was about ready to dock in New York. An army officer, stopping at the bedside of a wounded soldier, inquired if there were any items he wanted to be sure were included with his belongings as the injured were moved ashore. "Nothing at all, sir," the young man responded. "Do you mean to tell me that after all you've been through and suffered," asked the officer, "you have no souvenirs to help you remember the war?" "No sir, I don't," the scarred veteran replied. "All I want of that war is a faint recollection!"

I think we may feel something like that in heaven. When we reach our eternal home, we'll be ready to forget the trials, heartaches, hardships, and sufferings of this present life. We'll focus instead on the joys of being with Jesus, for the "former things have passed away." Someday, when finally at home in heaven and forever freed from the conflicts and pains of this earthly life, battle-scarred soldiers of Jesus Christ may well say, "All I want of that world is a faint recollection!"—R. W. D.

**THE GLORIES OF HEAVEN WILL TOTALLY
ECLIPSE THE TRIALS OF EARTH.**

Hold such men in esteem.

PHILIPPIANS 2:29

The distinguished congressman Claude Pepper was called by his colleagues "a national treasure." He was a valiant champion of the elderly and the poor. A few days before Pepper's death in 1989, President Bush visited him in Walter Reed Hospital to present him with the nation's highest civilian award, the Medal of Freedom. Rep. Silvio Conte recalls, "Despite what was obviously a great deal of pain, Claude apologized to the president and first lady that he couldn't stand up." Said Conte, "He didn't have to stand up. He was a giant."

God's Word tells us of many giants—some named, some anonymous (Heb. 11:32–40). They are measured by their willingness to serve the Lord's cause and others. Their faithfulness in fulfilling their place in His plan marks them out as great.

God is not primarily concerned about bigness, all-time records, or status. His giants are ordinary people who do their best at whatever God calls them to do because they love Christ.—D. J. D.

**GOD IS LOOKING FOR ORDINARY PEOPLE
WHO WILL DO EXTRAORDINARY WORK.**

The father of the righteous will greatly rejoice.

PROVERBS 23:24

David Wilkerson, author of *The Cross and the Switchblade*, said, "Good parents do not always produce good children, but devoted, dedicated, hardworking mothers and fathers can weigh the balance in favor of decency and moral character."

To assist in your quest to be a good parent, here are 10 commandments for guiding your children.

1. Teach them, using God's Word (Deut. 6:4–9).
2. Tell them what's right and wrong (1 Kings 1:6).
3. See them as gifts from God (Ps. 127:3).
4. Guide them in godly ways (Prov. 22:6).
5. Discipline them (Prov. 29:17).
6. Love them unconditionally (Luke 15:11–32).
7. Do not provoke them to wrath (Eph. 6:4).
8. Earn their respect by example (1 Tim. 3:4).
9. Provide for their physical needs (1 Tim. 5:8).
10. Pass your faith along to them (2 Tim. 1:5).—J. D. B.

**HOW OUR CHILDREN LIVE TOMORROW
DEPENDS ON WHAT WE TEACH THEM TODAY.**

Casting all your care upon Him, for He cares for you.

1 PETER 5:7

When Donald Grey Barnhouse was in London, he gave some important papers to a secretary to type and mail to a man in another part of the city. It was Friday and the matter was urgent. On Monday morning she discovered that the person to whom she had given the envelope had not mailed it. So a courier was sent to deliver it by hand across London. The address was 5 Eaton Place. But no one at that location had even heard of the person to whom it was addressed.

The messenger phoned the office, only to learn that the letter was to go to 5 Eaton Gate. If it had been mailed, it would have been delivered to the wrong place and eventually returned to the sender. God had overruled human failure to make sure that the right person at the right address received it on time.

Delays, detours, disappointments, surprising turn of events, joyous fulfillment—are these chance? No, the child of God has the assurance that providential provision is always being made for him. He who knows the end from the beginning cares for His own.—P. R. V.

**NOTHING IS TOO BIG FOR GOD TO ACCOMPLISH;
NOTHING IS TOO SMALL FOR HIM TO NOTICE.**

Let each one give . . . not grudgingly or of necessity;
for God loves a cheerful giver.

2 CORINTHIANS 9:7

I like the story about the church that was having a problem meeting its budget. The pastor suggested to the board that a special fund be established, and he recommended that the leaders set a good example by being the first to contribute to it.

As he made the suggestion, he looked straight into the eyes of one of the wealthiest, but also one of the stingiest, men in the church. The man hesitated, then said rather grudgingly, "I'll give $25.00." Just then a small piece of plaster fell from the ceiling and hit him on the head. "I'll make that $50.00," he quickly declared. At that point, someone was overheard praying, "Hit him again, Lord. Hit him again."

Now, we know that God doesn't beat His children into giving generously. Rather, He takes great delight when the offerings of His children are willingly and cheerfully given. God could accomplish His work in the world without our help, but He has allowed us to have a part in the great things He is doing. Remember, the Lord loves cheerful givers.—R. W. D.

MANY CHEERFULLY GIVE GOD CREDIT;
FEW GENEROUSLY GIVE HIM CASH.

283

Let each of you look out . . . also for the interests of others.

PHILIPPIANS 2:4

Billy, a nine-year-old boy, had a dog he loved very much. One day as he was playing with his pet, the dog gave him a great big lick on the face. Billy responded by kissing the dog on the tip of his cold, wet nose. The boy's mother, seeing what had happened, was horrified. Billy noticed her shocked expression and commented, "Don't worry, Mom, I won't give the dog my cold. I'm over it." Billy never gave a thought to the germs he might get from his pet. His concern was focused entirely on his dog.

That's a far cry from the "me first, others last" philosophy of so many people today. We are told, "Don't worry about the other person. Do what's best for you. Your own happiness is the important thing." Look out for number one—you!"

Christ never displayed such a self-centered attitude. He was willing to leave the glories of heaven, become a man, take our sin on Himself, and pay its awful price at Calvary. He did it all because of His deep love for us.—R. W. D.

**LOOKING OUT FOR THE INTERESTS OF OTHERS
PAYS ETERNAL DIVIDENDS.**

Do not be afraid, but speak, and do not keep silent.

ACTS 18:9

*A*re you discouraged because the work that God has called you to do is off to a slow start? Remember, some of our most wonderful inventions got off to slow starts as well.

The first electric light was so dim that a candle was needed to see its socket. The first steamboat took 32 hours to chug its way from Buffalo to Albany, a distance of 522 miles. Wilbur and Orville Wright's first airplane flight lasted only 12 seconds. And the first automobiles traveled 2 to 4 miles per hour and broke down often. Carriages would pass them with their passengers shouting, "Get a horse!" But look what these inventions are capable of today.

Are you off to a slow start? Don't let a rough beginning in your endeavor for the Lord get you down. When you know you're in God's will and you're obeying His call, stick with it!—D. C. E.

GOD CAN MAKE A GREAT FINISH OUT OF A SLOW START.

Flee also youthful lusts.

2 TIMOTHY 2:22

Little Jeff was trying his best to save enough money to buy his mother a present. It was a terrible struggle because he gave in so easily to the temptation to buy goodies from the ice cream man whenever the brightly colored van came through the neighborhood.

One night after his mother had tucked him in bed, she overheard him praying, "Please, dear God, help me to run away when the ice cream man comes down our street tomorrow." Even at his young age he had learned that one of the best ways to overcome temptation is to avoid what appeals to our weaknesses.

All believers are tempted to sin. Yet they need not give in. The Lord provides the way to be victorious over evil enticements (1 Cor. 10:13). But we must do our part. Sometimes that involves avoiding situations that would contribute to our spiritual defeat. If possible, we should never let ourselves be in the wrong places or with people who will tempt us to do the things we should be avoiding. Be quick to run from the "ice cream man"!—R. W. D.

WE FALL INTO TEMPTATION WHEN WE DON'T FLEE FROM IT.

*Christ died for our sins . . . , He was buried,
and . . . He rose again the third day.*

1 CORINTHIANS 15:3–4

Crosses decorate church steeples. They designate burial places. They sometimes mark the spot where people died in highway accidents. They are worn as jewelry. Crosses remind people of Jesus Christ. I was made aware of this when a Jewish businessman, seeing a small gold cross on the lapel of my jacket, asked me, "Why are you a believer in Christ?" I was glad for the opportunity to share my faith with him.

Jesus died on the cross for us, but He did not remain there. We don't worship a dead Savior. Our Lord's body was taken from the cross and placed in a tomb, and then on the third day He emerged in a glorified body.

The cross speaks to us of the total picture—our Lord's atoning death to pay the price for our sins and His glorious resurrection to deliver us from the power of death.—H. V. L.

AT THE CROSS WE STAND AT THE CROSSROAD TO HEAVEN OR HELL.

Be thankful to Him, and bless His name. For the LORD is good.

PSALM 100:4–5

Bible teacher Leon Tucker told about taking a trip to Europe and promising his little daughter that he would bring her a doll from each country he visited. He purchased them in Ireland, Scotland, Belgium, France, and several other countries. But on the way back to the States, the luggage containing these gifts was delayed and didn't arrive with him.

When Tucker got home, his little daughter greeted him with love and expectation. The look on her face said, "Did you bring the dolls, Daddy?" Gently he told her about the mix-up. Momentarily her lip quivered and her eyes filled with tears, but then she threw her arms around his neck and said, "I'd rather have you, Daddy, than all the dolls in the world!"

Is God more precious to us than all of His gifts? Our love and devotion should be centered on the Giver, not His gifts.—P. R. V.

NO GIFT IS GREATER THAN THE GIVER HIMSELF.

I delight to do Your will, O my God.

PSALM 40:8

A Hebrew slave had the legal right to be set free after six years. But if he was dedicated to his master, he could decide not to accept his freedom. He would then remain a servant for the rest of his days. If a Hebrew servant chose to do this, a rather strange ceremony took place. The master would take him to a doorpost, place his ear against the wood, and pierce the earlobe with an awl. The opening in the ear marked him as a bondservant, one who would willingly and lovingly serve his master for life.

Referring to His heavenly Father, the Lord Jesus said, "I always do those things that please Him" (John 8:29). In His earthly ministry and redemptive work, Jesus took "the form of a servant . . . and became obedient to the point of death, even the death of the cross" (Phil. 2:7–8). Having purchased us by His sacrifice at Calvary, He now becomes our Master.

Are you a slave of Jesus Christ by choice?—P. R. V.

CHRIST FREED US FROM SLAVERY THAT WE MIGHT SERVE HIM FREELY.

I am the way, the truth, and the life.
No one comes to the Father except through Me.

JOHN 14:6

Sir Alexander Mackenzie is a Canadian hero. An early fur trader and explorer, he accomplished a magnificent feat when he led an expedition across Canada from Fort Chippewyan on Lake Athabasca to the Pacific Ocean. His incredible journey was completed in 1793, eleven years before Lewis and Clark began their famous expedition to the west.

Mackenzie's earlier attempt in 1789, however, had been a major disappointment. His explorers had set out in an effort to find a water route to the Pacific. The valiant group followed a mighty river (now named the Mackenzie) with high hopes, paddling furiously amid great danger. Unfortunately, it didn't empty into the Pacific but into the Arctic Ocean. In his diary, Mackenzie called it the "River of Disappointment."

Many people are following religions that will lead to ultimate disappointment. Because they are not based on Christ, they are false and will not lead to heaven. Only Jesus, the eternal Son of God, can take us to the waters of eternal life.—D. C. E.

RELIGION MAY INFORM AND REFORM,
BUT ONLY CHRIST CAN TRANSFORM.

Judge nothing before the time, until the Lord comes.

1 CORINTHIANS 4:5

A Persian king wanted to teach his four sons never to make rash judgments. So he told the eldest to go in winter to see a mango tree, the next to go in spring, the third in summer, and the youngest in the fall.

After the last son had returned from his autumn visit, the king called them together to describe what they had observed. "It looks like a burnt old stump," said the eldest. "No," said the second, "it is lacy green." The third described it as "beautiful as a rose." The youngest said, "No, its fruit is like a pear." "Each is right," said the king, "for each of you saw the tree in a different season."

What a lesson this fable holds for Christians! We quickly forget that our brothers and sisters in the faith are at different stages of growth and come from many different backgrounds and cultures. Conversion to Christ is just the beginning of a lifetime of replacing old thoughts, habits, and actions with new ones created by the indwelling Holy Spirit. God sees the whole picture, and He never draws hasty conclusions. Neither should we.—D. J. D.

IT IS EASIER TO THINK YOU ARE RIGHT THAN TO BE RIGHT.

Be kindly affectionate to one another . . . ,
in honor giving preference to one another.

ROMANS 12:10

The story is told about two monks, Andrew and Thomas, who lived in a cave. They got along so well that not a cross word passed between them. In fact, life was so harmonious it seemed monotonous at times.

One day Andrew came up with an idea to break the boredom. "Let's have a good quarrel," he suggested, "like people in the outside world!" Thomas responded, "But we don't have anything to argue about." Andrew thought for a moment, and then suggested, "Let's find a rock and place it on the ground between us. I'll say, 'This rock is mine!' And you'll say, 'No, it isn't, this rock is mine!' Maybe that'll get a good argument started."

So, finding a rock, and placing it on the ground between them, Andrew exclaimed, "This rock is mine!" Thomas, pausing for a moment, responded meekly, "I think, brother, that the rock is mine." "Oh, very well, then," Andrew said agreeably, "if the rock is yours—take it."

A sure cure for quarreling is to give honor and preference to one another.—R. W. D.

TWO CANNOT QUARREL WHEN ONE WILL NOT.

Not by works of righteousness which we have done,
but according to His mercy He saved us.

TITUS 3:5

Helene Madison was a 1932 Olympic champion. Royal Brougham of the *Seattle Post-Intelligencer* wrote, "She could out-swim any woman on earth." But after winning twenty-three national championships and breaking every world record, she dropped from sight.

Thirty years later Brougham wrote a different story. He told of finding Helene sitting in a one-room basement apartment, a despondent woman. Forgotten by the world and desperately ill, the former champion was planning to drive her car to some dead-end road, close the windows, and by piping in carbon monoxide snuff out the life that still remained in her cancer-ravaged body. Brougham convinced her to change her mind and seek help.

A year later she died, but not without hope. In recounting her death, Brougham wrote, "At long last, Helene Madison placed her thin, frail hand into the hand of a bedside counselor and asked the Lord Jesus to come into her heart. She found the peace she had unsuccessfully sought in so many byways."—H. G. B.

LIFE WITH CHRIST IS AN ENDLESS HOPE.
LIFE WITHOUT CHRIST IS A HOPELESS END.

*Then we who are alive and remain shall be caught up
together with them in the clouds to meet the Lord.*

1 THESSALONIANS 4:17

William L. Pettingill told of the time he visited a great steel plant. The owner was a devoted Christian. Together they walked out into the scrap metal yard. Motioning to the operator of the electric crane, the owner instructed him to lower a huge magnet over a wide dirt road beaten hard by truck traffic.

"Watch," he said as he gave the signal to turn on the current to the magnet. Up from that cracking road leaped pieces of metal, long covered and out of sight. They were caught up to meet that powerful magnet in the air! It attracted the metal having the same nature as itself. Pettingill knew what his friend was illustrating—the truth of 1 Thessalonians 4:17.

A great event awaits the child of God! When Christ descends from heaven, He will draw all believers to Himself—those who have died in the Lord, and those who are alive at His coming. The anticipation of that event should thrill the heart of every person who knows Jesus as Savior.
—R. W. D.

**ALL WHO WANT TO MEET CHRIST IN THE AIR
MUST FIRST MEET HIM AT THE CROSS.**

SEPTEMBER 30

*One of them . . . returned, . . . and fell down
on his face at His feet, giving Him thanks.*

LUKE 17:15–16

*A*retired school teacher in her eighties was overjoyed to get
a letter from a former student thanking her for her role in
his life. She responded immediately: "I can't tell you how much your
letter meant to me. You will be interested to know that I taught school
for fifty years, and yours is the first note of appreciation I have ever
received. It filled me with cheer."

The story of the ten lepers highlights the fact that we are prone to
accept blessings without saying, "Thank you." We are too often like the
nine lepers who never returned to give thanks to the Lord Jesus.

God delights in hearing His children say, "Thank You."—H. V. L.

AN ATTITUDE OF GRATITUDE CAN MAKE YOUR LIFE A BEATITUDE.

October

Whom having not seen you love.

1 PETER 1:8

William Drummond told a story of a young woman he knew whose face always seemed to radiate Christian joy. Her actions too made it evident that she was a devout follower of Christ. But she also had one other identifying feature—she always wore a little gold locket around her neck. Such oval or heart-shaped cases usually contain the picture of a loved one, which the wearer gladly shows to anyone who inquires. This girl, however, never showed anyone what was inside hers.

One day, during a time when she had become seriously ill, one of her closest friends was permitted to open the locket. Drummond said, "Instead of seeing the photograph of the girl's mother or of some male admirer, she found inscribed the words, 'Whom, having not seen, I love.' The secret of her consecrated life was revealed. She had given her full devotion to Jesus, the Lover of her soul, and all her actions had been beautified by His presence."—H. G. B.

A LIFE GIVEN FULLY TO GOD BECOMES A GOD-FILLED LIFE.

298

He did not waver at the promise of God through unbelief,
but was strengthened in faith.

ROMANS 4:20

I like the story about old Uncle Oscar and his first airplane ride. His friends asked him, "Did you enjoy the flight?" "Well," Uncle Oscar replied, "it wasn't as bad as I thought it might be. But I'll tell you this, I never did put all my weight down!"

That sounds a little like some of us. As Christians, we know that our sins have been forgiven, and we rejoice in the assurance of going to heaven, but we fall short of entrusting other areas of our lives to the Lord. We never put all our weight down. As a result, we are beset by doubts, fears, and uncertainties. We don't "enjoy the trip" to heaven as much as we could. We have complete confidence in the Lord for eternity, but we don't dare trust Him for the here and now.

The Lord is trustworthy. That's why we can put "all our weight down."—R. W. D.

FAITH KNOWS THAT GOD ALWAYS PERFORMS WHAT HE PROMISES.

Now you yourselves are to put off all these:
anger, wrath, malice, blasphemy, filthy language.

COLOSSIANS 3:8

One winter a resort in Breckenridge, Colorado, posted signs instructing skiers to keep off a certain slope. The signs, large and distinct, said, "Danger! Out of Bounds!" In spite of the warnings, however, several skiers went into the area. The result? A half-mile-wide avalanche buried four of the trespassers beneath tons of snow and rock. This tragedy never would have happened if the signs had been heeded.

God has posted clear warning signs in the Bible to tell us what kinds of behavior and attitudes are off-limits. The Lord loves us and wants to spare us from tragedy. He warned us about lying, stealing, blasphemy, filthy language, adultery, murder, drunkenness, and a host of other sins. Yet, many times we ignore His warnings and intentionally wander into a forbidden area. We convince ourselves that nothing bad will happen to us or that we can turn back if we sense danger.

But God is not kidding, nor is He being authoritarian. Sinning guarantees His disapproval and opens the door to remorse and tragedy. Don't be foolish. Heed God's warning signs that say, "Danger! Out of Bounds!"—D. C. E.

THE COST OF OBEDIENCE IS SMALL COMPARED
WITH THE COST OF DISOBEDIENCE.

[Jesus] said to them, "It is I; do not be afraid."

JOHN 6:20

Thomas Kelly told about his first voyage down the St. Lawrence River. The Long Sault Rapids came into view with their rushing, foaming, tossing waters. While still a safe distance away, the boat was anchored and a new pilot was taken on board. He was a strong and stalwart American Indian, and was the only man who had brought a vessel safely through those raging waters.

The pilot put his hand on the wheel and headed the boat toward the center of the rapids. With eyes riveted on an object beyond the torrent, he held the vessel steady as it moved through the rushing current. Huge rocks protruded from the water, little more than an arm's length from the hull of the boat. But the pilot knew precisely what he was doing, and soon the danger was behind them.

Life is much like the perilous waters of those rapids. How can anyone navigate such a hazardous, uncharted voyage? There is but one way. First we must put out the anchor of faith and receive the Lord Jesus as our personal Savior. Then we must trust Him as the Pilot of our life and let Him take complete control.—P. R. V.

WE NEED NOT FEAR SHIPWRECK WHEN JESUS IS AT THE HELM.

Abide in Him, that when He appears,
we may have confidence and not be ashamed.

1 JOHN 2:28

A wealthy young man had gone away to war soon after he was married. His new bride wrote him of the demanding schedule she had to keep as a nurse in a certain hospital. Apologizing for her infrequent writing, she explained that she was spending a great deal of time with the wounded.

Some months later when the man was scheduled for leave, a friend suggested, "Don't announce your coming. Slip in quietly." Arriving in London, the young man went directly to the hospital, but his wife was not there. He then went to their house, where he was told by the servants, "Oh, she will probably be at the tea dance at the Ritz." Going there, he found her in the company of another man. How shocked and ashamed she was at her husband's appearing!

When our Lord returns, we won't want to be found flirting and preoccupied with the world. What if He comes for us today?—P. R. V.

THOSE WHO BELONG TO CHRIST SHOULD BE LONGING TO SEE HIM.

*To be carnally minded is death,
but to be spiritually minded is life and peace.*

ROMANS 8:6

A small boy was taken to the barbershop for a haircut. The room was filled with cigar smoke. The lad pinched his nose and exclaimed, "Who's been smoking in here!" The barber sheepishly confessed, "I have, son." The tyke responded, "Don't you know it isn't good for you?" "I know" the barber replied. "I've tried to quit a thousand times but I just can't." The boy thought for a moment and then commented, "I understand, sir. I've tried to stop sucking my thumb, but I can't either!"

Those two remind me of the way believers sometimes feel about their struggle with the sins of the flesh. Paul summed it up well by crying out, "Oh, wretched man that I am! Who shall deliver me from the body of this death?" (Rom. 7:24).

Are you struggling to break some stubborn habit? Like Paul, you can be an overcomer. You don't have to say with that barber and that little boy, "I've tried to quit a thousand times, but I just can't." If you know the Lord Jesus as your Savior, victory is possible through the power of the indwelling Holy Spirit.—R. W. D.

**THINK LESS OF THE POWER OF THINGS OVER YOU
AND MORE OF THE POWER OF CHRIST IN YOU.**

I have uttered what I did not understand, things too wonderful for me.

JOB 42:3

While working on his book *Disappointment with God*, Philip Yancey interviewed a young man named Douglas who was enduring much suffering. "Could you tell me about your own disappointment?" asked Yancey. After a long silence, Douglas said, "To tell you the truth, Philip, I didn't feel any disappointment with God. I learned, first through my wife's illness [cancer], and then especially through the accident [he was hit by a drunk driver], not to confuse God with life. I'm no stoic. . . . I feel free to curse the unfairness of life and to vent all my grief and anger. But I believe God feels the same way about that accident—grieved and angry. I don't blame Him. . . . God's existence, even His love for me, does not depend on my good health."

Job, it seems, did for a time confuse life with God (14:19; 16:9). So God asked him more than seventy questions (chs. 38–40) about what he knew of the world and the universe. The implication? "Job, if you can't grasp My great power in the visible world, how can you know My wonderful ways in the unseen world? Trust Me!"—D. J. D.

IN OUR TRIALS, LET'S NOT CONFUSE LIFE WITH GOD.

A bishop then must be . . . one who rules his own house well.

1 TIMOTHY 3:2, 4

A boy was given a world globe for his birthday. He liked it so much that he kept it beside his bed. One night his father wanted to study the globe. Thinking his son was asleep, he tiptoed into his room, picked it up, and started for the door. He had just about reached it when the child, sitting up in bed, called out, "Hey, Dad, what are you doing with my world?"

Most of us are not in positions to influence world affairs. Every father, however, can make a tremendous difference in his own home—his children's "world." It is his privilege and responsibility to make it the best place possible for their development. Fathers are to create an environment that provides a sense of belonging. They are to exercise loving discipline that reflects the care of the heavenly Father for His children.

If your child asked, "Hey, Dad, what are you doing with my world?" what would you have to say?—R. W. D.

HAPPY IS THE HOME WHERE JESUS' NAME IS SWEET TO EVERY EAR.

You are the light of the world.
A city that is set on a hill cannot be hidden.

MATTHEW 5:14

How much light does it take to push away the darkness? Only a little.

During World War II, my wife's father was an air raid warden in St. Clair Shores, Michigan. Because it was on the flight pattern to Selfridge Air Force Base, he said that it was vitally important during a blackout that every light was out to avoid the possibility of giving help to an enemy plane. This included putting blankets over radios, since even the dim glow of those early radio tubes could be seen from the sky.

What areas of spiritual darkness do you encounter? Your place of employment? Your neighborhood? Your family? You can be a light in that dark place. God didn't call us all to be giant searchlights or 1,000-bulb chandeliers. You can, however, give a quiet word of testimony backed up by a consistent life.

Remember, darkness can be dispelled by even a little light.—D. C. E.

THE SUREST WAY TO DRIVE OUT DARKNESS IS TO BRING IN LIGHT.

I have fought the good fight, I have finished the race,
I have kept the faith.

2 TIMOTHY 4:7

One of the most grueling of all bicycle races is the Tour de France. A contestant in that event, Gilbert Duclos-Lassalle, describes it in a *National Geographic* article titled, "An Annual Madness." The race covers about 2,000 miles, including some of France's most difficult, mountainous terrain. Eating and drinking is done on the run. And there are extremes of heat and cold. To train for the event, Lassalle rides his bicycle 22,000 miles a year.

What kind of prize makes people endure so much hardship and pain? $10,000? $100,000? No. It's just a special winner's jersey. What then motivates the contestants? Lassalle sums it up: "Why, to sweep through the Arc de Triomphe on the last day. To be able to say you finished the Tour de France."

The apostle Paul, expecting his soon departure to be with Christ, declared, "I have finished the race." He had completed the work God had given him. As a reward, he was anticipating not a mere jersey, but "the crown of righteousness" (2 Tim. 4:8).—R. W. D.

**WE ARE REWARDED NOT FOR RUNNING THE RACE
BUT FOR FINISHING THE RACE.**

Bless the LORD, O my soul, and forget not all His benefits.

PSALM 103:2

Moses Montefiore, the British philanthropist, had this motto in his home: Think and Thank. It reflects the fact that the word *thankfulness* comes from an old Anglo-Saxon term that meant "thinkfulness."

If we pause to think about the abundance that God has showered on us, we will discover many reasons to express our gratitude to Him. Unfortunately, it's all too easy to take God's goodness for granted. For example, most of us have food, clothing, and shelter. Yet in some parts of the world, even in highly developed countries, many people fight hunger, poverty, and homelessness.

God in His goodness keeps on blessing us with an abundance far beyond what we need or deserve. In addition to our material blessings, we as Christians receive so many spiritual blessings. Today and every day, let's take time to think of all the blessings we have received from God, lest we become unthankful.—H. G. B.

OUR PRAISES SHOULD BE AS ENDLESS AS GOD'S BLESSINGS.

Love suffers long and is kind; . . . does not behave rudely.

1 CORINTHIANS 13:4-5

The *Sunday School Times* told of an elderly Christian who was a shut-in. She said, "I have two daughters who take turns cleaning my small home. Jean comes and makes everything shine. Yet she leaves the impression that I'm an awful burden. But when Mary comes, no matter how dull the day or how low my spirit, she's so cheery that my heart is tuned to singing. Above all, she makes me feel that she loves me. They're both good Christians, you understand, but what a difference in their attitudes! Mary has the extra touch of grace that this old world so badly needs. She does everything with a loving heart."

What is our attitude in helping others? Do we assist people grudgingly, making them feel like a burden, or do we demonstrate heartfelt concern that leaves them uplifted and blessed?

Today, for Jesus' sake, let's serve one another with that extra touch.

—H. G. B.

LOVE IS GOOD WILL FOR THE GAIN OF ANOTHER.

Whatever you do, in word or deed, do all in the name of the Lord Jesus.

COLOSSIANS 3:17

During World War II, Great Britain needed to increase her production of coal, so Winston Churchill called labor leaders together to enlist their support. He asked them to picture a great parade through the streets of London at the end of the war. First would come the sailors who kept the vital sea lanes open. Then would come the soldiers who had safely returned from Dunkirk and who had eventually gone on to defeat Rommel. Then would come the pilots who had driven off the German air force.

Finally, Churchill said, there would come a long line of sweat-stained, soot-streaked men in miner's caps. Someone in the crowd would ask where they were during the critical days of struggle. And from thousands of mouths would come the answer, "We were deep in the earth with our faces in the coal."

Maybe your part in the Lord's work is like those coal miners—no publicity and no prominence. Just remember, when Christ returns in victory, you'll be a part of the parade!—D. C. E.

NOTHING IS LOST THAT IS DONE FOR THE LORD.

Walk circumspectly, not as fools but as wise, redeeming the time.

EPHESIANS 5:15–16

A government agent was sent to a remote and undeveloped area of his country to tell the people about plans to build a road through their territory. They objected strenuously. Trying to reason with them, the official asked, "How long does it now take you to deliver your goods to market by donkey using the existing trail?" "Three days," they replied.

The agent, thinking he had a convincing argument, said with an air of confidence, "If we build that road through here, you'll be able to go to market and come back home all in a single day." A man who had been listening carefully responded, "But tell me, sir, what are we ever going to do with all that extra time?"

Don't you wish you had a "problem" like that? For most of us, it seems there just aren't enough hours in a day. That's why we must make wise use of the time we do have. Yes, let's spend time wisely.—R. W. D.

IF YOU VALUE ETERNITY, MAKE GOOD USE OF TIME.

The righteous cry out, and the LORD hears,
and delivers them out of all their troubles.

PSALM 34:17

Aquilla Webb told of a friend who asked a lifeguard this question: "How can you tell if someone is in need of help when thousands of bathers on the beach or in the water are all combining their voices in a hubbub of noise?" He replied, "No matter how great the sounds of confusion may be, there has never been a time when I couldn't distinguish a cry of distress above them all. I could always tell when there was an actual emergency."

Webb concluded, "That's exactly like our heavenly Father. In all the babel and confusion here below, He never fails to hear the soul that cries out to Him for help amid the breakers and storms of life."

The psalmist David found that in his hour of trouble he could call on the Lord and be confident of receiving His help. If you are encountering troubles today, cry out to the Lord. Then praise Him for the help that He brings to you.—H. G. B.

GOD TAKES HEED TO YOUR EVERY NEED.

Let those who suffer according to the will of God
commit their souls to Him.

1 PETER 4:19

Years ago *The Chaplain* magazine told how the noted preacher Charles Spurgeon and his wife were called miserly because they sold all the eggs their chickens laid and wouldn't give any away. Because they always made a profit on their butter, milk, and eggs, rumors circulated that they were greedy.

The Spurgeons, however, took the criticism graciously, and only after the death of Mrs. Spurgeon was the truth revealed. The records showed that their entire profits had been used to support two needy, elderly widows whose husbands had spent their lives in serving the Lord. Yet because the Spurgeons did not want to call attention to their giving, they had refused to defend themselves.

Christian friend, are you being misunderstood in spite of your pure motives and faithful service? Don't be discouraged. God knows the motives of your heart. Commit your situation to Him and keep on doing good.—H. G. B.

GOD JUDGES US NOT BY WHAT OTHERS SAY, BUT BY WHAT WE DO.

Jesus Christ is the same yesterday, today, and forever.

HEBREWS 13:8

An unusual phenomenon can be seen at the Bay of Fundy on the eastern coast of Canada. Near the mouth of the St. John River, where it flows into the bay, are the Reversing Falls Rapids. They are created by the rise and fall of the extreme tides in the Bay of Fundy, and the flow of water from the St. John River.

At low tide the river flows in thundering rapids out to the sea. But at high tide that great current is changed and water surges upstream, reversing the flow of the falls. In the period of time when the tide is slack and the river and bay are at equal levels, that mighty torrent appears as calm as a mill pond.

How like human nature are those changing tides. Our emotions and actions vary with the day—and sometimes by the hour. But this is not so with our immutable God, who has revealed Himself in His Son Jesus Christ. His truth, grace, mercy, and love for us remain constant.—P. R. V.

THE BEST WAY TO FACE LIFE'S CHANGES IS TO LOOK TO THE UNCHANGING GOD.

*All the paths of the LORD are mercy and truth,
to such as keep His covenant and His testimonies.*

PSALM 25:10

As a boy, Sir Walter Scott was left weak and lame by a severe attack of fever. Some people thought he would never amount to anything in life.

When Scott was a teenager, he visited in a home where some famous writers were being entertained. The poet Robert Burns was among them. In one room was a picture under which was written a beautiful bit of verse. Burns asked who wrote it, but no one seemed to know. Timidly, Scott gave the writer's name and quoted the rest of the poem. Burns was impressed. Laying his hand on young Walter's head, he said, "Ah, my boy, I'm sure you'll be a great man in Scotland someday!" That brief conversation was the affirmation Walter Scott needed to set him on the road to greatness.

We never know what effect a well-timed word of encouragement may have. Ask God to guide you today to someone who needs an encouraging word.—H. G. B.

A LITTLE ENCOURAGEMENT CAN SPARK A GREAT ENDEAVOR.

Let patience have its perfect work,
that you may be perfect and complete, lacking nothing.

JAMES 1:4

nstant cash. Ten-minute oil change. One-hour photo processing. Same-day dry cleaning. You would think waiting is one of life's most trying experiences. We've created for ourselves instant lifestyles. If things don't happen right now, a turbulence of impatience blows through our inner world.

As Christians, we tend to direct our impatience toward God—especially when we are undergoing a trial. If He can create something out of nothing in an instant, why doesn't He act? Yet He seems to take His time. Look how long He delayed before sending Jesus into the world. Yet in "the fullness of the time" He came (Gal. 4:4). And there is for us a "right time" to bring us to maturity and a strong faith.

When our patience is being stretched, we are being given opportunity to expand. That's what James 1 is all about—becoming "perfect and complete." And a lot of expansion is needed to become like Christ.
—D. J. D.

GOD IS NEVER IN A HURRY.

A man's heart plans his way, but the LORD *directs his steps.*

PROVERBS 16:9

Frank W. Boreham said, "It was not by chance that Elijah and Ahab met on the grassy slopes of Carmel. It was not by chance that Herod and John met on the highways of Galilee. It was not by chance that Pilate and Jesus met in the judgment hall at Jerusalem. It was not by chance that Peter and Cornelius met on the Syrian seaboard. It was not by chance that Philip and the Ethiopian met on the sandy road to Gaza. It was not by chance that Nero and Paul met amid the antique splendors of ancient Rome. . . . No, our meetings are no more by chance than the meeting of Stanley and Livingstone in Central Africa."

As we begin each day, we should, with a sincere desire to please the Lord, gladly anticipate God's appointments for us. They may be the people we meet or unplanned circumstances. But we should welcome them as opportunities to witness, to serve others, and to grow spiritually. —R. W. D.

THE INCIDENTS IN OUR LIVES DO NOT HAPPEN BY ACCIDENT.

The LORD shall preserve your going out and your coming in.

PSALM 121:8

In his book *Where in the World Is God?* Richard Harding tells of a British liner headed to America during the dangerous days of World War II. The captain had orders which stated, "Keep straight on this course. Do not turn aside for any reason. If you need help, radio a message in code."

A few days out at sea, the lookout spotted an enemy ship. The captain dispatched a coded message: "Enemy sighted! What shall I do?" Back came the reply, "Keep straight ahead. Help is standing by." The captain obeyed orders and kept on course.

Soon after they had arrived safely, the passengers and crew were surprised to see a great British man-of-war steam into the harbor. That battleship, though out of sight, had followed them from England to America, prepared to help if necessary.

We cannot see God. At times we do not even feel His presence. But in the daily uncertainties of life, amid the dangers around us, in our most pressing hour, God is standing by to help. He will see us safely to the other shore.—P. R. V.

GOD IS PRESENT, EVEN WHEN WE FEEL HE IS ABSENT.

Be anxious for nothing, but . . .
let your requests be made known to God.

PHILIPPIANS 4:6

Imagine the daily grind that faced the mother of evangelist Paul Rader. She raised ten children. Here's how he described his growing-up years when things got tough: "I have seen Mother so perplexed! She would roll that gingham apron up and say, 'Paul, watch the potatoes and don't let them burn.'" She would then leave the room for a few minutes.

One day Paul decided to find out where his mother went when the little Raders got to her. He followed her to her room, where she got down on her knees and prayed, "Jesus, I want to meet You. I am getting nervous, and it is kind of hard; but You are tender and understand the whole business." Then she got up, went back downstairs, and resumed her work—singing as she went. Rader commented, "It is a mighty sweet thing when the mother of ten children can come back with the worry all chased away."

Are you looking at another day of hectic routine? Take a prayer break, and "let your requests be made known to God."—J. D. B.

WHEN SWEPT OFF YOUR FEET, BETTER GET ON YOUR KNEES.

Lo, I am with you always, even to the end of the age.

MATTHEW 28:20

A young Chinese Christian named Lo was given a New Testament, and he began to read it. When he found in Matthew 28:20 the words, "Lo, I am with you always," he was greatly excited because he took this verse as a personal promise to him.

Although he misinterpreted the first word of that text for his own name, Lo didn't miss the impact of the verse. In fact, it became all the more real to him.

We who have received Christ as our Savior and are committed to serving Him may read our name into this promise as well. "Mary, John, Gloria, David, Helen, I am with you always!"

As you walk the Christian pathway, remember that Jesus is always with you.—H. G. B.

WHERE CHRIST SENDS US, HE ALWAYS GOES WITH US.

*He knelt down on his knees . . . and prayed . . . ,
as was his custom since early days.*

DANIEL 6:10

In one region of Africa, the first converts to Christianity were very diligent about praying. In fact, the believers each had their own special place outside the village where they went to pray in solitude. The villagers reached these "prayer rooms" by using their own private footpaths through the brush. When grass began to grow over one of these trails, it was evident that the person to whom it belonged was not praying very much.

Because these new Christians were concerned for each other's spiritual welfare, a unique custom sprang up. Whenever anyone noticed an overgrown "prayer path," he or she would go to the person and lovingly warn, "Friend, there's grass on your path!"

Have you met with the Lord yet today? Do you regularly come to "the throne of grace" to "obtain mercy and find grace to help in time of need"? (Heb. 4:16). Is there any "grass on your path"?—R. W. D.

NO DAY IS WELL SPENT WITHOUT SPENDING TIME WITH GOD.

You were . . . redeemed with . . . the precious blood of Christ.

1 PETER 1:18–19

A miner came to British pastor and author G. Campbell Morgan at the close of a service and said, "I'd give anything to believe that God would forgive my sins. But I just can't accept the idea that all I have to do is trust Him. It's too cheap."

Morgan asked, "Have you been working today?"

"Yes, I was down in the pit."

"Did you pay to get back out?"

"Of course not!" the miner replied. "It didn't cost me anything. I just got in the cage and was pulled to the top."

"Weren't you afraid to trust yourself to that cage? Wasn't it too cheap?"

"Oh, no. The ride was free. But the company paid a lot of money to sink the shaft and make it safe."

Suddenly the truth dawned on the miner. He saw that salvation was free, but he also realized that it had cost the Son of God a tremendous price to come down from heaven and rescue fallen man.—P. R. V.

SALVATION, THOUGH FREE, WAS PURCHASED AT INFINITE COST.

I will lift up my eyes.

PSALM 121:1

A woman who did a lot of research at home began to have difficulty with her vision, so she went to see an eye doctor. After a thorough exam, he said, "Your eyes are extremely tired. They need rest."

"But that's impossible," she replied. "My work requires that I use them all the time."

After thinking for a moment, he said, "Do you have any wide views of the countryside from your home?"

"Yes," she answered. "From the front porch I can see the peaks of the Blue Ridge Mountains."

The specialist replied, "The next time your eyes get tired, gaze steadily at the mountains for ten to twenty minutes. That will rest your eyes."

What is true in the physical realm is also true in the spiritual. The eyes of the soul grow tired from focusing on our problems. But if we turn our attention to the far horizon of God's love, we gain a new perspective. We experience the rest we so desperately need.—H. G. B.

WHEN YOUR BURDEN IS TOO MUCH TO BEAR, TRUST GOD'S TENDER CARE.

He spoke a parable to them,
that men always ought to pray and not lose heart.

LUKE 18:1

A wealthy woman phoned the manager of a concert hall and asked, "Have you found a diamond pendant? I think I lost it in your building last night." The manager replied, "No, we haven't found it, but we'll look. Please hold the line." During a quick search, the valuable diamond was located. When the manager returned to the phone, however, the woman was no longer on the line. She had hung up. She never called again, and the expensive jewelry went unclaimed.

We would fault that woman for her impatience and lack of persistence, but we sometimes act just like that when we pray. And in doing so, we give up something much more precious than diamonds. We lose the opportunity to have the God of the universe help us with our problems, meet our needs, or lead us to do His will. If your request is in keeping with God's will, keep praying and don't fail to "hold the line."—P. R. V.

DELAY IS NOT DENIAL—KEEP PRAYING!

Power belongs to God.

PSALM 62:11

*Y*ears ago, workmen were building a bridge across a portion of the New York harbor. While seeking a base for one of the supporting towers, they hit a submerged barge full of stone that had sunk deeply into the mud at the bottom of the bay. Divers attached chains to the flatboat, but no crane was powerful enough to lift it.

At last a special engineer was called to solve the problem. He ordered two barges brought to the spot. Cables were fastened to them and tightly secured to the sunken boat when the waters were at low tide. As the water rose higher and higher, it began to move the two barges. The submerged boat shook and then responded, breaking free of the mud on the harbor floor. It had been released by the power of the Atlantic Ocean!

So too, lives mired in sin are raised out of their plight by the Holy Spirit's heavenward "lift." With the psalmist we can say triumphantly, "Power belongs to God."—H. G. B.

THE SOURCE OF OUR STRENGTH IS OUR CREATOR AND REDEEMER.

*You will keep him in perfect peace, whose mind is stayed on You,
because he trusts in You.*

ISAIAH 26:3

Tivoli Gardens, a famous amusement area in Copenhagen,
Denmark, has a very unusual attraction. For a small charge,
customers can try to shatter pieces of chinaware by hitting them with
small wooden balls. Flawed products from area manufacturers are hung
on racks at the end of the gallery, and each participant gets five chances
to smash the plates, cups, saucers, and other items of china into
smithereens. Touted as a great tension breaker, the activity is supposed to
rid the person of unwanted anxiety.

Breaking china may be fun and may soothe frayed nerves, but the
Christian has a better means of experiencing relief from tension and
worry. There's nothing quite like the relaxation that comes through a
deep and abiding trust in God. That's the best "tension breaker."—R.W.D.

**WHEN WE KEEP OUR MIND ON GOD,
HE WILL GIVE US PEACE OF MIND.**

They bowed their faces to the ground . . . ,
and worshiped and praised the LORD.

2 CHRONICLES 7:3

It wasn't a normal, run-of-the-mill morning worship service when Solomon dedicated the temple. There was the sacrifice of countless animals (2 Chron. 5:6). Special music was provided by the Levites on stringed instruments, cymbals, and harps, and by 120 trumpet-playing priests (5:12). There was the thick cloud in which dwelt the glory of the Lord (5:14). There was the dedicatory prayer of Solomon (6:12–42).

The most dramatic event occurred, however, when fire fell from heaven and consumed the offerings (7:1). The people, awed by God's presence, bowed low in worship (7:3). Two weeks later, when Solomon sent them home, they were "joyful and glad of heart for the good that the LORD had done" (7:10).

Although we cannot duplicate the majesty of such a celebration, from it we can learn about the transforming power of worship. And we can be challenged as believers and as churches to seek to worship God more effectively. Let's joyfully worship the Lord.—J. D. B.

TRUE WORSHIP ACKNOWLEDGES THE TRUE WORTH-SHIP OF GOD.

The fire will test each one's work.

1 CORINTHIANS 3:13

Driving through the city one day, I decided to swing by three of the rental houses I lived in as a small boy. Two were gone, but one stands just as straight and tall as it did sixty years ago. It had a good foundation and was constructed with high-quality materials.

The apostle Paul used the metaphor of building to warn us that we who have made Jesus Christ the foundation of our faith can still build a poor superstructure. We do this when we use materials like "wood, hay, straw," which cannot stand the fire test. These combustibles represent wrong doctrines and careless conduct—every thought and deed that is false, impure, or worthless. If we build with these, our lives will accomplish little of eternal value.

How different if we use gold, silver, and precious stones! These valuable elements stand for materials of a lasting quality—putting Christ first in our lives, living purely, and serving God faithfully. If we construct our lives this way, we will be rewarded at the judgment seat of Christ (2 Cor. 5:10).—H. V. L.

**WHAT IS DONE RIGHT FOR CHRIST NOW
WILL BE REWARDED IN ETERNITY.**

November

What do you want Me to do for you?

MARK 10:51

atherine Marshall compared generalized, non-focused prayers to window-shopping. She wrote, "Window-shopping can be enjoyable—but there it ends. It costs nothing. We are just looking, have no intention of buying anything; so we bring nothing home to show for the hours of browsing. Too many of our prayers—private and public—are just browsing among possible petitions, not down to cases at all."

We can learn from Bartimaeus. He knew that the Lord had the ability to grant his request. He knew exactly what he wanted. When the Lord turned to this blind man and gave him an opportunity to make a request, Bartimaeus said without hesitation, "I want to be able to see." He believed that Jesus could heal him. Bartimaeus asked—and received. His plea was specific.

May we too have the faith and courage to ask the Lord for our specific needs and trust Him to do what is best for us.—D. C. E.

**YOU WON'T GET AN ANSWER AT GOD'S DOOR
IF YOU AREN'T KNOCKING.**

When I bring a cloud over the earth, . . .
the rainbow shall be seen in the cloud.

GENESIS 9:14

After the flood, God told Noah that the rainbow would symbolize His gracious pledge never again to destroy the earth with water. Out of the clouds the deluge came; yet it is in the clouds that God places this colorful arch of promise. The rainbow reminds me that little beauty can enter our lives without the clouds of trial. And when the sunshine of God's love floods our sorrow with light, there a shining rainbow of hope appears. God does more than offer hope, however. Amid the troubling clouds, He sends His angels to help us (Heb. 1:14).

In one of Germany's famous art galleries, a painting called "Cloud Lane" hangs at the end of a long dark hall. It appears at first to be a huge, ugly mass of confused color—unattractive and foreboding. Upon closer examination, however, you see an innumerable company of angels.

If clouds hang heavy over your life today, look for the rainbow of hope. You can be sure that God's angels will be there to meet your needs.—H. G. B.

NO CLOUD OF AFFLICTION IS WITHOUT GOD'S RAINBOW OF PROMISE.

Beloved, do not think it strange concerning the fiery trial . . . ;
but rejoice.

1 PETER 4:12–13

read about a godly woman who had suffered for several months with a lingering illness. One day while her pastor was visiting, she said, "I have such a lovely robin that sings outside my window. In the early mornings, as I lie here, he serenades me." With a smile that radiated a deep joy within her weakened body, she added, "I love him because he sings in the rain."

This trait of the robin, singing when the storm has silenced other songbirds, should be evidenced in a similar way by every child of God. I think I hear the song in Paul's heart as he writes concerning his ministry: ". . . as dying, and behold we live; as chastened, and yet not killed; as sorrowful, yet always rejoicing; as poor, yet making many rich; as having nothing, and yet possessing all things" (2 Cor. 6:9–10).

Anyone can sing in the sunshine. But those who know the Savior can experience joy in the darkness because their confidence is in God's goodness and power.—P. R. V.

EVEN WHEN THE RAINS COME, WE STILL HAVE REASON TO REJOICE.

Though by this time you ought to be teachers,
you need someone to teach you again.

HEBREWS 5:12

When a young bird leaves the nest, it usually knows how to fly. But as a rule, it requires plenty of help in finding food. It may take pride in its new independence, but its first solo flights are quickly followed by cries of, "Feed me! Feed me!" Gradually this pattern begins to change as the helpless young bird matures and becomes capable of feeding not only itself but also its own brood.

A similar development should be just as predictable in the spiritual lives of believers. Unfortunately, many of God's children spend their entire lives crying to their pastors and teachers, "Feed me! Feed me!" That's not to say church leaders shouldn't be instructing their people all the time. But there must come a point of maturity when we search the Scriptures for ourselves, apply the truth to our lives, exercise our senses to discern between good and evil (Heb. 5:14), and teach others what we have learned.—M. R. D. II

NOT UNTIL WE KNOW TRUTH CAN WE BESTOW TRUTH ON OTHERS.

When the king heard the words of
the Book of the Law, . . . he tore his clothes.

2 KINGS 22:11

*P*erhaps you think "anything goes" on TV these days. Not
true, according to columnist Cal Thomas. He uncovered one TV
taboo when he was asked to appear on a network news program. Just
before the taping began, the producer said to Thomas, "Please don't use
any Bible verses tonight." On another occasion he was dropped from an
appearance on the same network's morning show. The producer
expressed concern that he "might quote some Bible verses."

Those producers are clearly justified in their fear of the Bible. They
do need to fear the book inspired by a holy God—a God who demands
obedience.

Josiah displayed a better response to the Bible when Hilkiah read
from the rediscovered Book of the Law. Instead of silencing Hilkiah,
Josiah "tore his clothes" in repentance (2 Kings 22:11). His people had
"not obeyed the words of this book," but had stirred "the wrath of the
Lord" because of their evil behavior (v. 13). How do you respond to the
Word of God?—J. D. B.

DON'T FAIL TO LOOK IN GOD'S BOOK.

When the south wind blew softly, supposing that they
had obtained their desire, . . . they sailed.

ACTS 27:13

In Acts 27 we read that Paul, a prisoner headed for Rome, warned the centurion of disaster if they set sail. The man, however, listened to contrary advice and gave orders for the ship to leave port. When a gentle south breeze got them off to a favorable start, it looked as if Paul had been wrong. But soon the sky darkened. The breeze turned into a howling wind. Waves battered the ship with merciless fury. Several days later the vessel ran aground and was broken into pieces by the storm. Paul had been right!

J. C. Macauley used this story to show what happens to a young person who is lured by the soft south wind of pleasant circumstances that may temporarily accompany wicked conduct. He described five stages of decline in Acts 27. A youth leaves (v. 13) the moorings of home and church, is caught (v. 15) in a whirl of excitement, is driven (v. 17) by the winds of passion, is lightened (v. 18) of his or her former virtues, and finally is broken by the storm (v. 41).

Don't be lured by the "soft south wind."—H. V. L.

IT IS ONLY WHEN WE ARE DECEIVED BY SIN,
THAT WE TAKE DELIGHT IN SIN.

Abstain from fleshly lusts which war against the soul.

1 PETER 2:11

've cleaned out the garage again. It meant making some painful decisions. I had accumulated enough junk to make a pack rat blush. Yet something had to go; I couldn't get the car in. In its place were the leftover remains of a few home repair jobs. Broken tools and toys were hanging on the walls. Then there were all those old tires. My wife kept asking why I was keeping them. So I finally did it—I got rid of the junk. Now I can get the car in its place again, and I don't even miss what I got rid of.

That experience reminds me of today's Scripture reading. The apostle Peter suggested that the children of God have been made for a purpose (Pet. 2:9). But they can lose sight of this purpose if their lives become cluttered with sinful desires and worldly concerns (vv. 11–12).

I don't know about you, but all too often I lose sight of the purpose for which God saved me. I let my life get cluttered with nonessentials. That's why I have to keep asking Him to help me make space for Him.—M. R. D. II

WE HAVE TO GET RID OF THE JUNK TO LEAVE ROOM FOR JESUS.

He said to me, ". . . go, speak to the house of Israel."

EZEKIEL 3:1

A teenager told me, "Dad lashes out at me when I do wrong, but he rarely shows me that he loves me. I get angry whenever he tries to correct me."

A woman in the hospital said, "My pastor comes to pray with me, but he seems to do it as a duty. He never gives me a chance to express my concerns."

God called Ezekiel to proclaim His message to the Israelites in exile. The task would be difficult because the people were rebellious. Therefore, God prepared Ezekiel by giving him a vision in which he was told to eat a scroll. He was to receive into his heart the words of God (v. 10). Then, when Ezekiel came to the captives by the River Chebar, he sat in silence among them for seven days. This gave him an understanding of their circumstances so that he could speak with sympathy.

If we are led to rebuke, comfort, or counsel people in need, we must first feed on God's Word and empathize with their situation. Only then will we be spiritually prepared to minister to them.—H. V. L.

WHEN GOD'S WORD RULES YOUR HEART IT WILL GUIDE YOUR WORDS.

*[They] searched the Scriptures daily to
find out whether these things were so.*

ACTS 17:11

C hildren sometimes do unusual things to song lyrics. One child
sang a verse of the "Battle Hymn of the Republic" as follows:
"He has trampled on the village where the great giraffe is stored." And my
preschooler Melissa likes to sing the familiar spiritual, "Joshua Fit the
Battle of Jericho." Only she sings it, "Joshua fit the battle of Cherry Coke."

Word-twisting stops being funny, though, when adults alter
Scripture to make it say what they want it to say. Maybe they take a verse
out of its context to prove a pet teaching. Some use Jeremiah 10:2–4 to
prove that we should not have Christmas trees. Or it may be reinterpreting
Scripture to make it support a belief that is not orthodox. Some alter the
wording of John 1, for example, to make it say that Christ is not God.
When we study the Bible, we must be careful to get the words right—to
let Scripture say what it says. And even more, we must make sure we do
not read into it what is not there.—J. D. B.

WE MUST MAKE SURE WE ARE HEARING WHAT GOD HAS SPOKEN.

God loves a cheerful giver.

2 CORINTHIANS 9:7

The Christians in a Haiti church service were all smiles as they put their coins in the offering plate. When I remarked about this, I was told that these country people, most of whom lived in small huts, were delighted to have something to share with others. This concept of freely sharing had become part of the fabric of their lives since they became believers.

One of the Haitian believers said, "We have a saying: 'If I have something today, I'll share it with others. Then tomorrow, when I have nothing, they may be able to share with me.'" They gave cheerfully, knowing that God would take care of their needs.

The believers in Macedonia, who were poor, amazed Paul by the amount they gave for the needy saints in Jerusalem (2 Cor. 8:1–5). And they did it because they wanted to; they actually begged Paul to allow them a chance to give (v. 4).

We too can be part of the circle of blessing. And we will be if we are cheerful givers!—H. V. L.

WHEN LOVE OPENS THE HEART, IT OPENS THE HAND.

The LORD has heard the voice of my weeping.

PSALM 6:8

*S*ometimes it doesn't take much to get us down, does it? Even on the sunniest day, an unkind remark from a friend, bad news from the auto mechanic, a financial setback, or even a misbehaving child can put a cloud of gloom over everything, making simple tasks a struggle. You know you should be joyful, but everything seems to be against you.

David must have been feeling that way when he wrote Psalm 6. He felt weak and sickly (v. 2), troubled (v. 3), forsaken (v. 4), weary (v. 6), and grief-stricken (v. 7). But he knew what to do when he was down. He looked up and trusted God to take care of him and to see him through.

When we look up and begin to focus on God, something good begins to happen. We get the focus off ourselves and gain a new appreciation for Him. Next time you're down, try looking up to God.
—J. D. B.

THINGS LOOKING DOWN? TRY LOOKING UP!

Those who were scattered went everywhere preaching the word.

ACTS 8:4

Because of the intense competition in the automobile industry, carmakers like to keep their design breakthroughs secret. A company that can offer a new and desirable feature on its cars gains a coveted selling edge in a tough market.

I guess that's why I was surprised when I saw a Mercedes-Benz commercial on television. It showed one of their cars being crashed into a brick wall during a safety test. The way it withstood the impact revealed why its energy-absorbing construction has saved lives. Even though Mercedes-Benz holds the patent on the safety design, competitors are free to use it because the company does not enforce its claim. When asked why, the Mercedes-Benz spokesman replied, "Because some things in life are too important not to share."

The message of salvation is the best news mankind has ever received. Yet all too often that good news is not shared. So tell someone. The gospel is too good to keep secret!—D. C. E.

THE GOSPEL IS TOO IMPORTANT NOT TO SHARE.

Blessed is the man who walks not in the counsel of the ungodly.

PSALM 1:1

According to the *1992 World Almanac*, tourists are now welcome to visit Chernobyl. This is the site of the nuclear accident that occurred in 1986, releasing deadly radiation throughout the area. The tourist bureau has invited travelers to tour the city of Chernobyl, the radioactive waste dump at Kopachi, and the concrete sarcophagus that is built around the reactor. All visitors will be given a free radiation test at the beginning and end of the tour. If medical treatment is needed, it will be provided "at no extra charge."

Most of us would think twice before taking advantage of an offer like that. We value our lives too much to go to a place that would expose us to nuclear danger needlessly.

But wait. Are there places we might be tempted to visit that could do us great spiritual harm? It could be anywhere: a bar, an apartment, a restaurant, a casino, a gym. To those invitations we must send firm regrets!—M. R. D. II

STAY AWAY AND YOU WON'T GO ASTRAY.

A fool's mouth is his destruction,
and his lips are the snare of his soul.

PROVERBS 18:7

The cranes in the Taurus mountains of southern Turkey tend to cackle a lot, especially while flying. All that noise gets the attention of eagles, who swoop down and seize them for a meal. The experienced cranes avoid this threat by picking up stones large enough to fill their mouths. This prevents them from cackling—and from becoming lunch for the eagles.

Are you having a problem with your tongue? Try this: Ask the Lord for His help. Think before speaking. Let your words be few. Following that formula can be as effective as a stone in the mouth.

Lord, help me watch the words I say,
To keep them few and sweet,
For I don't know from day to day
Which ones I'll have to eat.—Anonymous

—R. W. D.

DON'T BREAK THE SILENCE UNLESS YOU CAN IMPROVE IT.

Casting all your care upon Him, for He cares for you.

1 PETER 5:7

Author Lucretia Hanson noticed a mistake in a caption she was proofreading. Instead of "Used Cars" it read, "Used Cares." Hanson wrote, "It made me stop short and reflect on how many of our cares are used ones, dredged up from past memories.

"There are the *cares of self-pity*: the long illness we had, or the unreasonable way people treated us on a certain occasion. . . . Then there are the used *cares of regrets*. If I had only gone on to school or been more careful in the selection of my life mate.

"We think too of the *unavoidable cares*. The accident for which we were not to blame. We have used these cares so long that they have depressed us and left us powerless." Many of us have "used cares"—past problems that we review and lament. But instead of carrying the burdens of used cares, let's give them to Jesus.—H. G. B.

**BECAUSE GOD CARES ABOUT US,
WE CAN LEAVE OUR CARES WITH HIM.**

Evening and morning and at noon I will pray,
and cry aloud, and He shall hear my voice.

PSALM 55:17

One of the most fascinating technological gadgets on my desk is my modem. It allows my computer to talk to another computer anywhere in the country. All I have to do is turn it on, punch in the right numbers, and my information goes immediately through phone lines to another computer.

Well, there is one small catch. The person who operates the computer at the other end has to turn his or her computer on. Otherwise, nothing gets communicated. So, the reception of my data is not fully automatic.

If you think the modem is a rather fantastic way to communicate, consider something even greater: prayer. Not only do we not have to depend on electricity or phone lines or satellite uplinks, but we also never have to wonder if the Person receiving the message is going to be there.—J. D. B.

OUR GOD IS ALWAYS THERE—RECEIVING EVERY PRAYER.

Daniel purposed in his heart that he would not defile himself.

DANIEL 1:8

Christians without goals are a little like Alice in the fairy tale *Alice in Wonderland*. In a conversation with the Cheshire Cat, Alice asked, "Would you tell me please, which way I ought to go from here?" "That depends a good deal on where you want to get to," said the Cat. "I don't much care where," said Alice. "Then it doesn't matter which way you go," said the Cat.

That way of living may be okay in Wonderland, but it doesn't work in the real world. If I am going to make spiritual progress, I must be specific. It's not enough, for example, to say, "I'm going to try to be a better Christian." That's far too general. I need to say, "I'm going to set up a plan to battle my tendency to think that other people always have life easier than I do."

If we do not establish specific spiritual goals for ourselves, we will make little if any real progress. We'll wander aimlessly from one experience to another. Realistic goals stretch our faith.—D. C. E.

IF YOU AIM FOR NOTHING, YOU'RE SURE TO HIT IT.

346

Whoever exalts himself will be humbled.

LUKE 14:11

What did King Nebuchadnezzar of ancient Babylon and Nikolai Ceausescu of modern-day Romania have in common? Both were ruthless dictators who fell after boldly exalting themselves.

Nebuchadnezzar brazenly declared that he had built the great city of Babylon by his own power and for the honor of his majesty (Dan. 4:30). God humbled him by driving him into the wilderness with a mental illness. Ceausescu, after years of cruelly persecuting Christians and killing all potential threats to his power, instructed the National Opera to produce a song in his honor that included these words: "Ceausescu is good, righteous, and holy." He wanted this song to be sung on his 72nd birthday on January 26, 1990, but on December 25, 1989, he and his wife were executed.

Of course, God does not always send immediate judgment on all who claim deity or try to take the honor that rightly belongs to Him. But sooner or later the truth of God's Word prevails: "Whoever exalts himself will be humbled."—H. V. L.

THOSE WHO WOULD RULE MEN MUST BE RULED BY GOD.

He who is greedy for gain troubles his own house.

PROVERBS 15:27

Advertisers constantly appeal to consumer greed, trying to convince us that we need their products. An executive of an electronics firm boasted that his company had created the demand for transistor radios. He said, "When we introduced pocket radios years ago, nobody needed them, so they didn't sell. We had to convince the consumer that he needed our products. Sales have boomed ever since."

The desire for more and more money, things, or power isn't unique to our day. Thousands of years ago, Gehazi, Elisha's servant, saw a chance to get money from wealthy Naaman. He would be able to buy clothing, olive groves, vineyards, sheep and oxen, and servants (2 Kings 5:26). Greed took over.

We are all susceptible to the powerful grip of greed. We must often pray, "Lord, help me to be most concerned about how I can please You, not how I can gain more for myself."—D. J. D.

GREEDY PEOPLE ALWAYS LOSE MORE THAN THEY GAIN.

The dead were judged . . .
by the things which were written in the books.

REVELATION 20:12

Rom Eaton spent sixteen years in prison even though he was innocent. At the end of that time behind bars, he made this observation: "I didn't have a dime in my pocket or a friend in the world when they put me on trial for armed robbery. That's why I spent sixteen years in prison for a crime committed by two other men while I was 1,700 miles away. I am free now, completely vindicated. Life played a dirty trick on me in Circuit Court."

Such an injustice will never occur in God's "courtroom." No one will ever bear the penalty of another person's guilt. No one will be able to claim he or she got a "bad rap" or was the victim of a "dirty trick."

Unlike Rom Eaton, who did suffer a cruel injustice, those who appear at the great white throne judgment will agree with the verdict. That's why we must urge all people to accept Christ's offer of pardon now before it's too late. With God there is perfect justice.—R. W. D.

TO REJECT GOD'S GRACE IS TO INCUR HIS JUDGMENT.

Do I seek to please men? For if I still pleased men,
I would not be a bondservant of Christ.

GALATIANS 1:10

At one point in his ministry, English evangelist George Whitefield (1714–1770) received a vicious letter accusing him of wrongdoing. His reply was brief and courteous: "I thank you heartily for your letter. As for what you and my other enemies are saying against me, I know worse things about myself than you will ever say about me. With love in Christ, George Whitefield." He didn't try to defend himself. He was much more concerned about pleasing the Lord.

Such an attitude prevailed in the life of the apostle Paul. He said, "For if I still pleased men, I would not be a bondservant of Christ" (Gal. 1:10). He also prayed that the Colossian believers would be "fully pleasing" to God (Col. 1:10).

If we are faithfully serving Christ, we don't need to waste time defending ourselves when harsh, hurtful, and untrue things are said about us. We can take comfort in knowing that we are walking "worthy of the Lord" (Col. 1:10).—D. L. B.

WHAT GOD KNOWS ABOUT US IS MORE IMPORTANT
THAN WHAT PEOPLE SAY ABOUT US.

They sang a new song, saying: "You are worthy."

REVELATION 5:9

A great celebration was staged in Boston in 1869 to commemorate the end of the American Civil War. A man who was there wrote a letter to a friend and described some of the events.

He told of a 10,000-voice choir supported by a 1,000-piece orchestra. The violin section included 200 musicians, led by the world's greatest violinist, Ole Bull. And when the soloist sang "The Star Spangled Banner" and hit high C with the full orchestra and chorus, her voice was so loud and clear that it seemed to soar above everything else.

With those memories flooding his mind, the letter writer concluded, "I am an old man now, but I am looking forward to the music of heaven —music infinitely superior to the marvelous chorus I listened to that day."

Yes, as thrilling as that music was, who can imagine the sound in heaven when "ten thousand times ten thousand, and thousands of thousands" join in praise to our Lord! (Rev. 5:11).—R. W. D.

**WHEN CHRIST PUTS A NEW SONG IN YOUR HEART,
YOU WILL SING HIS PRAISE FOREVER.**

Let us come before His presence with thanksgiving.

PSALM 95:1–2

When the American colonies were first settled, the newcomers suffered many hardships. They spent much time in fasting and prayer, asking the Lord to help them in their distress.

According to Tom Olson in *Now* magazine, on one occasion when some New England settlers were discussing their hardships, one person suggested that they set aside a special day for fasting and prayer. Another man stood up and said they had been dwelling too much on their problems. It was time, he emphasized, to focus on their blessings.

The man pointed out that the colony was making good progress. The harvests were becoming more abundant. The streams were full of fish, and the forests provided plenty of game. But more important than that, he reminded them that they now had what they had been seeking when they had left their homeland—liberty. He recommended that instead of a day of fasting they have a day of thanksgiving!—R. W. D.

IF WE PAUSE TO THINK, WE WILL HAVE CAUSE TO THANK.

NOVEMBER 24

The things which are seen are temporary,
but the things which are not seen are eternal.

2 CORINTHIANS 4:18

When evangelist Pat Kelly played major league baseball for the Baltimore Orioles, his manager was the fiery, successful Earl Weaver. Weaver, like many top sports skippers, kept his mind on one thing—winning baseball games.

One day Kelly stopped to talk with his manager. "Weave," Pat said, "it sure is good to walk with Jesus." "That's nice," the manager replied, "but I'd rather you would walk with the bases loaded."

That exchange is a good example of the difference between two views of life—the temporary and the permanent. When we have the first, we can become preoccupied with the things of this earth. We can forget that this life is only a time to prepare for eternity. With the permanent view, however, we recognize the importance of getting ready for eternity by trusting in and living for Jesus Christ.—J. D. B.

NOW IS THE TIME TO INVEST IN ETERNITY.

Surely, in vain the net is spread in the sight of any bird.

PROVERBS 1:17

Birds sometimes have more sense than people. A farmer learned that some crows were stealing his corn. So he went out and strung twine about five feet from the ground between the trees surrounding the area where he had planted his crop. He thought that the black-feathered thieves were probably watching him and would become leery. He was right. They stopped eating his corn. They wouldn't take a chance on being captured.

How strange that we are less wary! Even when we recognize dangerous temptations, we indulge in sins that appear inviting, thinking it won't matter or that we won't get caught.

Perhaps you've considered doing a little shoplifting. Maybe you have been tempted to cheat on a test or to lie to your boss. You may even be thinking of being unfaithful to your spouse. Beware! Don't yield to these evil urges. The devil is setting a trap for you. Learn a lesson from the birds.—H. G. B.

**A WISE MAN FLEES TEMPTATION AND
DOESN'T LEAVE A FORWARDING ADDRESS.**

Set your mind on things above, not on things on the earth.

COLOSSIANS 3:2

A watchmaker told me that because he used his fingers to pick up very small parts of a watch, it was extremely important to protect them from becoming calloused. He then recounted an incident early in his career that made him keenly aware of this danger. He was mowing his lawn one day when his employer, the owner of a fine jewelry store, came by and asked, "Do you usually mow your own lawn?"

"Every week," he replied.

"Well," said the owner, "this will be the last time. I'll get someone to mow it for you. No watchmaker of mine will be doing this kind of work."

The jewelry store owner was not belittling hard, manual labor, but merely trying to protect the watchmaker's hands from losing their great sensitivity. Something of that same caution must be shown in our walk with the Lord. We must never do things that will diminish our love for God's Word or dull our appetite for prayer and Christian service.—P. R.V.

AVOID WHATEVER DULLS YOUR SENSE OF SIN.

A merry heart makes a cheerful countenance,
but by sorrow of the heart the spirit is broken.

PROVERBS 15:13

Can changing our facial expression help to change our heart? According to an article in *The New York Times*, the act of smiling can contribute to pleasant feelings. Writer Daniel Goleman says there is a relationship between facial expression and resulting mood. He cites experiments in which researchers found that pronouncing the word *cheese* prompted a smile and pleasant feelings, while pronouncing the word *few* tended to create another expression, resulting in negative emotions.

Smiling isn't the only thing we can do to change the way we feel. In Psalm 4, we find many actions that troubled people can take. When distress grips our soul, we can ask the Lord for relief and mercy (v. 1). We can take comfort in knowing we are among those who are favored by Him, remembering that He hears us when we call (v. 3). We can acknowledge our feelings and be quiet before Him (v. 4). We can do what is right (v. 5) and trust in Him to give us overflowing gladness (v. 7). And we can rest in the assurance of His peace and safety (v. 8).—M. R .D. II

A HEART TOUCHED BY GRACE BRINGS JOY TO THE FACE.

I will praise You, O LORD, . . .
I will sing praises to You among the nations.

PSALM 108:3

In the early 1970s, Brazilians found themselves singing and humming catchy tunes that urged patriotism, a strong work ethic, cleanliness, and other national goals. According to a report that appeared in *The Calgary Herald*, propaganda was not new in Brazilian politics, but observers agreed it had never before been used so skillfully.

The whole campaign was run by a soft-sell agency called the Special Bureau of Public Relations. One person was quoted as saying: "Let me compose the songs a nation sings, and I care not who writes its laws."

Think of the music of the world. So many songs contain demoralizing lyrics that have a degrading effect on the millions who are captivated by their catchy tunes and rhythmic beat. By contrast, God gifted David, that sweet singer of Israel, who provided many of the great expressions of praise that we find in the book of Psalms. The words of those songs extol the Lord. How uplifting and inspiring they are!—R. W. D.

YOU ARE THE CHOSEN OF THE LORD TO SING HIS HIGHEST PRAISE.

Esau ran to meet [Jacob], and embraced him.

GENESIS 33:4

For sixty-one years, piano virtuoso Vladimir Horowitz refused to visit his native Russia. After he fled the country in 1925, he seemingly turned his back forever on his homeland. He declared, "I never want to go back, and I never will." Yet after all those years he changed his mind. Early in 1986, at age eighty-one, Horowitz returned to the Soviet Union and gave a truly remarkable concert. His willingness to rethink his position led to a most memorable musical performance.

What Horowitz did when he reversed his longstanding position can be a good example for any of us. If we were wrong or if conditions change, we must be willing to change our mind.

Esau had every reason to be upset with Jacob for stealing his blessing. One translation of Genesis 27:41 says that Esau "held a grudge" against Jacob. In fact, he threatened to kill him. Yet when it came time for the brothers to be reunited, Esau had a change of heart. He swallowed his words and did what was right. Are we willing to do the same?—J. D. B.

FORGIVENESS IS THE KEY THAT OPENS THE DOOR TO RECONCILIATION.

The time will come when they will not endure sound doctrine.

2 TIMOTHY 4:3

For years, scaffolding in the Sistine Chapel has partially obscured the view of Michelangelo's sixteenth-century frescoes. Restorers have been carefully removing the dulling residue of candle smoke, incense, and dust.

Some people are critical of the project and feel that the colors on the ceiling are now too strong. But officials insist that the restoration enables visitors to see what the Renaissance master wanted them to see.

The debate is sure to continue, especially when the even sootier painting *The Last Judgment* is restored. The renewing of that scene, with its crowded figures crying out in hell, has a spiritual parallel that is just as soiled. Our generation has become accustomed to a very dim portrayal of the last judgment described by Jesus. Countless jokes and profanities have obscured the vivid picture Christ gave us. To restore Christ's picture of hell, we need to look at what He said and sense its reality.—M. R. D. II

A CLEAR VISION OF HELL GIVES US COMPASSION FOR THE LOST.

December

You have been my defense and refuge in the day of my trouble.

PSALM 59:16

The city of Lucerne has long been important in Switzerland's history because of its strategic location. It guards a natural passageway through the Alps. In the fourteenth century, the people of Lucerne built a massive wall around the city. From its nine towers they could see the approaching enemy, and sharp-shooting defenders with arrows could easily repel invaders.

In medieval days, Lucerne was impregnable. But with the increasing use of gunpowder, the walls became obsolete. A few well-placed artillery shells would demolish them quickly.

We as Christians often try to protect ourselves from being hurt by building "thick walls" and "high towers" around our lives. They may take the form of keeping silent, criticizing, or rationalizing our actions. But these defenses turn out to be as useless as the walls of Lucerne. We still get wounded, discouraged, defeated. We need to learn the secret of the psalmist. Instead of fighting his own battles, he discovered that if he let the Lord be his defender he would be safe.—D. C. E.

**WE MAY FACE SITUATIONS BEYOND OUR RESERVES
BUT NEVER BEYOND GOD'S RESOURCES.**

Rejoice with those who rejoice.

ROMANS 12:15

orty thousand fans were on hand in the Oakland stadium when Rickey Henderson tied Lou Brock's career stolen-base record. According to *USA Today*, Lou, who had left baseball in 1979, had followed Henderson's career and was excited about his success. Realizing that Rickey would set a new record, Brock said, "I'll be there. Do you think I'm going to miss it now? Rickey did in twelve years what took me nineteen. He's amazing."

The real success stories in life are with people who can rejoice in the successes of others. What Lou Brock did in cheering on Rickey Henderson should be a way of life in the family of God. Few circumstances give us a better opportunity to exhibit God's grace than when someone succeeds and surpasses us in an area of our own strength and reputation. Let's "rejoice with those who rejoice."—M. R. D. II

YOU CANNOT BE ENVIOUS AND HAPPY AT THE SAME TIME.

Man looks at the outward appearance,
but the LORD looks at the heart.

1 SAMUEL 16:7

Have you checked the labels on your grocery items lately? You may be getting less than you thought. According to *U.S. News & World Report*, some manufacturers are selling us the same size packages we are accustomed to, but they are putting less of the product in the box. For example, a box of well-known detergent that once held sixty-one ounces now contains only fifty-five. Same size box, less soap.

How something is wrapped doesn't always show us what's on the inside. That's true with people as well. We can wrap ourselves up in the same packaging every day—nice clothes, big smile, friendly demeanor— yet still be less than what we appear to be.

We live in a world that often measures the value of products—and people—by their packaging. But let's not become preoccupied with outward appearance and neglect what's on the inside. In God's eyes, it's the contents that count!—J. D. B.

REPUTATION IS WHAT OTHERS THINK YOU ARE;
CHARACTER IS WHAT GOD KNOWS YOU ARE.

Let each of you look out not only for his own interests,
but also for the interests of others.

PHILIPPIANS 2:4

Ours is a self-serving age. That's what George Sweeting, former president of Moody Bible Institute, told graduating seniors at Taylor University. To illustrate, he told of a farmer who was single and wanted a wife. So he put an ad in a newspaper that read: "Man 35, wants woman about 25, with tractor. Send picture of tractor."

All of us are infected with selfishness. That's why Paul told us to look out not only for our own interests but also for the interests of others. The "not only . . . but also" phrase keeps a proper balance.

We need the outward look. Psychiatrist Dr. Carl Menninger was asked what he would do if he knew he was on the verge of a nervous breakdown. His reply: "I'd go out, find somebody in need, and help him."

Christ is the greatest example of the outward look. Even though He is God, He humbled Himself as a man and became obedient to the point of death. He was looking out for you and for me.—D. J. D.

WE ARE AT OUR BEST WHEN WE ARE GOOD TO OTHERS.

The fool and the senseless person perish,
and leave their wealth to others.

PSALM 49:10

A few years ago, eighteen percent of Americans said they had a great fear of flying. Only nine percent said that driving or riding in a car was their greatest fear. Research shows, however, that traveling in a commercial airliner is actually safer than going the same distance with all wheels on the ground. A study group at the University of Michigan calculated that if a person were traveling from Detroit to Chicago, flying would be seven times safer than driving. While more of us might feel safer on the ground than in the air, those feelings are misleading.

We can be misled by other feelings as well. Psalm 49 says that the rich often trust in their wealth and boast about their riches (v. 6). They think their houses will last forever (v. 11). They congratulate themselves for what they have (v. 18). Money makes them feel secure, powerful, and almost immortal. But they are deceived!

If we want something solid under our feet, we need to place our trust in God.—M. R. D. II

THE CHRISTIAN'S GREATEST SECURITY IS
HIS INVISIBLE MEANS OF SUPPORT.

Do not fear therefore; you are of more value than many sparrows.

LUKE 12:7

arly one summer, city workers in Hamilton, Ontario, were trimming limbs from trees along the streets. In one tree marked for cutting they found a nest of baby robins. The workers decided not to touch the limb until the young birds had flown away.

Later when the nest was abandoned, they examined it and discovered in the bottom a little scrap of paper. The robins had used it, along with the dried twigs, to build their nest. On the paper were these words: "We trust in the Lord our God." Now, we don't know if the workers saw the remarkable significance of those words, but their concern for sparing those tiny robins was God's way of caring for His creatures.

Likewise, our heavenly Father takes special care to protect us from dangers we cannot foresee. Sometimes we are not even aware of His guarding hand, and at other times His care is evident in unusual ways. Therefore we can "trust in the Lord."—P. R. V.

**THE ONE WHO NOTES THE SPARROW'S FALL,
PREPARES EACH DAY FOR ME.**

Do not be afraid to take to you Mary your wife,
for that which is conceived in her is of the Holy Spirit.

MATTHEW 1:20

*P*oor Joseph. He was trying to be the right kind of Jewish husband-to-be when he discovered that Mary, his bride-to-be, was going to have a baby. What could he do but call off the marriage! Surely this was the only way to avoid the ridicule they both might receive.

Then came a new twist in the story. As Joseph was contemplating his next move, an angel appeared and told him not to be afraid to take Mary as his wife. Things weren't the way they seemed. Neither he nor Mary had anything to be ashamed of because they had done nothing wrong. The baby she was carrying had been conceived by the Holy Spirit. She would bear the Messiah, and there was nothing to hide.

What a lesson we can learn from those two young people! If we are steadfast in our desire to please the Lord and remain true to Him, we will have a clear conscience. We won't have to spend our time trying to cover our tracks. We'll have nothing to hide.—J. D. B.

A CLEAR CONSCIENCE, LIKE A SOFT PILLOW, HELPS YOU SLEEP WELL.

Look now toward heaven, and count the stars.

GENESIS 15:5

T. C. Roddy Jr. from Rusk, Texas, wrote, "In my front yard are six huge oak trees that must be over 100 years old. I look at them and realize that the leaves must have barrels of fresh water each day to stay green. God causes their roots to exert a working pressure of more than 3,000 pounds per square foot just to move the water up to the leaves—not considering the resistance of the wood. That is just another of God's 'miracles' that occur every day unnoticed."

God didn't ask Abraham to look at trees but directed his attention to the stars. As Abraham contemplated the vast numbers of stars, God said, "So shall your descendants be." I believe that was more than a promise of large numbers. To me it implies that if God could create and maintain all those stars, He would have no trouble fulfilling His promise that Abraham would have a son in his old age. And Abraham got the picture, for we read that "he believed in the LORD" (Gen. 15:6).—D. J. D.

THE WONDERS OF CREATION TELL OF THE WONDERFUL CREATOR.

*Be an example to the believers in word, in conduct,
in love, in spirit, in faith, in purity.*

1 TIMOTHY 4:12

A pastor was on a guided tour of a mission field. The leader of the group asked him if he would be willing to greet the believers and deliver a brief message when they arrived. He consented, but was somewhat reluctant because of the language barrier.

The guide, who was familiar with the country, tried to put him at ease by explaining, "I'll interpret for you. We'll practice a few times before the service. I'm sure you'll have no difficulty."

"I'll try," replied the pastor, "even though I'm not in the habit of practicing what I preach!"

We may smile at what the pastor said, but his words express a problem we all face as Christians: We don't always practice what we "preach." What we claim to believe and what we teach to others doesn't always match the way we live. Our actions sometimes contradict all our good words. And what people see in our lives can make a bigger impression on them than what they hear from our lips. Lord, help us to practice what we preach.—H. G. B.

AN OUNCE OF EXAMPLE IS WORTH A TON OF ADVICE.

Do not be deceived, . . . for whatever a man sows,
that he will also reap.

GALATIANS 6:7

A children's book titled *The Chance World* describes an imaginary planet where everything happens unpredictably. For example, the sun might rise one day or it might not, and it might appear at any hour. Some days the moon might come up in its place. One day you might jump up and not come down, and the next day find gravity so strong you can't even lift your feet.

Henry Drummond, Scottish biologist, writer, and lecturer, read *The Chance World*. He commented that in such a place where natural law was annihilated, "reason would be impossible. It would become a lunatic world with a population of lunatics."

We should be thankful for the dependability of the natural laws the Creator has set in motion. They can be a great benefit to us if we recognize and respect them. That is also true of God's spiritual laws. The person who ignores God's standards and caters to sinful appetites can expect destruction. But the person who follows the leading of the Spirit will experience the blessings of everlasting life.—R. W. D.

WE CHOOSE WHAT WE REAP WHEN WE CHOOSE WHAT WE SOW.

*"Your word I have hidden in my heart,
that I might not sin against You"*

PSALM 119:11

There is a story of an Oriental prince who received from a magician a ring set with diamonds, rubies, and pearls. "This ring," said the magician, "has more value than the beautiful gems with which it is adorned. You will discover that it has a rare and mystic property." The prince soon found that whenever he had a bad thought or committed an evil action, the ring would press painfully on his finger.

Commenting on that legend, the nineteenth-century Scottish clergyman Thomas Guthrie wrote, "Such a ring, thank God, is not the peculiar property of kings. The poorest of us may possess this inestimable jewel; for the ring of the fable is like the voice of God within us when we do wrong."

The psalmist declared, "Your word I have hidden in my heart, that I might not sin against You" (Ps. 119:11). The conscience must be guided by the Word of God if it is to be trusted as a warning of evil. Does your conscience ring true?—H. G. B.

CONSCIENCE IS A SAFE GUIDE ONLY WHEN GUIDED BY GOD.

God so loved the world that He gave His only begotten Son.

JOHN 3:16

A poignant story is told about children of Untouchables in a Christian school in India before World War II. Each year the students received Christmas presents from children in England. The girls got a doll, and the boys a toy.

On one occasion, the doctor from a nearby mission hospital was asked to distribute the gifts. In the course of his visit, he told the youngsters about a village where the boys and girls had never heard of Jesus. He suggested that maybe they would like to give them some of their old toys as presents. They liked the idea and readily agreed. A week later, the doctor returned to collect the gifts. The sight was unforgettable. One by one the children filed by and handed the doctor a doll or a toy. To his great surprise, they all gave the new present they had received a few days earlier. When he asked why, a girl spoke up, "Think what God did by giving us His only Son. Could we give less than our best?"—P. R. V.

GOD'S HIGHEST GIFT CALLS FOR OUR DEEPEST GRATITUDE.

O My Father, if it is possible, let this cup pass from Me.

MATTHEW 26:39

Sitting majestically atop the highest hill in Toledo, Spain, is the Alcazar, a sixteenth-century fortress. In the civil war of the 1930s, the Alcazar became a battleground when the Loyalists tried to oust the Nationalists, who held the fortress. During one dramatic episode of the war, the Nationalist leader received a phone call while at the Alcazar. It was from his son, who had been captured by the Loyalists. The ultimatum: If the father didn't surrender the Alcazar, they would kill his son. The father weighed his options. After a long pause and with a heavy heart, he said to his son, "Then die like a man."

Harsh? Tragic? Yes. But in the commander's view, the life of one person—even his own son—was worth the sacrifice if it saved the lives of others and kept their cause alive.

On the night before Jesus died, He prayed to His Father, asking if there was any way to avoid the agony of the cross. But His Father's silence told Him that there was no other way. In order to defeat the enemy and preserve the lives of all who would someday come into His kingdom, the Son had to die.—J. D. B.

THE HEAVENLY FATHER'S PAIN BECAME OUR ETERNAL GAIN.

DECEMBER 14

This grace was given, that I should preach . . .
the unsearchable riches of Christ.

EPHESIANS 3:8

An extremely wealthy man was being interviewed for a magazine article. The extent of his vast holdings in industry and commerce was being discussed. Finally the writer asked, "We'd be interested in knowing, just what is your net worth?" The interviewer seemed surprised when the man responded, "I have no idea. I just know it's more than I can count."

I was thinking about that statement. It sounds like the kind of situation I know I'll never be in. Imagine having more money than you can count! Then I thought, on a spiritual level that does apply to me.

Writing to the believers in Ephesus, Paul spoke of "the unsearchable riches of Christ." Our spiritual wealth is so vast that it cannot be measured. The word *unsearchable* literally means, "that which cannot be tracked."

Feeling poor? Helpless? Then read Ephesians 3:8 again. You have access to the unfathomable, inexhaustible, eternal riches of God. You can say about your riches in Christ, "I have more than I can count!"—D. C. E.

THE PRICELESS TREASURES IN CHRIST
MAKE US RICH BEYOND COMPARE!

Every part does its share.

EPHESIANS 4:16

It's not easy to keep a country going. In the United States, for instance, the workforce stands at about 120 million. That includes 14 million salespeople, 5 million construction workers, 1.3 million farmers, and 5 million transportation workers who get everything where it is supposed to be. If any one group were to stop working, the rest would have a hard time functioning.

Now think about the workforce that is needed to keep a large church and all the related Christian ministries going—the Sunday school, the youth work, children's outreaches, the Christian day school, the counseling center for unwed mothers. To make sure that all these important ministries function properly, a wide variety of "job skills" is needed.

Just as each segment of the workforce in a nation is vital to its functioning, so too your special skill is vital to the success of your church and its ministries. The church works only if "every part does its share." Are you doing yours?—J. D. B.

EVERY CHURCH MEMBER CARING MEANS EVERY MEMBER SHARING.

Rest in the LORD, and wait patiently for Him; do not fret.

PSALM 37:7

In 1832, French engineer Ferdinand Marie de Lesseps was traveling on the Mediterranean Sea. When a fellow passenger became sick with a contagious disease, the ship was quarantined. The confinement was terribly frustrating for de Lesseps. To help pass the time he read the memoirs of Charles le Pere, who had studied the feasibility of building a canal from the Red Sea to the Mediterranean. That volume led the engineer to devise a detailed plan for the construction of the Suez Canal, which was completed under his leadership in 1869. That quarantine thirty-seven years earlier proved to be immensely valuable to de Lesseps—and to the world.

Likewise, Christians sometimes undergo a "spiritual quarantine" to prepare them for further usefulness in God's service. God does not forsake His own but draws them aside so that they can get to know Him and understand His purposes better. What can we do in these periods? The psalmist said, "Rest . . . wait . . . do not fret."—P. R. V.

GOD SHUTS US IN TO HELP US, NOT TO HURT US.

You are the light of the world. . . . Let your light so shine before men.

MATTHEW 5:14, 16

At the end of a radio commercial for a motel chain, a voice reassuringly says, "We'll leave the light on for you." My mother used to say the same thing. Sometimes I worked the late shift at the factory. Or I would come home late from college. No matter what time I got home, the porch light was burning. Its warm beams seemed to say, "This is where you belong. Someone loves you here. You are home."

One night the porch light wasn't on. I remember my feelings. Were my parents angry with me? Had I done something wrong? Was I no longer welcome? The explanation was simple: the bulb had burned out. Everything was okay.

Jesus is the true light, but as His followers we reflect His light. Our faithful walk of obedience is a beacon of God's love and truth. Our testimonies are beams of warm light piercing the cold darkness of this world. We are like a porch light, drawing unbelievers to Jesus, assuring them that Someone loves them and waits to welcome them home.—D. C. E.

OUR SHINING LIGHT IS A GUIDE TO THOSE LOST IN SIN'S NIGHT.

Jesus . . . saw a great multitude;
and He was moved with compassion for them.

MATTHEW 14:14

It was a tragic mistake. On July 3, 1988, the navy cruiser *USS Vincennes* shot down an Iranian airliner with 290 aboard. All were lost. The ship's captain mistakenly thought they were under attack by an F-14 Iranian fighter.

Public opinion polls showed that most Americans opposed paying compensation to the victims' families. The cruel treatment of American hostages in Iran was still fresh in many minds. But President Reagan approved compensation. Asked by reporters if such payment would send the wrong signal, he replied, "I don't ever find compassion a bad precedent."

To many people, the principle of revenge is so much simpler to practice. Yet compassion is Christ's way—a deep caring for the physical, emotional, and spiritual needs of the whole person. It reveals the heart of God for sinful people—for you and for me. As Christians, we must look at the whole person through the eyes of Jesus. Being moved by compassion always sends the right signal.—D. J. D.

COMPASSION IS LOVE IN ACTION.

I will bless the L<small>ORD</small> who has given me counsel.

P<small>SALM</small> 16:7

By now, most of the Christmas presents have been lovingly purchased and carefully wrapped. Some have been mailed to friends and family who live far away. But it all started with a list. You wanted to get the right gifts, so you carefully wrote a list, making sure to match each person with the right present. It was a giving list—based solely on the desire to give to those you love.

It's good we do that, because it's so easy for us to fall into the trap of making lists of what we want to receive rather than what we can give. Unfortunately, this happens all too often in our prayer life. There are so many times when we need God's help that we tend to make a prayer list like a child's Christmas list.

To avoid being one-sided in our praying, perhaps it would be helpful to keep two kinds of prayer lists: the needs list in which we bring our problems to the Lord, and the giving list in which we offer our praise to the Lord. In prayer, as in all of life, we need a giving list. And first on the list is praise to God.—J. D. B.

**A GOOD ATTITUDE TOWARD LIFE
BEGINS WITH GRATITUDE TOWARD GOD.**

Let your conduct be without covetousness;
be content with such things as you have.

HEBREWS 13:5

What would it take to make you happy? Inheriting a fortune? Winning $14 million in the lottery and being able to purchase anything you want?

A psychologist named Denier did a study on the effect that a major life change would have on a person's happiness. Half the people tested were big lottery winners. The other half suffered severe injuries in bad car accidents. To his amazement, Denier discovered that a few weeks after these drastic life changes both groups were about equally happy and satisfied with their lives. Denier concluded that we "evaluate our lives on the basis of other people in similar circumstances" and feel about the same degree of fulfillment.

Christians, however, have another explanation. If we accept ourselves the way God made us, if we are grateful for whatever He has given us, and if we trust in His unending goodness, we can experience a joy that does not depend on changing circumstances.—D. C. E.

TRUE HAPPINESS IS KNOWING THAT GOD IS GOOD.

Defend the poor and fatherless;
do justice to the afflicted and needy.

PSALM 82:3

It was one of the most touching displays of human compassion and love my family had ever seen. We watched with tears of joy as the ABC News program *20/20* reported on the stunning rescue of children from an ill-equipped Romanian orphanage.

Because the Romanians were unable to care for these neglected children, they agreed to let American couples adopt them. Blind children. Malnourished children. Children who had been given up as worthless. Family after family—hundreds of them—put up with endless red tape, crossed the ocean, and welcomed these needy children into their hearts and homes.

That scene brought to mind the words of Psalm 68:5. David wrote, "A father of the fatherless, a defender of widows, is God in His holy habitation." God cares for those who can't care for themselves. He has rescued us, so we can sympathize with the fatherless and oppressed of this world.—J. D. B.

OUR HEAVENLY FATHER'S LOVE REACHES OUT TO ALL.

*I cried out to the L*ORD *because of my affliction,*
and He answered me.

JONAH 2:2

When was the last time you heard anything good about the prophet Jonah? He disobeyed God when He told him to go to the wicked city of Nineveh to preach His message of judgment. The Lord called him to go northeast, but Jonah boarded a ship heading west. God had to send a storm and a fish to help him change his mind—and his direction! When Jonah finally did go to Nineveh, he didn't fare very well there either. He had hoped God would destroy the cruel Ninevites. But when he preached God's message of judgment, the people repented and God spared them. So Jonah pouted.

In spite of all this, one good thing can be said for Jonah: He did the right thing when he got into trouble. When he was swallowed by the fish and found himself in the worst mess he had ever been in, he turned to God and prayed.

Have you been running away from God? Are you in a mess of trouble? Cry out to God. The One who delivered Jonah can also deliver you.—D. C. E.

GOD'S HELP IS ONLY A PRAYER AWAY.

DECEMBER 23

Whoever loses his life for My sake and the gospel's will save it.

MARK 8:35

A wealthy young man came to Jesus and inquired, "Good Teacher, what shall I do that I may inherit eternal life?" (Mark 10:17). Jesus told him to give up everything and follow Him (v. 21). But this was far more than the rich young man had bargained for. It seems that he wanted a level of religious commitment that would not upset his secure lifestyle. Jesus, however, required that he hold nothing back.

As a young man, Jim Elliot determined to invest his life for eternity by serving God on the mission field. Along with four other young missionaries, Jim ventured into the jungles of Ecuador to take the gospel to the savage Auca Indians. On January 8, 1956, Auca tribesmen killed all five missionaries in a surprise attack.

"What a loss!" some might say. Yet, in the intervening years, many of the Aucas have become believers in Jesus Christ. Jim Elliot and his colleagues lost their lives but gained eternal dividends. In his journal Jim had written, "He is no fool who gives what he cannot keep, to gain what he cannot lose."—D. L. B.

**HOLD LIGHTLY TO THE THINGS OF EARTH
BUT TIGHTLY TO THE THINGS OF HEAVEN.**

Jesus said to him, "I am the way, the truth, and the life."

JOHN 14:6

Mr. Brown was driving his car in an unfamiliar city and was having trouble finding a certain address. So he stopped and asked a pedestrian how to get to his desired destination. The man replied, "Well, let's see. Go two blocks north, turn right, proceed six blocks, and—wait, no—go four blocks south to the first light. Turn right and stay on—no, that won't work either. Just turn at the corner and go west—no, that won't do. The new interstate is going through there." The man finally blurted out, "I'm sorry, Mister. I guess you just can't get there from here!"

This story reminds me of the tragic situation in which we would find ourselves if the Savior had not been born. It would have been necessary to say to a world of sinners searching for the way to heaven, "Sorry, you just can't get there from here." Because of sin, which separates us from God, we were all lost and unable to make it to heaven on our own.

Jesus came into the world to provide forgiveness by dying on the cross. He alone could be the perfect sacrifice to pay the penalty for our sins. And by rising from the grave, He is now the way to heaven for all who put their trust in Him. Because of Jesus, we can get there from here!—R. W. D.

**PEOPLE CAN GO TO HELL THEIR OWN WAY,
BUT MUST ENTER HEAVEN GOD'S WAY.**

When the fullness of the time had come, God sent forth His Son.

GALATIANS 4:4

Several years ago a group of historians authored a book called *If—Or History Rewritten.* Some of the *ifs* they considered were these: What if Robert E. Lee had not lost the battle of Gettysburg? What if the Moors in Spain had won? What if the Dutch had kept New Amsterdam? What if Booth had missed when he shot at Abraham Lincoln?

The attempt to reconstruct the past on the basis of these *ifs* was only a historian's game. But apply it for a moment to the central event in history—the birth of Jesus Christ. It was foretold with pinpoint accuracy hundreds of years before by the prophet Micah. The greatest *if,* therefore —the most startling question to the imagination—is, "What if Jesus had not been born?"

Such an *if* staggers the mind. It is like imagining the earth without a sunrise or the heavens without a sky. On this Christmas day, try to think of the world without Christ. What would history have been without Him? And at a personal level, what would your life be without Him? Thank God that there are no *ifs* in history.—H. W. R.

A WORLD WITHOUT CHRIST WOULD BE A WORLD WITHOUT HOPE.

As newborn babes, desire the pure milk of the Word,
that you may grow thereby.

1 PETER 2:2

A person who is "born again" starts a new life similar to that
of a newborn infant. Seven rules that promote good health
in babies can be adapted and applied to a Christian's spiritual growth.

1. **Daily Food.** Take in the "pure milk of the Word" through study
   and meditation.
2. **Fresh Air.** Pray often or you will faint. Prayer is the oxygen of
   the soul.
3. **Regular Exercise.** Put into practice what you learn in God's
   Word.
4. **Adequate Rest.** Rely on God at all times in simple faith.
5. **Clean Surroundings.** Avoid evil company and whatever will
   weaken you spiritually.
6. **Loving Care.** Be part of a church where you will benefit from a
   pastor's teaching and Christian fellowship.
7. **Periodic Checkups.** Regularly examine your spiritual health.

Are you growing?—H. G. B.

THERE ARE NO SHORTCUTS ON THE WAY TO MATURITY.

Love does not envy.

1 CORINTHIANS 13:4

A huge diamond was on display at Cartier's Fifth Avenue store in New York. This perfect 69.42 carat stone was purchased for over a million dollars. Large crowds came to view it, and many interesting comments were made. One man remarked, "They said it was perfect, but I see a flaw." A woman said disparagingly, "It isn't really that beautiful." Another concluded, "It's too large." Someone else commented, "I think it's vulgar."

A guard at the store, hearing many such comments, observed, "I've heard more sour grapes in the last two days than in my whole life!"

Isn't it strange how jealousy makes people speak with authority on matters that others spend much of their life mastering! And how boldly jealous people express their negative opinions!

Got sour grapes? Replace bitter envy with the sweetener of love (1 Cor. 13:4). It works!—R. W. D.

WHEN YOU TURN GREEN WITH ENVY, YOU ARE RIPE FOR TROUBLE.

A wise man will hear and increase learning.

PROVERBS 1:5

Many years ago an old man took a class at the University of Berlin. It was an unusual sight to see this small, white-haired gentleman sitting among nineteen- and twenty-year-old students. But what made this most unusual was that the old man was Alexander von Humboldt (1769–1859), the renowned German naturalist and scientist. In fact, during a lecture on physical geography, the professor, who was an eminent scholar himself, quoted as his authority something von Humboldt had written.

When Alexander von Humboldt was asked why he, with all his learning, was taking that class, he replied, "To help me review what I had neglected in my youth." With such a hunger for knowledge, he was not too proud to take notes and learn right along with his younger classmates.

The desire to learn about our physical world is commendable. But nothing is more important than to increase our knowledge of God's Word. A wise person never stops learning about God and His world.—R. W. D.

THE WISDOM WE NEED FOR LIFE COMES FROM GOD'S OWN MIND.

The LORD is my rock and my fortress and my deliverer.

PSALM 18:2

The story is told about the time an earthquake struck a small village and caused great fear. One of the residents, however, seemed so calm through it all that the neighbors wondered how she could remain so peaceful and undisturbed.

"What is your secret?" someone asked her. "We want to know what keeps you so relaxed while the ground we stand on is shaking under our feet. Aren't you afraid?"

The woman simply replied, "No, I'm not. I'm just glad that I have a God who is strong enough to shake the world!"

We who know Him as our heavenly Father through faith in His Son, the Lord Jesus Christ, can also find comfort and courage in threatening circumstances. We are in the hands of One who is all-powerful. Nothing is too strong for Him to control. He is able to care for and protect His own no matter what happens. With the psalmist David, we too can say, "The Lord is my rock and my fortress and my deliverer; my God, my strength, in whom I will trust."—R. W. D.

GOD IS THE ROCK ON WHICH WE STAND.

I, even I, am He who blots out your transgressions.

ISAIAH 43:25

I don't know where they go. One minute the computer screen is full of words that I have typed. Then, with one stroke of a key on my keyboard, I can eliminate them all. Suddenly they are gone. It's not like a wad of paper that I throw away—I can still keep track of that as it goes from waste can to garbage truck to landfill. Computer words, when deleted, are gone for good and can't be recalled.

Isn't that the way it is with our sins that have been forgiven by God? In Isaiah 43, the Lord says something about sin that seems like the Old Testament equivalent of deleting something on a computer: "I, even I, am He who blots out your transgressions" (v. 25). Just as an Old Testament writer would scribe something on a papyrus scroll and then get rid of it forever by blotting it out, so God wipes our sin from His record.

If God has blotted out your sins, it's time for you to delete them too.—J. D. B.

WHEN GOD DELETES A SIN, LET'S NOT SAVE IT IN OUR MEMORY.

391

Let us lay aside every weight,
and the sin which so easily ensnares us.

HEBREWS 12:1

Shelby Foote tells of a soldier who was wounded at the battle of Shiloh during the American Civil War and was ordered to go to the rear. The fighting was fierce and within minutes he returned to his commanding officer. "Captain, give me a gun!" he shouted. "This fight ain't got any rear!"

Have you ever felt that way as a Christian—pressured from every side? You want to stay true to Christ, but you constantly feel the allurement of the world from without and the almost irresistible pull of sinful inclinations from within. It seems that there is no rear—no rest from the battle.

In Hebrews 12:1, the Greek word translated "ensnares" literally refers to being surrounded or hemmed in. When we feel pressured to give in to the sin that surrounds us, we are to look to Jesus, the author (literally "captain") of our faith (v. 2). He is our example. As He approached the hour of His crucifixion, Jesus was encircled by the most powerful forces of darkness known to any human, yet He came through to victory.—D. J. D.

THE POWERS OF EVIL ARE NO MATCH FOR THE POWER OF JESUS.

Notes

Prayers

OUR DAILY BREAD

Enjoy it everyday!

You can continue to make *Our Daily Bread* part of your regular time with God. Every month, you can receive a new booklet of devotional articles. Each day's topic is timely and the Bible teaching is reliable—just like the articles you've enjoyed in this book.

To receive *Our Daily Bread* each month at home, with no cost or obligation, just write to us at the address below, or visit us at **www.odb.org/guide** to order online.

As part of the *Our Daily Bread* family, you'll also get opportunities to receive Bible-study guides and booklets on a variety of topics, including creation, the church, and how to live the Christian life.

To order your copy of Our Daily Bread, write to us at:

USA: PO Box 2222, Grand Rapids, MI 49501-2222
CANADA: Box 1622, Windsor, ON N9A 6Z7

Notes

Prayers

Notes